A Social History of the Bakwena and Peoples of the Kalahari of Southern Africa, 19th Century

A SOCIAL HISTORY OF THE BAKWENA AND PEOPLES OF THE KALAHARI OF SOUTHERN AFRICA, 19TH CENTURY

Gary Y. Okihiro

African Studies
Volume 52

The Edwin Mellen Press
Lewiston•Queenston•Lampeter

Library of Congress Cataloging-in-Publication Data

Okihiro, Gary Y., 1945-
  A social history of the Bakwena and peoples of the Kalahari of southern Africa, 19th century / Gary Y. Okihiro.
    p. cm. -- (African studies ; v.52)
  Includes bibliographical references and index.
  ISBN 0-7734-7839-6
  1. Kwena (African people)--Kinship.2. Kwena (African people)--Genealogy. 3.Kwena (African people)--History--19th century. 4. Molepolole (Botswana)--Genealogy. 5. Molepolole (Botswana)--History--19th century. 6. Kalahari Desert--Genealogy. 7. Kalahari Desert--History--19th century. I. Title. II. African studies (Lewiston, N.Y.) ; v. 52.
DT2458.K84 O37 2000
968.83--dc21

99-057090

This is volume 52 in the continuing series
African Studies
Volume 52 ISBN 0-7734-7839-6
AS Series ISBN 0-88946-175-9

A CIP catalog record for this book is available from the British Library.

The Edwin Mellen Press
Box 450
Lewiston, New York
USA 14092-0450

The Edwin Mellen Press
Box 67
Queenston, Ontario
CANADA L0S 1L0

The Edwin Mellen Press, Ltd.
Lampeter, Ceredigion, Wales
UNITED KINGDOM SA48 8LT

Printed in the United States of America

For

Magatelo Mokgoko and Nkwane Gaealafshwe

CONTENTS

ACKNOWLEDGMENTS

A grant from the Social Science Research Council and the American Council of Learned Societies enabled the research that resulted in this book. However, the conclusions, opinions, and other statements in this work are those of the author and not necessarily those of the Council.

To kgosi Bonewamang Sechele II, who gave me permission to work among his people and who gave active support to my project, I extend my heartfelt thanks. My translator and friend, Selebatso G. Masimego, gave me able assistance, without which the research in Molepolole would have been vastly more difficult. Although I acknowledge my informants in the bibliography, the following deserve special recognition: Keakele Sechele II, Ditloung Kusi, Pepere Gabaraane, Kabelo Kebakae, Ratlou Ketshabile, Samokwati Kgakge, Gagonthone Kgari, Phutego Kotonyane, Sepotoka Mafuri, Semetsataola Maselesele, Serare Matong, Phutego Mokaka, Koama Motlhale, Matome Mpusang, Thukhwi Segaetsho, and Kebopeleng Tshomane, all of Molepolole; Tome Baitsadi, Moloiwa Molale, Matlho Reokwaeng, and Gakenne Tshipa of Letlhakeng; Pense Tshaila of Luzwe; and Kereke Seipone of Kang.

Our neighbor, Mma Thobo of Ntloedibe, supplied us with meat, *bojalwa*, and *mabele*, and cheerfully volunteered to re-smear our compound whenever our dog, Chils, got carried away playing on its smooth surface. When the *kgosi*'s cattle trampled down our fence and destroyed our maize crop, Mma Thobo argued on our behalf and the *kgosi* gave us a chicken as recompense. We cherish her friendship.

The author's photograph was taken by Libby Okihiro, the map, drawn by Sean Sachio Ritch Okihiro, and the cover photograph, taken by the author.

Finally, I would like to thank my wife, Libby, for her assistance and companionship throughout this project, from the scorching sands of the Kalahari to the frigid waters of the Orkneys.

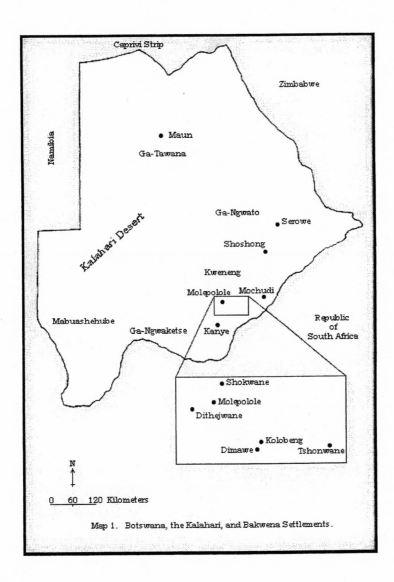

Map 1. Botswana, the Kalahari, and Bakwena Settlements.

1

The Bakwena of Molepolole

"Tell me about Bakwena history," I asked the assembled historians of the Bakwena "nation" when I began my research in 1975. I had returned to Molepolole, the Bakwena capital on the edge of the Kalahari desert, where I had lived for three years, from 1969 to 1971, as a Peace Corps volunteer and teacher at the secondary school. The question was carefully framed, based upon my five years of graduate training in African history at the University of California, Los Angeles, to be as value-neutral as possible and to avoid asking a leading question that would influence the answer. I had been tutored in "scientific" history, often termed "objective" history to distinguish it from its other -- polemics, and I was of a generation of historians bent on "Afro-centrism," or the re-centering of Africans within the discourse (although we didn't use those terms at the time) to allow the historical actors to "speak for themselves."

What befuddled me were the blank stares, the stammerings, the pained silences that followed my "learned" question from the group of elite men chosen by the *kgosi* or "king" or "chief" for the occasion. My "informants" suffered through several days of my persistent, though weakening resolve, trying to fill me in on their "national" history prompted by my vaguest of questions. Walking home one day after nearly a week of such agonizing sessions, my shoulders sagged more than usual in the midday heat and I began thinking the unthinkable, that I was not going to find enough evidence to sustain my intended study -- the economic history of the Bakwena before the arrival of Europeans. Perhaps human memory was indeed fragile among the Bakwena, I surmised, and I harbored secret notions that I knew more about their past than the people themselves. It never occurred to me that I might be asking the wrong questions.

Eventually, after a particularly exasperating exchange, I thought to "humor" my interviewees by asking them about their individual pasts. Much to my surprise, the question unleashed a veritable stream of historical information centered around their genealogies that sometimes reached back thirteen and more generations. That "discovery" on my part revealed some of the troubling assumptions I held about the Bakwena past, and set me on a new path of historical reconstruction. I had assumed that the Bakwena were a unitary "tribe" with a "national" history or variants thereof. I had assumed that the Bakwena, like other Sotho-Tswana peoples, always lived in large, permanent villages comprised of thousands of people as described by nineteenth-century European travellers and by many skilled ethnographers in southern Africa. I had assumed that the Bakwena carried on, as a people, a mixed economy of cattle-herding and grains-cultivating from time immemorial. Bakwena genealogies would lead me to question and ultimately reject all of my bookish assumptions, but also allow me to create new verities and traditions that must surely be subjected to critical thinkings and rethinkings.

My renewed quest, pursued for nearly the entire year, shifted from collecting bits of information to fill-in the blanks of my formalist economics to gathering the genealogies of every lineage in every corner of Molepolole. With that data, I was able to see the Bakwena of Molepolole in their entirety, all of their constituent parts and when and how they fitted together into the whole called the "nation" (*morafe*). My tireless teachers also disabused me of some of the "rules" and "processes" by which groups separated and came together that I had learned from others who had studied and formalized African behavior into sets of "laws" and "customs." Traditon, my African tutors told me, often served the ends of the tradition-holder, and tidy generalizations became messy on the ground where individuals, historical agents operated. But they also generously gave me vibrant, living pasts from which sprang their identities as persons and collectivities, and I bent and twisted them into the shapes we call history in the U.S. scarcely recognizable to those who had entrusted me with their stories. I wept, long ago, over my imperious arrogance.

Kgotla Formation: Theory

The "people of the crocodile," or "Bakwena," organized themselves through *kgotla* and cluster formation. Both of those social processes were stimulated by population changes that derived from population increase and redistribution. Reproduction, or increase that was internally driven, and the absorption of foreigners, or increase externally driven, were the two principal ways by which the Bakwena population grew. Marriage and reproduction theoretically led to the establishment of a *kgotla*.

A man and his wife were said to have founded a *kgotla*, when they built a *lelwapa* (household) consisting perhaps of several dwelling and other structures together with a *kgotla* (meeting place) set in front of the *lelwapa*. That household compound, in Sekwena (a literal translation of *ka Sekwena*, referring to language or meaning but also to "rules"), was properly called a *lelwapa*, a *kgotla*, or even a *motse* (village), and the man was the *kgosi* of the *kgotla*. The settlement was usually named after its male founder or most prominent issue. That was the simplest, most elemental form of a *kgotla*. Sometimes a man had several wives. In that case, each wife was entitled to her own *lelwapa* which was referred to by its order of seniority. Thus, the "first wife" established the "first household," the "second wife" formed the "second household," and so forth. The group of such households still constituted a single *kgotla*.

Reproduction increased the numbers and created generations, both of which added to the complexity of the *kgotla*. Sons generally remained within the *kgotla*, and daughters became members of their husband's households. Under patriarchal primogeniture, the first-born son of the senior *lelwapa* succeeded his father as *kgosi* and occupied his *lelwapa*, and his junior brothers, when they married, built their *malwapa* (plural of *lelwapa*) next to the founder's household, forming a *sebeso* or circle of households. This second-generation *kgotla* contained autonomous units, each household directed by its male head, but their authority was ultimately delegated and circumscribed by the senior male or *kgosi* who was accordingly called the *mong wa kgotla* or "owner of the *kgotla*." Marriage, generally exogamous with a cross-cousin preference, created ties and sustained relations outside the male-headed households that reduced somewhat the insularity of the *kgotla*.

A *kgotla*'s composition enlarged and diversified through reproduction and marriage, but it also diminished through separation. Divisions were common within *makgotla* (plural of *kgotla*) where the *kgosi* had more than one wife, each of whom had sons. The senior son of each wife or household, together with his younger brothers, generally left their father's *sebeso* and built their *malwapa* elsewhere, thereby establishing new *makgotla*. In Sekwena, my teachers told me, the senior son of each household had the right to form his own *kgotla*, whereas junior sons had no such rights and had to secure permission from their seniors. The rule served to preserve the male hereditary seniority structure, while allowing for the integrity and continuation of each *lelwapa*. Further, it gave to seniors the right to repress competition from ambitious juniors, but also offered a mechanism whereby juniors might shield themselves from overbearing seniors.[1]

Kgotla Formation: Practice

Succession took place with the heir inhabiting the office and household of his father and his junior brothers of his mother's *lelwapa* building their households within his *sebeso*. The senior son of his father's second household, however, could choose to move away and establish his own *kgotla* with his junior brothers of his mother's *lelwapa* building their households within his new *sebeso*. The *kgosi*, when that separation of his *kgotla* occurred, ordinarily handed over cattle to his departing half-brother and named them. The new *kgotla* was known by the name of that cattle. When Kgakge, the *kgosi* of Ntlheng-ya Godimo, a section (*motse*) of Molepolole, created a *kgotla* for the senior son of his second *lelwapa*, he named the cattle "Dilemana" because they posssessed a variety of beautifully shaped horns. The new *kgotla* henceforth bore the name, Dilemana.[2]

But there were ways by which juniors managed to form their own *makgotla*, thereby showing that the "rules" of succession and *kgotla* formation provided guidelines but were also situational and elastic. When the Bakwena *kgosi*, Sechele, appointed Mosimane his counselor (*ntona*) in charge of the Ntlheng-ya Tlhase area of his capital, Mosimane's *kgotla*, Senyadima, was moved from Ntlheng-ya Tlhase to Kgosing, Sechele's section (*motse*) of the town. Perhaps because of that move and his heavier responsibilities, Mosimane divided

---

[1]H/M/61.
[2]H/M/46.

his *kgotla* handing over a portion named Sekamelo, from *go sekama* meaning "to recline one's head" or "to rest," to his junior brother, Mmutlanyane.[3]

Seniors, in some cases, might defer to their juniors. Legojane, the founder of the *kgotla* Goo-Ra-Mmoopi, had two sons Mosimanegape and Mmoopi. Although the heir, Mosimanegape chose not to succeed his father, and so handed over the *bogosi* ("chiefship") to his junior brother. Henceforth, the descendants of Mmoopi became the "owners of the *kgotla*," as reflected in the name of the *kgotla* which means, "the people of Mmoopi."[4] In another situation, juniors might override their seniors by popular demand. During the early nineteenth century, a mass assembly of the people within the *kgotla* Matlhalerwa voted to install Ikalafeng over the heir, Sebekedi, ostensibly because the latter's mother was from the Bangwaketse, a people living to the south of and junior to the Bakwena, while Ikalafeng's mother was a Mokwena.[5]

Women also "owned" *makgotla*. Tumagole, the junior brother of the Bakwena *kgosi* Sebele (*a* Sechele), was *kgosi* of the *kgotla* Senyadimana. Tumagole had two daughters but no sons. Phetogo, the elder daughter, inherited the *kgotla* from her father, but did not administer its affairs and willed it to her sons. Senyadimana is accordingly known as a *kgotla ya dipitsana*, or "inherited *kgotla*," implying inheritance from a woman. Phetogo married Kealeboga, her uncle Sebele (*a* Sechele)'s heir, and her senior male descendants in turn became the Bakwena *kgosi* and head of her *kgotla*. In 1975, Bonewamang, Bakwena *kgosi* and Phetogo's grandson, was the "owner" of Senyadimana.[6]

The older the *kgotla*, the greater the opportunities for diversification. But even the youngest *makgotla* show the complexities of *kgotla* formation, on the ground, as opposed to in theory. To illustrate, I will trace the development of Kgosidintsi's *kgotla* which constitutes the nucleus of Mokgalo, perhaps the least differentiated section (*motse*) of the Bakwena capital. Table 1 shows the lineages and seniorities of Kgosidintsi's sons.

[3]H/M/105.

[4]H/M/43.

[5]H/M/46. See, Gary Y. Okihiro, "Genealogical Research in Molepolole: A Report on Methodology," *Botswana Notes & Records* 8 (1976), pp. 53-54, for a fuller explanation of the succession and its variant accounts.

[6]H/M/102; H/M/123; and H/M/125.

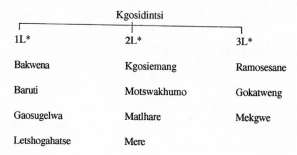

*1L designates first *lelwapa*, 2L, second *lelwapa*, and 3L, third *lelwapa*.

Table 1. Kgosidintsi and His Sons.[7]

Kgosidintsi might have received his *kgotla*, Serame, from his father, the Bakwena *kgosi* Motswasele (*a* Legwale), or Serame might have been instead created by Sechele (*a* Sebele), Kgosidintsi's senior brother, or formed by Kgosidintsi himself when the Bakwena were scattered and disorganized in the period following Motswasele's death, from about 1822 to 1831. When Kgosidintsi died, his heir, Bakwena, inherited Serame. Bakwena, although the most senior of Kgosidintsi's sons, was eclipsed in popularity, wealth, and some maintained, even in political power by his juniors, Baruti, said to be the most popular, Kgosiemang, and Motswakhumo, believed to be the wealthiest.[8]

The circumstance gave rise to four new *makgotla*, all independent from the original *kgotla* of Kgosidintsi, but theoretically under its jurisdiction in collective activities and in cases of appeal. Bakwena's juniors, Baruti, Gaosugelwa, Kgosiemang, and Motswakhumo built their own *makgotla* away from Serame, and took with them some of their juniors. Thus, Gaosugelwa absorbed Letshogahatse's household, and Matlhare, Mere, and Ramosesane joined Motswakhumo's *kgotla*. With his enormous wealth and popularity, Motswakhumo was able to attract a considerable following both at his *kgotla* in Molepolole and his cattlepost at Lentswe-le-Tau.[9] Ramosesane's juniors of his

---

[7]H/M/89; H/M/91; and H/M/93.
[8]H/M/93.
[9]H/M/95.

mother's *lelwapa*, Gokatweng and Mekgwe, died before marrying.[10]   Those developments in Kgosidintsi's *kgotla*   showed that even in one of the least differentiated of Molepolole's *makgotla*, the "rules" -- that juniors were circumscribed by their seniors and that each *lelwapa* formed a separate *kgotla* -- did not apply.

Cluster Formation

If *kgotla* formation was a vertical social organization, then cluster formation was a horizontal grouping of the Bakwena of Molepolole. *Makgotla* were formed by succeeding generations, while clusters were the collective *makgotla* of the children of a single man (*bana ba motho*). For example, the Bakwena *kgosi* Motswasele (*a* Legwale) had four sons, Sechele, Kgosidintsi, Basiamang, and Tebele, each from a separate *lelwapa*. Sechele, the senior son of the senior household, succeeded his father, and Kgosidintsi, Basiamang, and Tebele formed their own *makgotla*, named Serame, Moepetlo, and Botlhajana, which became the nucleus for the Mokgalo section (*motse*) of Molepolole. The people of Serame, Moepetlo, and Botlhajana were grouped together spatially and politically as the *bana ba* Motswasele cluster. Table 2 illustrates schematically the arrangement.

---

[10]H/M/91.

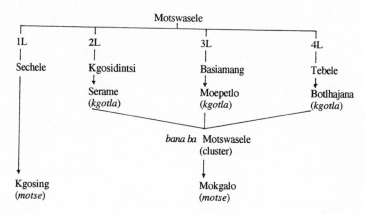

Table 2. Cluster Formation.

The process of *kgotla* formation could be viewed as political localization, as a devolution of authority, while clusters represented political centralization. Cases on appeal within the *bana ba* Motswasele cluster moved from Botlhajana to Moepetlo to Serame.[11]   In that way, the cluster consolidated and resisted the general thrust of *kgotla* formation that sought greater autonomy and the insularity of each *lelwapa*. Changes, nonetheless, occurred over time, as the original *kgotla* gave rise to new *makgotla*, as in the case of Serame, and as the kinship distance widened within each cluster. Eventually, for instance, appeals from Botlhajana by-passed entirely Moepetlo's jurisdiction and went directly to Serame.

The Bakwena of Molepolole at the time of *kgosi* Sechele were organized into five clusters, the *barwa* Kgabo, *bana ba* Motshodi, *barwa* Motswasele (*a* Legojane), *bana ba* Seitlhamo, and *bana ba* Motwasele (*a* Legwale). Table 3 shows the succession of Bakwena *dikgosi* (plural of *kgosi*) and the lineages and compositions of the five Bakwena clusters about the mid-nineteenth century.

[11]B. J. van Niekerk, "Brief Report of the Investigations Carried Out Under the Bakwena Re the Administrative Structure of the Bakwena-Tribe," BNA, S. 471/3.

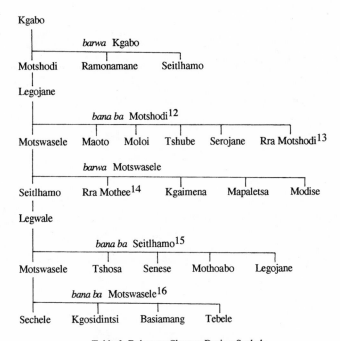

Table 3. Bakwena Clusters During Sechele.

Immigrants

Population increase was impelled by reproduction and especially by the absorption of immigrants (*baagedi*). Immigrants who were non-Bakwena were called *badichaba*, indicating that they were aliens or foreigners. Contrary to the

---

[12]This cluster bears the name of Motshodi, despite being the sons of Legojane, because Motshodi outlived his son, Legojane, who never became the Bakwena *kgosi*. Motshodi's fame, accordingly, exceeded that of his son.

[13]I was unable to ascertain this person's name, only that of his son, Motshodi. I herein refer to him as "Motshodi's father."

[14]See note 13.

[15]Although sons of Legwale, this cluster called themselves the children of Seitlhamo, their grandfather, because Legwale's rule was brief and uneventful while his father ruled for a long time and was more famous.

[16]Members of this cluster generally avoid the designation, "children of Motswasele," because Motswasele was extremely unpopular and was eventually overthrown in a revolt. Instead, they referred to themselves in 1975 as the "children of Kgosidintsi," who was an outstanding statesman.

prevalent notion of "tribes," conceived of as kinship groupings, immigrants comprised the majority of the Bakwena of Molepolole from the time of Sechele to the present. The large numbers of immigrants and aliens relative to the indigenous kin group profoundly affected the size of the population, the relations of power, and the physical layout of the Bakwena capital. The centrality of immigrants was recognized by anthropologists like Isaac Schapera, who observed in his landmark work, *A Handbook of Tswana Law and Custom* (1938), that four-fifths of the Bangwato were *baagedi*, but their social significance was generally missed or slighted.[17]

Most of the *baagedi* in Molepolole joined the Bakwena during the first half of the nineteenth century. A distinctive feature of immigration during this period was that the immigrants came to the Bakwena in large groups rather than as individuals or families.[18] Those *baagedi* were primarily refugees fleeing the *difaqane* and Afrikaner predations in the Transvaal. Their arrival, mainly between 1820 and 1860, more than quadrupled the Bakwena population, and although the estimates of European travellers must be scrutinized with a good deal of skepticism, they provide some indication of relative size.[19] In 1843, British missionary David Livingstone reported 300 people among Sechele's Bakwena at Tshonwane and 350 among Bubi's Boo-Ra-Tshosa section of Bakwena. Six years later, he estimated that the rejoined sections of Sechele and Bubi at Kolobeng numbered 2,384, an increase that must have included absorbed foreigners. Later that same year, an estimated 1,236 Bakaa arrived and settled with the Bakwena, and by 1857, just 14 years after Livingstone's first census, Sechele's capital at Dithubaruba had swelled to an estimated 20,000.[20]

---

[17]I. Schapera, *A Handbook of Tswana Law and Custom* (London: Oxford University Press, 1938); and I. Schapera, *The Ethnic Composition of Tswana Tribes* (London: London School of Economics, 1952).

[18]A notable twentieth century absorption of a large group was the immigration of the Baphalane in 1952-53 to the Bakwena under *kgosi* Kgari. See, "Bakwena Affairs: Request for Ba-Phalane people to remove from Vleischfontein (Zeerust Dist.) into Bakwena Reserve," BNA, S. 300/12.

[19]David Livingstone, for instance, explained some of the motivations and reasons for miscounting in a letter to A. Tidman, Kuruman, June 24, 1843, LMS-SOAS, Africa, Odds, Box 9, Folder 2A.

[20]David Livingstone to A. Tidman, Kuruman, June 24, 1843, LMS-SOAS, Africa, Odds, Box 9, Folder 2A; and Gary Y. Okihiro, "Resistance and Accommodation: baKwena-baGasechele, 1842-52," *Botswana Notes and Records* 5 (1973), pp. 111, 116.

Although just as imprecise as the nineteenth-century estimates and incapable of supplying absolute numbers, an ennumeration of Molepolole's *makgotla* reveals the magnitude and timing of immigration and some of its causes. In 1975, there were twenty-one major Bakwena *makgotla* as compared with thirty-seven major *baagedi makgotla*. Among all immigrant *makgotla*, seven were constituted before Sechele's rule, twenty-two during Sechele, five during Sebele (*a* Sechele), two during Kealeboga, and one during Sebele (*a* Kealeboga). Fifteen of the *baagedi makgotla* were formed as a result of the *difaqane* or Afrikaner incursions, while only five arose out of internal disputes and three because of wars between Batswana groups.[21]

Immigrants, as individuals or family groups, generally attached themselves to members of a *kgotla* with whom they had a chance encounter or were related or were friends. The largest number of immigrants by far were absorbed into the Bakwena *kgosi*'s section (*motse*), Kgosing. Within the five sections (*metse*, plural of *motse*) of Molepolole in 1975, twenty-three major immigrant *makgotla* were located at Kgosing, eight at Ntlheng-ya Tlhase, four at Ntlheng-ya Godimo, two at Ntloedibe, and none at Mokgalo.

At times, individuals and family groups were permitted to form their own *makgotla*. Immigrants with specialized skills, for example, were commonly allowed to build their own *makgotla* usually at Kgosing. Specialists included *dingaka* (physicians) and *baroka ba pula* (rainmakers), who possessed knowledge associated with and useful to the Bakwena *kgosi*. More often, however, individuals and families became members of existing Bakwena *makgotla*, and because of the large influx, immigrants predominated numerically even within Bakwena *makgotla*.

That preponderance is exemplified in Goo-Ra-Mokalake, a Bakwena *kgotla* within Ntloedibe, the oldest and most stable of the five sections (*metse*) of Molepolole. The *kgotla*'s inner circle (*sebeso*), when I visited it in 1975, housed the great-grandsons of Mokalake's sons, Kgosientsho, Mogapi, and Dikgang, whose households surrounded the central meeting place (*kgotla*). Situated behind that center were the *makgotla* of foreigners, consisting mainly of "Bakgalagadi" who were the former servants (*batlhanka*) of the Bakwena, numbering more than

---

[21]See Appendices B and C.

double that of Mokalake's descendants and calling themselves "Bakwena." In addition, among the foreigners was a large *kgotla* of Bahurutshe who had come to Ntloedibe and eventually to Goo-Ra-Mokalake as a "gift" (*ketleetso*) accompanying the Mohurutshe bride of Mokalake's junior uncle.[22]

The rise of *makgotla* comprised of former servants and people who came as "gifts" suggest that not all foreigners in the Bakwena capital were immigrants. Significant numbers were forcibly absorbed. The Baphalane of Goo-Ra-Mochina, and the Bakgatla of Magaba in Goo-Ra-Moeng were people who were captured in warfare by the Bakwena and who eventually established *makgotla* of their own.[23]

Individual and family immigrants were sometimes grouped together to form an entirely new *kgotla* called *makatlanathapong* from *katlana*, meaning "to adhere, to stick together" and *thapo* or "string."[24] Dikgori, a subordinate *kgotla* of Goo-Ra-Tshosa, consisted of three lineages. The most senior, the Boo-Ra-Koosentse, are Bangwaketse who probably immigrated during the time of Tshosa, the Boo-Ra-Dimpe, and the most junior, the Boo-Ra-Setilo. The latter two are Bakgatla (bagaKgafela) who were refugees of the *difaqane* joining the Bakwena during the time of Kgakge, the son of Tshosa.[25] It was probably Kgakge who grouped the three together to form Dikgori.

Once constituted, the *makatlanathapong kgotla* could be reduced and reconstituted by the *kgosi* of the section or *motse*. The Bakwena *kgosi* Sechele assigned the Basikwa of Namaneatau to Mosimane's *kgotla* Senyadima until his son, Tumagole, reached maturity and founded his own *kgotla* Senyadimana, the diminutive of Senyadima. When that happened, Namaneatau's Basikwa became members of Tumagole's Senyadimana. Similarly, Kgakge's son, Gaealafshwe, removed immigrants Baeti and Kudu of the Dimpe line and Senwedi of the Setilo line and made them members of the *kgotla* of his first-born son of his second

---

[22]H/M/130; H/M/133; H/M/136; H/M/137; H/M/142; H/M/143; H/M/145; H/M/147; and H/M/148.

[23]H/M/103; H/M/125; and H/M/147.

[24]H/M/106.

[25]The seniority of immigrants was determined by the order in which they arrived, by the seniority order prevailing among the immigrants themselves, and by "kinship" distance, with Bakwena and other Batswana immigrants having seniority over non-Batswana and *badichaba*.

wife. Later, Gaealafshwe's son, Gokatweng, reallocated Baeti, Kudu, and Lepodisi, a *moagedi*, to Gofetakgosi, also an immigrant, as a reward for his friendship and service as one of Gokatweng's councilors (*ditsotsoma*).[26]

Gokatweng's act resulted in further complicating the social relations. Previously, Gofetakgosi and Lepodisi served Gokatweng, and Baeti and Kudu were under Mmakadika, Gokatweng's junior brother. When the households of Lepodisi, Baeti, and Kudu were joined together under Gofetakgosi's *kgotla* Goo-Morakile, which was a subordinate *kgotla* to Gokatweng's Goo-Ra-Tshosa, their old obligations continued but they acquired additional responsibilities to their new *kgotla* and its head. Accordingly, Gofetakgosi and Lepodisi still paid tax (*sehuba*) to their former head, Gokatweng, and ploughed his field (*letsema*), and Baeti and Kudu, likewise, paid tax to and ploughed for Mmakadika. But as members of Goo-Morakile, Lepodisi, Baeti, and Kudu brought their first-fruits (*dikgafela*) to Gofetakgosi, who in turn took a portion to Gokatweng. Hearings and appeals followed that same path from Gofetakgosi to Gokatweng.[27]

Another kind of *makatlanathapong kgotla* was the consolidated *kgotla* formed by merging several *makgotla* into a single entity. The Bakwena *kgosi* Kealeboga created Goo-Ra-Letlamma for his son by bringing three existing immigrant *makgotla*, Goo-Meje, Goo-Ra-Molefe, and Ga-Mangwato, together into a single *kgotla*. Letlamma, Kealeboga's son, built his household within the circle of the Goo-Meje, the most senior lineage among the three, while the Goo-Ra-Molefe and Ga-Mangwato maintained their own *makgotla* outside of Goo-Meje. When Letlamma died without an heir or a replacement, the three *makgotla* drifted apart and formed a mere voluntary association while keeping their integrity as distinct *makgotla* intact. By 1975, the unit, "Goo-Ra-Letlamma," had begun to disappear.[28]

Immigrants who arrived as entire groups were sometimes permitted to form *makgotla* of their own, like the Goo-Modibedi *kgotla* in the Ntlheng-ya Godimo section (*motse*) of Molepolole.[29] Other immigrant groups, particularly

---

[26]H/M/2; H/M/102; H/M/105; H/M/118; H/M/123; and H/M/125.
[27]H/M/54.
[28]H/M/122.
[29]H/M/85.

well-organized and ambitious ones, posed a potential threat to the stability of the Bakwena state (*morafe*), and hence were divided and scattered by the *kgosi*. The Bakwena of Kgabo (*ya molelo*) fled to Sechele's Bakwena at Tshonwane as a result of the *difaqane* or Afrikaner presence in the Transvaal. Apparently, most of the immigrants were soldiers, well-disciplined, and tightly organized. In accepting them, Sechele wisely separated the senior lineages from their juniors, allocating the former to Kgakge of the Ntlheng-ya Godimo section (*motse*) of his capital and retaining the junior lineages within his Kgosing section (*motse*). Sechele thereby favored the juniors who were grateful to him, lowered the status of the senior lineage in relation to their juniors, and lessened the likelihood of a united Bakwena of Kgabo (*ya molelo*) challenge.[30]

Population redistribution featured immigrants who were moved from one *kgotla* to another, oftentimes at the bidding of a *kgosi*, but it also involved non-immigrant Bakwena who chose to leave the *makgotla* of their birth for that of a wealthy or politically powerful kinsman or non-kinsman. Another kind of redistribution occurred when there was a split caused by overcrowding as in the case of *kgotla* of Basimane. The physical separation of the *kgotla*'s two lineages led to the rise of two separate *makgotla*, Boo-Moitlhobo and their seniors, the Boo-Mhiemang. Overcrowding also led to the movement of people from one section (*motse*) of the capital to another. The Boo-Lebekwe left their home in Mokgalo to Ntloedibe for more space, and henceforth reported to Ntloedibe's *kgosi* for adjudication in matters of everyday life, but performed their kinship obligations to the *kgosi* of Mokgalo such as in observing "first-fruits" (*dikgafela*) and repairing the *kgosi*'s cattle fold and *kgotla*, taxed labor called *mokgalo*.[31]

Motse and Morafe

Kgotla and cluster formation, driven by the processes of population increase and redistribution, were the building blocks of nation-forming. Molepolole's Bakwena became a people when Kgabo (*a Tebele*) separated from his senior brother, Mogopa, perhaps in the Transvaal during the early eighteenth

---

[30]H/M/56; and H/M/58. The Babididi were likewise divided into two sections, one kept at Kgosing while the other sent to Ntlheng-ya Tlhase. H/M/123.

century, and with his followers gradually moved westward, eventually settling in present-day Botswana.[32]   The Bangwato and Bangwaketse, descendants of a junior line of Bakwena, left Kgabo's group perhaps about the mid-eighteenth century, and settled to the north and south respectively of the Kweneng (Bakwena territory) and became separate "nations" (*merafe*).[33] The Bakwena of Molepolole, accordingly, possibly began as Kgabo's household which had four *malwapa* organized as a single *kgotla* headed by a *kgosi*, Kgabo, and properly called a *motse* or village that became known as Kgosing ("place of the *kgosi*").

Kgabo had four sons, Masilo, Motshodi, Ramonamane, and Seitlhamo. Masilo, despite his seniority, lost the *bogosi* to his junior, Motshodi, because Masilo neglected his duties as *kgosi*, according to one account, or because Masilo was blind or without a male heir, as related by other versions.[34]   Whatever the reason, Phokotsea, Masilo's daughter and heir, and her sons were cut off from the line of Bakwena *dikgosi*, but Masilo's descendants retained their distinctiveness as the Bakwena of Masilo, or *barwa* Masilo, separate from the descendants of Motshodi, Ramonamane, and Seitlhamo, who were called the Bakwena of Masilonyane. "Masilonyane" is the diminutive form of Masilo, and designated the group's junior status.[35]

As evidence of their seniority, Masilo's Bakwena lived in a separate section (*motse*) of the capital called Ntloedibe, from *ntlo* ("house") and *dibe* ("sins"), and did not pay tax (*sehuba*) either in goods or labor to the Bakwena *kgosi*. If Ntloedibe's *kgosi* gave refuge to anyone, the Bakwena *kgosi* at Kgosing could not legally intervene.   On war or hunting campaigns or in "initiation schools," the age-regiment (*mophato*) of Masilo chose the camp site and

---

[31]H/M/105; H/M/113; H/M/114; H/M/121; and H/M/147.

[32]See Appendix A. For a survey of Botswana and the Kalahari from the late Stone Age to the eighteenth century, see Edwin N. Wilmsen, *Land Filled with Flies: A Political Economy of the Kalahari* (Chicago: University of Chicago Press, 1989), pp. 64-78.

[33]A. J. Wookey, *Dinwao Leha E Le Dipolelo Kaga Dico Tsa Secwana* (Vryburg: London Missionary Society, 1921), pp. 43-45; I. Schapera, ed., *Ditirafalo Tsa Merafe ya Batswana* (Lovedale: Lovedale Press, 1954), pp. 33-37; and I. Schapera, ed., *Praise-Poems of Tswana Chiefs* (Oxford: Clarendon, 1965), p. 123.

[34]H/M/10; H/M/130; and H/M/136.

[35]Refer to Appendix A, note 8.

were the first to light their campfires.[36]   That situation made for awkward
relations, especially during the nineteenth century when the Bakwena *kgosi*
sought to create a single, unitary state.   Perhaps in an attempt to reverse the
seniority order or to assimilate the *barwa* Masilo into the Masilonyane line,
Sechele formed Masilwana, a *kgotla* comprised of disparate lineages within
Kgosing, and appointed Mogotsi, a Masilo Mokwena, as head of the *kgotla*.
Later, however, Sechele placed his son, Motsatsi, in charge of Masilwana, and
thereafter Mogotsi and his line of Masilo Bakwena paid tax (*sehuba*) to Motsatsi's
Bakwena of Masilonyane.[37]   Despite attempts such as Sechele's designed to
subject the Ntloedibe section (*motse*) to the will of the Bakwena *kgosi* at
Kgosing, Masilo's Bakwena stoutly resisted and successfully maintained its
precedence over Masilonyane's line, and yet remained core members of
Molepolole's Bakwena.

Motshodi became the Bakwena *kgosi* after his father, Kgabo, and settled
at Kgosing. His juniors, Ramonamane and Seitlhamo, the *barwa* Kgabo cluster,
established their own *makgotla*, Maunatlala and Goo-Ra-Seitlhamo, in an area
called Ntlheng-ya Tlhase or "the lower side."[38]   During Motshodi's rule that
ended about 1770, thus, the Bakwena consisted of two groups, the Bakwena of
Masilo and of Masilonyane, who occupied two villages (*metse*), Ntloedibe and
Kgosing, with their respective *dikgosi*, and an area below Kgosing called
Ntlheng-ya Tlhase.   Table 4 shows the beginnings of the core Bakwena of
Molepolole.

---

[36]H/M/67; H/M/130; and H/M/132. See also, van Niekerk, "Brief Report."
[37]H/M/88.

[38]Goo-Ra-Seitlhamo split into two *makgotla*, Goo-Ra-Thipe and Goo-Ra-Monametsana,
during Sechele's rule. H/M/107; H/M/109; H/M/110; and H/M/112.

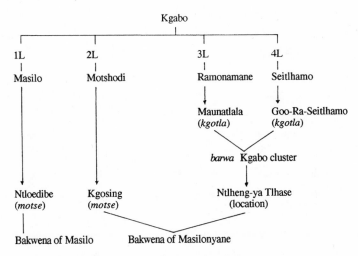

Table 4. The Core Bakwena of Molepolole.

Motshodi had a single son, Legojane, who had many sons but who died before his father and thus never ruled as *kgosi*. Instead, Legojane's senior son, Motswasele, succeeded his grandfather, and Legojane's junior sons, Maoto, Moloi, Tshube, Serojane, and Rra Motshodi, constituted the *bana ba* Motshodi cluster, and lived in an area of the capital called Ntlheng-ya Godimo or "the upper side."[39] The most senior member of the *bana ba* Motshodi cluster, Maoto, headed the group and established his own *kgotla*, Goo-Maoto. Moloi formed Goo-Moloi, and his son, Sereto, founded a *kgotla* named Goo-Moloinyana, the diminutive of his father's *kgotla*. Tshube had two sons, Moitoi and Moitoinyana, who established the *makgotla* of Goo-Moitoi and Goo-Moitoinyana, and Serojane formed the *kgotla* called Mogogoru, and Rra Motshodi founded a *kgotla* that divided into Goo-Molepolole and Goo-Mosarwa about the time of Tshosa.[40]

Immigrants were already a significant feature of that fledgling Bakwena settlement. Substantial numbers of Bataung, believed to have been refugees of

---

[39]H/M/51; H/M/59; H/M/60; H/M/65; H/M/66; H/M/68; H/M/82; H/M/98; H/M/117; H/M/127; H/M/128; and H/M/129.
[40]H/M/50; H/M/51; and H/M/60.

war (*bagaladi*), arrived during Motshodi's reign. They were divided by the Bakwena *kgosi*, into groups that were allocated to and absorbed by Goo-Maoto and Goo-Moitoi, and the most senior of the Bataung immigrants were allowed to form in Ntlheng-ya Godimo their own *kgotla* named Goo-Thato.[41]

Motswasele (*a* Legojane), who served as regent during the final years of Motshodi's rule, moved the Bakwena farther west to Shokwane, about nine miles northeast of Molepolole, then to Dithejwane, a few miles west of Molepolole, and finally back to Shokwane where he died in *c.*1785.[42] Motswasele had several sons, Seitlhamo, his heir who ruled from *c.*1785 to 1795,[43] and his juniors, Rra Mothee, Kgaimena, Mapaletsa, and Modise. Rra Mothee founded the *kgotla* of Senyadima, Kgaimena, Goo-Ra-Kgaimena, Mapaletsa, Goo-Ra-Mapaletsa,[44] and Modise, Goo-Ra-Modise.[45] Perhaps to strengthen his hold over the Ntlheng-ya Tlhase side of Kgosing which had two *makgotla* of uncles twice removed, Motswasele, it appears, directed his junior sons, the *barwa* Motswasele, to build their *makgotla* at Ntlheng-ya Tlhase.

That move brought together for the first time two core Bakwena clusters, the original but junior *barwa* Kgabo with the newer but senior *barwa* Motswasele, in a single residential area, Ntlheng-ya Tlhase. Likely to avoid a conflict between those clusters over power and to underscore the primacy of central authority, they remained autonomous one from the other and subject only to the Bakwena *kgosi* at Kgosing. That strategy was followed in Ntlheng-ya Godimo, when Seitlhamo's junior sons, Tshosa, Senese, Mothoabo, and Legojane, constituting the *bana ba* Seitlhamo cluster, built their *makgotla* -- Tshosa's Goo-Ra-Tshosa, Senese's Matlhalerwa, Mothoabo's Majatsie, and Legojane's Goo-Ra-Mmoopi named for his son, Mmoopi -- on the upper side of Kgosing alongside the *bana ba* Motshodi cluster, uncles twice removed to Legwale, Seitlhamo's heir, who was

---

[41]H/M/43; H/M/65; and H/M/73.

[42]Schapera, *Praise-Poems*, p. 123.

[43]*Ibid.*, p. 124.

[44]Goo-Ra-Mapaletsa was known as Goo-Ra-Ntsono in 1975, named for Ntsono, the great-grandson of Mapaletsa. H/M/51.

[45]Goo-Ra-Modise became Goo-Ra-Ramabinyana, named for one of Modise's sons, and was moved from Ntlheng-ya Tlhase to Mokgalo. H/M/98.

kgosi from *c*.1795 to 1803.[46] Like the two clusters in Ntlheng-ya Tlhase, the *bana ba* Motshodi and *bana ba* Seitlhamo clusters, together with the immigrant Bataung *kgotla* Goo-Thato, in Ntlheng-ya Godimo conducted their own affairs and reported directly to the *kgosi* at Kgosing.

A schematic representation in Table 5 of the Masilonyane Bakwena settlement (*motse*) at the time of Legwale's son, Motswasele, summarizes its composition, with two clusters each in Ntlheng-ya Godimo and Ntlheng-ya Tlhase, the households in Kgosing, and all of the *makgotla* of core Bakwena and immigrants (*baagedi*). Taken together they formed three aggregations that constituted a single administrative unit -- a section and village (*motse*) and a nation (*morafe*).

Ntlheng-ya Godimo	Kgosing	Ntlheng-ya Tlhase
bana ba Motshodi	*kgosi*	*barwa* Kgabo
Goo-Maoto[47]	Motswasele	Maunatlala
Goo-Moloi		Goo-Ra-Thipe
Goo-Moloinyana	brothers	
Goo-Moitoi	Segokotlo	*barwa* Motswasele
Goo-Moitoinyana	Molese	Senyadima
Mogogoru		Goo-Ra-Kgaimena
Goo-Molepolole	sons	Goo-Ra-Ntsono
Goo-Mosarwa	Sechele	Goo-Ra-Ramabinyana
	Kgosidintsi	
bana ba Seitlhamo	Basiamang	
Goo-Ra-Tshosa	Tebele	
Matlhalerwa	Sekwene	
Majatsie		
Goo-Ra-Mmoopi		
baagedi		
Goo-Thato		

Table 5. Masilonyane Bakwena *Makgotla* During Motswasele (*a* Legwale).

---

[46]Schapera, *Praise-Poems*, p. 125. H/M/42; H/M/43; H/M/45; H/M/46; H/M/50; and H/M/51. Cf., Schapera, *Ditirafalo*, pp. 39-40.

[47]Goo-Maoto's Bakwena, during Motswasele (*a* Legwale), had been driven into exile, and only returned after Motswasele's death. The *kgotla*, accordingly, consisted of the Bataung immigrants who had been assigned to Goo-Maoto by *kgosi* Motshodi. A large number of Maoto's Bakwena remained among the Bangwaketse, and in 1975 comprised a major *kgotla* in Kanye, the Bangwaketse capital. H/M/65; and Schapera, *Ditirafalo*, pp. 37-39.

Seitlhamo's brief rule and Legwale's death a mere eight years after having succeeded his father left an heir, Motswasele (*a* Legwale), who was a minor. His uncle, Maleke, served as regent, but Maleke died before the child reached adulthood, so Tshosa acted as regent until Motswasele became the *kgosi* in *c.*1807.[48] During his regentship, Tshosa repulsed two raids by the Bangwaketse, moved the Bakwena back to Shokwane, and he and his *bana ba* Seitlhamo cluster grew in influence and popularity, especially later when contrasted with Motswasele's misrule and abuse of the *bogosi*. Table 6 provides a simplified genealogy of the main characters in the revolt that toppled Motswasele.

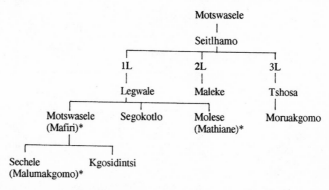

*Indicates *mophato*. See Appendix D.

Table 6. Motswasele (*a* Legwale) and His Kin.

In *c.*1822, Motswasele was assassinated at a public assembly by plotters led by Moruakgomo, Tshosa's son, and Segokotlo, the *kgosi*'s junior brother. A Bakwena faction, called the Boo-Ra-Tshosa, remained with Moruakgomo and Tshosa at Shokwane and then to Dithejwane, while those who fled with Segokotlo and Motswasele's young sons to the Bangwato later became known as the Bakwena of Sechele. The Boo-Ra-Tshosa consisted of the four *makgotla* of its *bana ba* Seitlhamo cluster, and attracted Goo-Moitoinyana, Mogogoru, Goo-Molepolole, and Goo-Mosarwa of the *bana ba* Motshodi cluster, along with the Bataung of Goo-Thato, to their side. In effect, with the exception of four

---

[48]Schapera, *Ditirafalo*, pp. 41-49; and Schapera, *Praise-Poems*, pp. 126-27.

makgotla, the senior cluster in Ntlheng-ya Godimo led its neighbors in a breakaway from Kgosing.

Among the Boo-Ra-Tshosa, the *kgotla* Goo-Ra-Tshosa assumed the functions of Kgosing, subordinating all of the *makgotla* that remained with them.[49] In 1824, two years after having established a new polity, the Boo-Ra-Tshosa were attacked and dislodged from their mountainous defences at Dithejwane by Sebetwane's Makololo, who pushed them into the desert and occupied Dithejwane until they were driven from the site by the Bangwaketse in 1826.[50] The Boo-Ra-Tshosa, from 1824 to 1826, lived in small, scattered villages in the Kalahari, seeking to repulse the raids of the Makololo to their south and the Ndebele to their east.

The *difaqane* similarly affected Sechele's Bakwena, who had suffered from Ndebele attacks along with their Bangwato hosts and who were dispersed throughout the desert. That pattern among both the Boo-Ra-Tshosa and Bakwena of Sechele might have been induced equally by invasions as well as by a leadership hiatus, particularly after the deaths of Tshosa and Moruakgomo in *c.*1828 at the hands of the Makololo, and the minority and capture of Sechele by the Makololo. During this period, Legwale moved his Majatsie *kgotla* south to the Marico river, the Boo-Moitoinyana migrated west to Ga-Tawana near Lake Ngami, Senese separated his *kgotla* Matlhalerwa from the Boo-Ra-Tshosa, Kgosidintsi and Molese stayed at Lephephe, Tebele settled in Bokaa, and Sechele, after his release, travelled east to Moilwe's Bahurutshe because his uncle, Molese, refused to relinquish the *bogosi* to him.[51]

In *c.*1831, Sechele became the *kgosi* of Molese's faction of Bakwena at Tshonwane, and around 1840 attacked the Boo-Ra-Tshosa led by Moruakgomo's half-brother Bubi in an attempt to reunite the sides that had separated after his father's assassination. He failed, but in 1846, after Bubi's death, he defeated Kgakge, Bubi's successor, and most of the Boo-Ra-Tshosa rejoined his

---

[49]H/M/43; H/M/50; H/M/51; H/M/59; H/M/60; H/M/65; H/M/66; H/M/68; H/M/82; H/M/98; H/M/117; H/M/127; H/M/128; and H/M/129.

[50]A. Sillery, *Sechele, The Story of an African Chief* (Oxford: George Ronald, 1954), pp. 61-63; David Livingstone, *Missionary Travels and Researches in South Africa* (London: John Murray, 1857), p. 13; and Margaret Hermina Lister, ed., *Journals of Andrew Geddes Bain* (Cape Town: van Riebeeck Society, 1949), pp. 58-70.

[51]Wookey, *Dico*, pp. 47-48; and "History of the Bakwena Tribe," BNA, S. 3/1.

Bakwena, although Kgakge led a small group to Mabotsa to join Mosielele's Bakgatla Mmanaana. In 1852, the Bakgatla fled to Sechele for protection against the Transvaal Afrikaners, and the following year the final remnants of the Boo-Ra-Tshosa, including Kgakge, returned to join Sechele's Bakwena [52]

Sechele faced several challenges in his attempt to build a nation (*morafe*) from the remains of the internal fractures of the immediate past and the sudden diversity brought about by the externally-driven influx of immigrants. The absorption of the Boo-Ra-Tshosa and immigrants added to the productive capacities of the Bakwena and thereby increased Sechele's power, but they also posed a latent and potentially disruptive presence insofar as the Boo-Ra-Tshosa had instigated the coup against his father and the immigrants arrived in large, organized groups and introduced foreign cultures. Sechele's solution employed both continuity and innovation, and it laid the foundation of the capital, Molepolole, that I found in 1975.

In 1847, at the urging of David Livingstone, Sechele had moved west to Kolobeng, and in 1851, to Dimawe where the Bakwena were attacked and plundered by an Afrikaner commando and their Bahuruthse allies. After the sacking of Dimawe in 1852, Sechele's Bakwena moved to the rocky fastness of Dithubaruba in the Dithejwane hills, that was described in 1854 by the missionary Robert Moffat as consisting of "different villages in the hills" surrounded by walls "piled up of loose stones, about five feet high," and "two very large villages on the small plain at the foot of a very precipitous part of the hills" each having about 3,000 inhabitants.[53] Sechele's Bakwena had swelled from a mere 300 at Tshonwane in 1843 to 3,620 at Dimawe in 1852 to an astonishing 20,000 just five years later.

Sechele's restructuring occurred amid those extraordinary circumstances. Ntlheng-ya Tlhase retained its identity as a place of settlement, where several clusters and *makgotla* carried on their own affairs subject only to Kgosing. On the other side, Ntlheng-ya Godimo constituted a political entity, a section (*motse*), where Goo-Ra-Tshosa functioned as a kgosing for the aggregation of clusters and

---

[52]Schapera, *Ditirafalo*, pp. 50-52; Schapera, *Praise-Poems*, p. 129; and Okihiro, "Resistance," pp. 104-116.

[53]J. P. R. Wallis, ed., *The Matabele Journals of Robert Moffat, 1829-1860*, I (London: Chatto & Windus, 1945), pp. 160-71.

makgotla there, and its head became the *kgosi* of the section, but who was, nonetheless, subordinate to the *kgosi* at Kgosing. Keeping Ntlheng-ya Tlhase's pre-Motswasele form avoided conflicts over seniority and power between its two Bakwena clusters, and changing Ntlheng-ya Godimo's structure to its post-Motswasele shape gave greater independence to the former dissidents of the Boo-Ra-Tshosa.

Self-rule, however, could undermine cohesion and prove dangerous to a *kgosi* who stood virtually alone against entire sections (*metse*) of his capital -- Ntloedibe and Ntlheng-ya Godimo. In addition, kinship united, but it also prompted and legitimated revolts. Although a potential problem, the large number of immigrants provided an opportunity. Sechele absorbed many of those immigrants into Kgosing, organizing them into *makgotla* that owed their existence to him, because *baagedi* had no legal claims to community membership or privileges, especially non-Batswana immigrants like the Ndebele and "Bakgalagadi." Accordingly, at a time when the Bakwena considered "Bakgalagadi" as inferiors and servants, Sechele formed a *kgotla*, Difetlhamolelo, in Kgosing for Segakisa, a "Mokgalagadi" and son of a servant, and appointed him counselor (*ntona*) to oversee a section (*motse*) of the capital.[54] By absorbing immigrants, Sechele transformed Kgosing into a true section (*motse*) of the capital, comprised mainly of the *makgotla* of immigrants, and thereby achieved a counter to Ntloedibe and Ntlheng-ya Godimo. Another boost generally to Sechele's paramountcy was the creation of a fourth section (*motse*), Mokgalo, comprised of the *kgosi*'s junior brothers, the *bana ba* Motswasele cluster, and led by Kgosidintsi.

Immigrants and contacts with non-Bakwena introduced novel ideas and institutions and divergent cultures. The *motse* configuration, like other Bakwena structures, possessed simultaneously inclinations toward integration and separation. To centralize authority and reduce fissiparous tendencies, Sechele introduced the *dintona* system which he might have learned from the Makololo or

---

[54]Segakisa's father, Rampena, was a servant of Ngakaemang of the *bana ba* Motshodi. After receiving his *kgotla* from Sechele, Segakisa invited Kgalaeng, a son of his father's master, to join him in Difetlhamolelo. In that way, the roles of master and servant were inverted. H/M/53; H/M/127; H/M/129; and H/M/149.

Ndebele.[55] The four *dintona* were appointed by Sechele to supervise the three sections (*metse*) and one area of the Masilonyane portion of the Bakwena capital. As appointees, the *dintona* owed their allegiance to Sechele and could not instigate a hereditary nest of privilege. His first *dintona* were Segakisa,[56] who was responsible for Kgosing, Mosimane, in charge of Mokgalo, Ketshabile, who oversaw Ntlheng-ya Godimo, and Magogwe, who headed Ntlheng-ya Tlhase. With the exception of Mosimane, all of the *dintona* were immigrants, and thus more dependent upon the *kgosi*, and all built their households within Kgosing and reported to Sechele daily. As a financial incentive for effective management, each *ntona* received a share of the annual tax (*sehuba*) collected in his respective section.[57]

Sechele's nation-building, his innovative state (*morafe*), was in truth an unfolding of the social processes set in motion by Molepolole's Bakwena that were delimited by norms, but responsive to situational changes.[58] The "rules" of *kgotla* formation provided guidelines that were modified by the personalities and circumstances of the time. Kinship and hereditary hierarchies located social relations, but immigration also determined the sites and trajectories of privilege. And the historical forces external to the formation impinged upon its shape and direction.

My naive question about individual pasts prompted answers that altered profoundly my understanding of "Bakwena history." My "discovery," of course, was a commonplace for my Bakwena teachers. When the Bakwena of Molepolole set out to establish their own nation, perhaps in the early eighteenth century, they were a small group of migrants making their way westward to the edge of the Kalahari desert. Their numbers diminished greatly when their juniors, the Bangwato and Bangwketse, left them about the mid-eighteenth century. And although reproduction increased their numbers, immigration as early as before 1770 was the most significant factor in the population changes, particularly of the

---

[55]H/M/2.

[56]Because Segakisa was old when he was appointed *ntona*, his son, Mhiko, replaced his father not long after Segakisa's installation. H/M/53.

[57]H/M/2.

[58]See John L. Comaroff and Simon Roberts, *Rules and Processes: The Cultural Logic of Dispute in an African Context* (Chicago: University of Chicago Press, 1981).

mid-nineteenth century, that resulted in the large, sprawling settlement of town-dwellers and farmers believed to have been "typical" of the Sotho-Tswana. A detailed description of Molepolole's Bakwena attests, I believe, to that unorthodox conclusion.

2

Connecting With the Ancestors

"To recite one's genealogy" (*go rulaganya* or *go tlhomaganya lesika*) is to connect onesself with one's ancestors (*badimo*). Genealogies provided the context for individual and collective identities. They located a person along a line that began with a point of origin and implied a continuity into the future. Genealogies, like history, were a very personal matter that explained and legitimized one's sites along the trajectories of social relations. As memory, genealogies were subject to lapses, and as identity, they were sometimes massaged and negotiated.[1] Those features of genealogies made them precarious documents, but their subject positions constituted trails to the Bakwena past.

Ntloedibe

At the core of Masilo's *motse* were four principal *makgotla*, in order of seniority -- Goo-Ra-Mokalake, Goo-Ra-Moleka, Goo-Ra-Moeng, and Matakala. A simplified genealogy shows their ancestry.

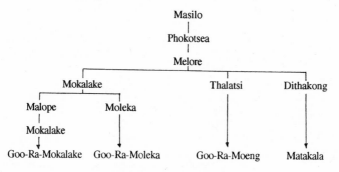

Table 7. Ntloedibe's Principal *Makgotla*.

---

[1]Gary Y. Okihiro, "Genealogical Research in Molepolole: A Report on Methodology," *Botswana Notes and Records* 8 (1976), pp. 47-62.

The Boo-Ra-Mokalake were the most senior of Masilo's descendants. Table 8 offers a version of Mokalake's genealogy.

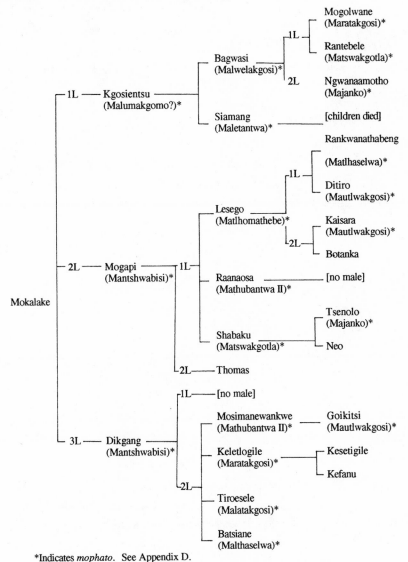

*Indicates *mophato*. See Appendix D.

Table 8. The Boo-Ra-Mokalake.

Successive generations of the Boo-Ra-Mokalake occupied the *kgotla's* center, along with their servants and illegitimate offspring like Mochubi and Dikgang, who were the sons of Mokalake and women servants (*batlhanka*). Mokalake appointed Mochubi the lighter of the *kgotla's* fires, and asked his legitimate sons to accept Mochubi as their brother.   Indeed, Mochubi (of the Mantshwabisi *mophato*) and his son, Lesole (Masitaoka *mophato*), and grandson Gabautlwane (Matlama *mophato*) built their households near Goo-Ra-Mokalake's center and were called "uncles" (*rrangwane*) by Mokalake's legitimate offspring, but they were still considered to be lesser uncles and inferiors.[2]   Dikgang's mother was a servant at Goo-Ra-Mmoopi in Ntlheng-ya Godimo. A genealogy of the Boo-Ra-Dikgang, not to be confused with the Dikgang of Mokalake's third *lelwapa*, appears in Table 9.[3]

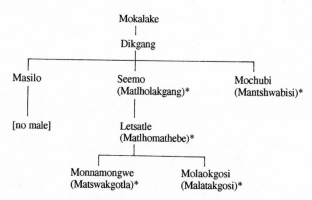

*Indicates *mophato*. See Appendix D.

Table 9. The Boo-Ra-Dikgang.

The Boo-Ra-Marobaphuti, Boo-Ra-Molatlwa, an offshoot of the former, and Boo-Ra-Lejage were Kgosientsu's servants (*batlhanka*), and the *kgotla* of Mathame consisted of a portion of the Bahurutshe who had accompanied the Mohurutshe bride of Mokalake's uncle, Moeng, as a "gift" (*ketleetso*).   Moeng

---

[2]H/M/148.

[3]H/M/137; H/M/145; H/M/146; H/M/147; and H/M/148.

ostensibly gave the Boo-Mathame to his senior, Mokalake, because he could not manage them. The Boo-Mathame, descendants of Dikolobe, are junior to the Bahurutshe of Letlhaku and Mogotsi in Goo-Ra-Moeng as shown in Table 10.[4]

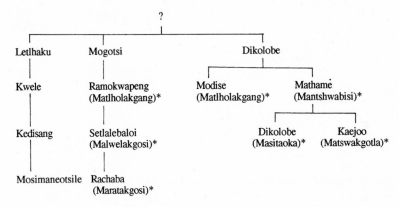

*Indicates *mophato*. See Appendix D.

Table 10. Bahurutshe *Makgotla* Mathame and Motokwane.

The Boo-Ra-Moleka were second in seniority to the Boo-Ra-Mokalake among Masilo's Bakwena in Ntloedibe. The *kgotla*, in 1975 and likely in the more distant past, was comparatively small, consisting only of the central circle (*sebeso*) and the adjacent *kgotla* of Nakedi, the son of Moleka's second *lelwapa*. Unlike Goo-Ra-Mokalake and Goo-Ra-Moeng, Goo-Ra-Moleka contained no large contingents of immigrants, perhaps reflecting its relative poverty, and the *kgotla* achieved little growth through reproduction. Moleka's genealogy appears in Table 11.[5]

---

[4]H/M/143; H/M/145; and H/M/147.
[5]H/M/145; and H/M/147.

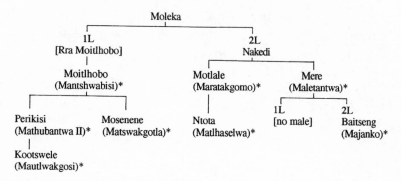

*Indicates *mophato*. See Appendix D.

Table 11. The Boo-Ra-Moleka.

Goo-Ra-Moeng, in contrast, although junior to Goo-Ra-Moleka, was more extensive and diversified than both its seniors.   Reproduction and particularly immigration stimulated the *kgotla*'s rise. A genealogy of the Boo-Ra-Moeng appears in Table 12.[6]

---

[6]H/M/133; H/M/136; and H/M/147.

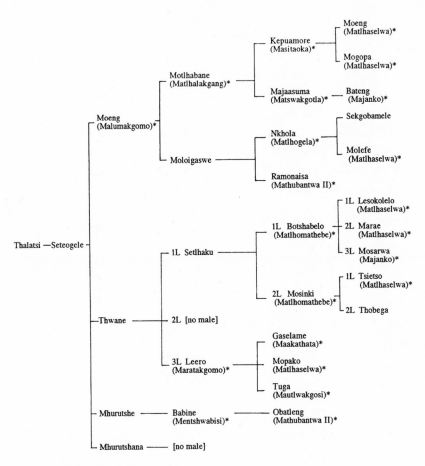

*Indicates *mophato*. See Appendix D.

Table 12. The Boo-Ra-Moeng.

The *kgotla* of Goo-Ra-Moeng comprised a hierarchy of *makgotla* that began with Goo-Ra-Moeng at the apex and successive *makgotla* of junior lineages and immigrants folded within. The head of Goo-Ra-Moeng, along with his juniors and their servants built their households around the central meeting place. Obatleng of the junior line of Mhurutshe maintained a *kgotla*, and Mosinki and Leerò, firstborn sons of subordinant households (*malwapa*), formed their own *makgotla*. Attached to Goo-Ra-Mosinki was Magaba, a *kgotla* of Bakgatla, that was subject to Mosinki's *kgotla*. The Bakgatla, believed to have been captives taken during Sechele's battles with the Bakgatla Kgafela of Mochudi, were divided into two groups, one forming the *kgotla* of Magaba and the other, the Boo-Ra-Motsenwane, reporting to Goo-Ra-Moeng.

Bokaa, Baphaleng, and Motokwane were major immigrant *makgotla* all subject to Goo-Ra-Moeng. Bokaa consisted of Bakaa, the Boo-Ra-Pheto of Ramokwelema, who were originally members of Bokaa, a *kgotla* in the Ntlheng-ya Tlhase area of the Bakwena capital. Because of a family dispute, those Bakaa left their seniors, the Boo-Ra-Pheto of Tsalaele, and joined the Boo-Ra-Motlhabane. Baphaleng arose as a result of Moeng's junior brother Thwane's marriage to a Mongwato woman. The Baphaleng came as "gifts" (*ketleetso*), and formed two sections within Goo-Ra-Moeng -- the Boo-Ra-Sibisibi and Boo-Ra-Ntetebale. Motokwane was the *kgotla* of the Boo-Ra-Rachaba, Bahurutshe who were the "gifts" (*ketleetso*) accompanying Moeng's Mohuruthse wife. Their juniors were the Boo-Mathame of Mokalake's *kgotla*, and their seniors, Letlhaku's lineage, were absorbed into Goo-Ra-Moeng. [See Table 10.]

Mathakala was the most junior *kgotla* of the *barwa* Masilo. A version of Mathakala's genesis appears in Table 13.[7]

---

[7]H/M/143; H/M/145; and H/M/147.

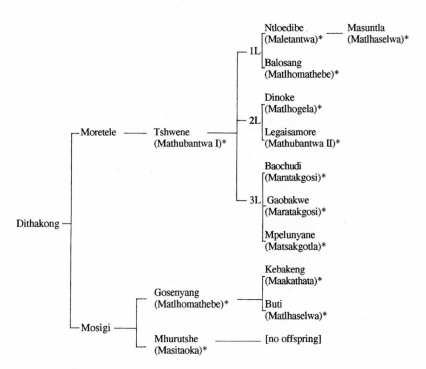

*Indicates *mophato*. See Appendix D.

Table 13. The Boo-Ra-Dithakong.

Mathakala, unlike its senior *makgotla*, consisted mainly of the male descendants of its founder Dithakong and their servants. The only significant group of immigrants were the Boo-Ra-Senokwe, who joined Mathakala during the time of Masilonyane Bakwena *kgosi* Kgari Sechele II, and who, despite their claim to have descended from Dithakong, were said to have been former servants by the Boo-Ra-Dithakong.

During my year of research in 1975, I lived in Ntloedibe. From my front porch, I could see the center of the Bakwena capital nestled on the side of a hill. As if to underscore their seniority and independence from the rest of Molepolole's Bakwena, Masilo's Bakwena built their *motse* on a slight rise some distance away from Masilonyane's Kgosing, separated by an expansive valley. When Sechele moved to Dithubaruba in the Dithejwane hills from 1852 to *c.*1865, the Boo-Ra-

Dithakong told me, Ntloedibe was situated to the west of Sechele's capital and between Dithubaruba and Mallakopie where the Boo-Ra-Tshosa lived. The Bakwena capital moved to Ntsweng near Molepolole in *c.*1865, and it appears that Ntloedibe moved with Masilonyane's Bakwena either to Ntsweng or to near Ntloedibe's current location. Around 1890, Masilo's Bakwena built their *motse* at its present site, making it the oldest, continually occupied section of Molepolole.[8]

Kgosing

Originally comprised only of the households of the Masilonyane Bakwena *kgosi* and his immediate circle of kin and servants, Kgosing acquired the features of a *motse* during the first half of the nineteenth century. Sechele's organization of immigrants into *makgotla* at Kgosing was still evident over a hundred years later when I visited the *motse* in 1975. I will describe, in alphabetical order, all of Kgosing's *makgotla* and their genealogies.

Basimane was an aggregation of three lineages, the Boo-Motlhabi, Boo-Mhiemang, and Boo-Moitlhobo, all of whom shared the same totem (*sereto*), the *phiri* (hyena). Both the Boo-Motlhabi and Boo-Mhiemang claimed seniority, and the latter denied a kinship with the former. All three lineages held that they were originally Bakwena who changed their totem from *kwena* (crocodile) to *phiri* (hyena) during the escape from wars in the Transvaal that led them to the Kweneng. But the evidence seems to suggest that the Boo-Motlhabi were the seniors in Basimane either because they joined the Bakwena before the Boo-Mhiemang or were of a senior line, and all three lineages were not Bakwena but Babolaongwe, a "Bakgalagadi" group, when they joined Motswasele (*a* Legwale). It also appears that the *kgotla* of Basimane was organized by Sechele, Motswasele's son, by bringing together divergent lineages under one administrative head. The Boo-Moitlhobo derived from Mhiemang's second household (*lelwapa*). The genealogies of Basimane's three sections, if the Boo-

---

[8]H/M/142; and H/M/143. From his observations made in 1972, the archaeologist R. Mason wrote that the "huts" and "general layout" of Ntloedibe were a "virtual duplicate" of parts of a Late Iron Age site at Platberg. R. J. Mason, "Background to the Transvaal Iron Age -- New Discoveries at Olifantspoort and Broederstroom," *Journal of the South African Institute of Mining and Metallurgy* 74:6 (January 1974).

Motlhabi and Boo-Mhiemang were not closely related, as I am inclined to believe, appear in Table 14.[9]

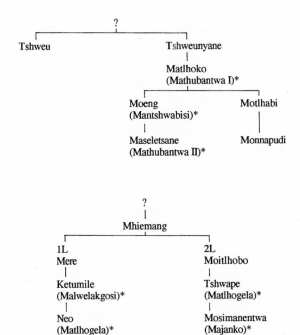

*Indicates *mophato*. See Appendix D.

Table 14. Basimane.

Bobididi was formed during Sechele's rule. The Babididi, whose totem was the *mhele* (water buck), were refugees fleeing from the Ndebele from an area east of the Bangwato. They came as a fairly large group and so were divided by Sechele into two sections, the senior Boo-Ra-Sekgwa whom he kept at Kgosing and the Boo-Ra-Ramasuana whom he assigned to Ntlheng-ya Tlhase. The Babididi came with skills as *dingaka* (doctors), both seers and healers, and as rainmakers (*baroka ba pula*), and consequently grew wealthy plying those trades and their *makgotla* grew in size. Administrative changes altered the kinship arrangements. Before Ntlheng-ya Tlhase's organization as a formal section

[9]H/M/105; H/M/113; H/M/114; and H/M/121. During *kgosi* Kgari, a man and his wife,

(*motse*), appeals arising within Goo-Ra-Ramasuana were taken for a hearing at
Goo-Ra-Sekgwa, and the former brought their first-fruits (*dikgafela*) to the latter,
but after Ntlheng-ya Tlhase's constitution as a separate *motse*, the Boo-Ra-
Ramasuana took their cases to that *motse*'s *kgosi* and their first-fruits directly to
the Bakwena *kgosi* at Kgosing.   When Moitelosilo, *kgosi* Sebele (*a* Sechele)'s
son, married, Sebele placed Bobididi under his direction, and henceforth the
people of that *kgotla* became known as *batho ba ga* Moitelosilo (the people of
Moitelosilo). Table 15 gives a version of the Boo-Ra-Sekgwa genealogy.[10]

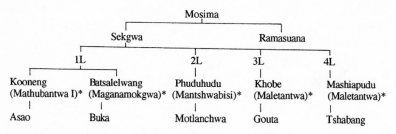

*Indicates *mophato*. See Appendix D.

Table 15. Bobididi.

Bokalaka was created by Sechele for Peshudi and Keleketu, who were
Bapedi refugees fleeing Afrikaners and the Ndebele. Both Peshudi and Keleketu
served as Sechele's herbalists (*dingaka*), but Peshudi eventually left to serve the
Bakgatla *kgosi* at Mochudi.   Other Bapedi immigrants, also refugees but who
arrived after Keleketu, the Boo-Ra-Koboatshwene, Boo-Ra-Malatsie, and Boo-
Ra-Kupane, were assigned to his *kgotla* called Bokalaka by Sechele's successor,
Sebele. Keleketu's genealogy appears in Table 16.[11]

Bakgatla Kgafela, joined the Boo-Motlhabi as immigrants.
[10]H/M/123.
[11]H/M/124.

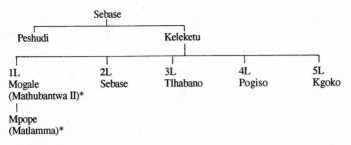

*Designates *mophato*. See Appendix D.

Table 16. Bokalaka.

Chadibe was established by Sechele for Mauana, a noted rainmaker (*moroka a pula*) from Chadibe, a village in Ga-Ngwato. The Bakwena *kgosi* had invited Mauana to serve him, and the Mongwato and his family moved to the Bakwena capital. The *kgotla* Chadibe was placed under Tumagole, Sechele's son, and eventually under the *kgotla* of Senyadimana in Kgosing. Table 17 gives Mauana's genealogy.[12]

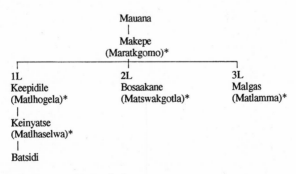

*Indicates *mophato*. See Appendix D.

Table 17. Chadibe.

Difetlhamolelo was created by Sechele for Segakisa, son of a "Mokgalagadi" servant, Rampena, and the *kgosi*'s counselor (*ntona*) overseeing Kgosing. Segakisa had been among the Bakwena delegation sent to accompany

---

[12]H/M/123.

Sechele back to the Kweneng following his release by the Makololo, and he
served the young *kgosi* well in many ways. His *kgotla*, thus, was named
Difetlhamolelo from *fetlha* ("to rub together") and *molelo* (heat or fire), meaning
persons who made the fire. The Boo-Ra-Kgalaeng, members of the core
Bakwena *bana ba* Motshodi cluster and the former masters of Rampena in
Ntlheng-ya Godimo, joined Segakisa's Difetlhamolelo at Kgosing.   There,
although retaining their hereditary seniority, the Boo-Ra-Kgalaeng were
subordinate to Segakisa and his successors. Similarly, the Boo-Ra-Nkane, Bakaa
immigrants, were moved from Goo-Ra-Tshosa in Ntlheng-ya Godimo to
Difetlhamolelo when Sechele created Segakisa's *kgotla*. Genealogies of the Boo-
Ra-Segakisa and Boo-Ra-Kgalaeng appear in Table 18.[13]

---

[13]The Boo-Ra-Segakisa have sought to erase their "Bakgalagadi" ethnicity by claiming to
have been born of Motshodi like their Boo-Ra-Kgalaeng subordinates. H/M/53; H/M/127;
H/M/129; and H/M/149.

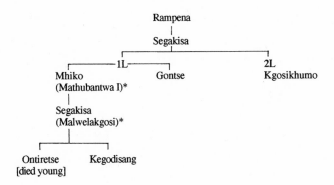

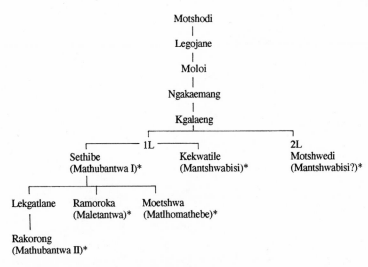

*Indicates *mophato*. See Appendix D.

Table 18. Difetlhamolelo.

Dikoloi was formed by Bakwena *kgosi* Kealeboga for his son, Sebele, by joining five separate groups, including Bakgatla, Bangwaketse, Bamalete, and Bakaa, into one *kgotla*. Of those groups, the Boo-Pule were the most senior having been the first to arrive during the time of Sechele, followed by the Bangwaketse, the Bamalete who immigrated during Sebele (*a* Sechele), and the Bakaa, the Boo-Morubisi who fled the Kgatleng during wars with the Afrikaners.

A fifth group, the Boo-Nope, were taken from the section (*motse*) Mokgalo, and moved to Dikoloi by Kealeboga. The *kgotla* was headed by Sebele (*a* Kealeboga), then Mosarwa, Sebele's younger brother, and finally by Kealetsang of the Boo-Pule. Brief genealogies of the Bakgatla Boo-Pule and Bakaa Boo-Morubisi appear in Table 19.[14]

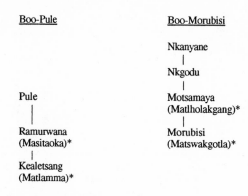

Boo-Pule	Boo-Morubisi
	Nkanyane
	|
	Nkgodu
	|
Pule	Motsamaya
|	(Matlholakgang)*
	|
Ramurwana	Morubisi
(Masitaoka)*	(Matswakgotla)*
|	
Kealetsang	
(Matlamma)*	

*Indicates *mophato*. See Appendix D.

Table 19. Dikoloi.

Ga-Mangwato was established by Bakwena *kgosi* Kealeboga after a visit from Mokutswane, a Mongwato, who brought him a servant, Rabaloi. Before Mokutswane returned to Ga-Ngwato, Kealeboga asked Rabaloi to remain among the Bakwena, because the servant was a gifted farmer and could grow European vegetables. Rabaloi agreed to stay, and Kealeboga gave him his own *kgotla*, that was later merged with Goo-Meje and Goo-Ra-Molefe to constitute Goo-Ra-Letlamma for his son. The Boo-Ra-Masuga, immigrants from Ga-Ngwato, joined Rabaloi's Ga-Mangwato. Table 20 shows Rabaloi's line.[15]

---

[14]H/M/115.
[15]H/M/122.

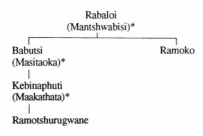

*Designates *mophato*. See Appendix D.

Table 20. Ga-Mangwato.

Ga-Maribana was created by Sechele for Magogwe, his counselor (*ntona*) who was responsible for Ntlheng-ya Tlhase and his herbalist (*ngaka e chochwa*) who specialized in making "medicine" (*peku*) for soldiers. The Boo-Ra-Magogwe were a section of the original Bakwena who had separated from Mogopa in the Transvaal during the early eighteenth century, but who had remained behind when Kgabo's group headed farther west, ostensibly to hunt for a species of red buck (*phala*). The people were thus called the "Baphalane," when they rejoined the Bakwena in the Kweneng possibly during the rule of Motswasele (*a* Legojane).   When Sechele became the *kgosi*, he split the Baphalane, leaving the Boo-Ra-Magogwe in their own *kgotla*, Ga-Maribana, and sending the others into Ga-Ranta, Goo-Kotwane, and Goo-Tsatsinyana in Ntlheng-ya Tlhase. Magogwe's *kgotla* received its name from Sechele because Magogwe, the story goes, had the audacity to pay a fine at the *kgosi's* *kgotla* with the short-horned variety of cattle instead of the usual long-horned type. Sechele, upon accepting the grudging payment, remarked that Magogwe had brought him "cattle with little, downturned horns that hid the face" (*dikgomo tsa maribanyana*), and so declared that his *kgotla* would be known as "Maribana."   Within Ga-Maribana were immigrants: the Boo-Ra-Mokone, who joined the *kgotla* from Ntloedibe during Sechele; the Boo-Ra-Monong, who came from Majatsi in Ntlheng-ya Godimo during Sechele; the Boo-Ra-Diphelesa, Balete who were with the Boo-Ra-Magogwe before they joined Sechele's Bakwena; and the Boo-Ra-

Mapharane, who came from Ga-Ngwato during Sebele (*a* Sechele). Magogwe's genealogy appears on Table 21.[16]

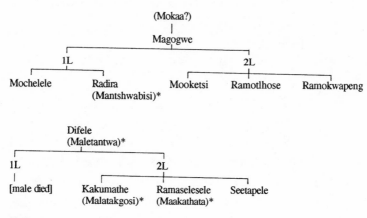

*Indicates *mophato*. See Appendix D.

Table 21. Ga-Maribana.

Ga-Morwa was formed by Sechele for his son, Kgari. The *kgotla*, although headed by Kgari, consisted of the households (*malwapa*) of his immediate family, but mainly of immigrants who were attached to Ga-Morwa. After Sechele's death, the struggle between Kgari and Sebele (*a* Sechele) and the accession of Sebele to the *bogosi*, Ga-Morwa was placed under the ruling Bakwena *kgosi* and contained only immigrants, because of the flight and exile of Kgari and his followers. After Baaname's return during Sebele (*a* Sechele)'s rule, Ga-Morwa was given back to Kgari's heirs. Originally, the *kgotla* was known as Disimakgosi, after the name of the cattle given to Kgari by Sechele at the *kgotla*'s formation. In 1975, Disimakgosi referred only to the central circle (*sebeso*), while the *kgotla* as a whole was called Ga-Morwa. The most prominent immigrants within Ga-Morwa were the Balete of Baga-Rakubu, Boo-Ra-Dikomane, and Boo-Ra-Mogaladi, who were already with the Bakwena in the years following Motswasele (*a* Legwale)'s assassination. Mogaladi, the most junior of the three, was Sechele's personal servant, and was given to Kgari when the *kgosi* created Ga-Morwa. Rakubu, the most senior of the brothers, asked to

---

[16]H/M/2; H/M/118; H/M/119; and H/M/125.

move from Mokgalo to Kgari's *kgotla* so he could join his kin. Two other immigrant lineages, the Boo-Ra-Nyetse and Boo-Ra-Koeshwang, became members of Ga-Morwa through the activities of the three brothers. Dikomane and Mogaladi were Sechele's messengers, and in the course of their travels met the Boo-Ra-Nyetse who were Bakaa displaced by wars and who returned with them to the Bakwena capital. Appeals arising from Goo-Ra-Nyetse were taken first to Goo-Ra-Dikomane and then to Disimakgosi. Koeshwang was captured by Mogaladi during a war campaign. Sechele assigned Koeshwang to Mogaladi who treated him like a son, and the Boo-Ra-Koeshwang adopted the cow (*kgomo*) as their totem (*sereto*), Mogaladi's totem. The final immigrant group within Ga-Morwa were the Boo-Ra-Chaka, Ndebele who joined Baaname during his years of exile and who accompanied him on his return to the Bakwena. Table 22 shows the heads of Ga-Morwa.[17]

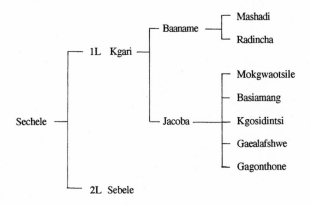

Table 22. Ga-Morwa.

Ga-Mosima was established by Sechele for his close confidant, Tsotso. During the years of dispersion following the assassination of Motswasele (*a Legwale*), when a Bakwena section, the Boo-Moitonyane, sought refuge in Ga-Tawana, they met and took in Tsotso, an Ndebele skilled in making earrings and bracelets and possibly a doctor (*ngaka*) or military tactician. Tsotso accompanied

---

[17]H/M/126.

the Boo-Moitonyane, upon their return to the Kweneng, after Sechele's accession
to the *bogosi*, and his fame and wealth grew as a metal worker or doctor and
soldier among the Bakwena. Sechele created Ga-Mosima for Tsotso by bringing
together several lineages, including the Boo-Kgabo, core Bakwena and
descendants of Tebele of the *bana ba* Motswasele cluster, and immigrant Bakwena
who were some of the offspring of Kodisa, Bolele, and Bolelenyane. The Boo-
Kodisa, Boo-Bolele, and Boo-Bolelenyane were among a large group of
Bakwena, descendants and peoples of Kgabo (*ya molelo*), who were made
refugees by the *difaqane* and Afrikaner advance in the Transvaal and who joined
Sechele's Bakwena at Tshonwane. Sechele divided them into several groups and
placed them within Ga-Mosima and Goo-Mabe in Kgosing and Goo-Kodisa and
Goo-Dinti in Ntlheng-ya Godimo. Apparently after Tsotso's death, neither of his
sons, Ngwanang and Ntloakhumo, was able to hold Ga-Mosima against the
ambitions of the Boo-Kgabo of Tebele who became the heads of Tsotso's *kgotla*.
His displaced lineage moved to Ntlheng-ya Godimo where they formed the Goo-
Ra-Suna *kgotla*, named for "Sune," after the nickname of Bolelenyane to whom
they were related by marriage.[18]

Ga-Sikwa consisted only of the Basikwa descendants of its founder
Ruele, who received his *kgotla* from Sechele. Like the Bakwena of Kgabo (*ya
molelo*), large numbers of Basikwa joined the Bakwena possibly as several mass
infusions, and were divided and allocated to various *makgotla* to reduce their
potential for collective revolt.   Thus, Basikwa were found in Ga-Sikwa,
Difetlhamolelo, and Senyadimana in Kgosing, Ga-Sikwa, Goo-Kotwane, Goo-
Moloi, and Goo-Tsatsinyana in Ntlheng-ya Tlhase, and Goo-Ra-Rambinyana in
Mokgalo. Ruele's group apparently arrived during Motswasele (*a Legwale*)'s
rule, although his genealogy, given in Table 23, does not appear to extend back
that far.[19]

---

[18] I believe that the *kgotla*'s name was chosen to disguise its founders' Ndebele origins and
to attach Tsotso's lineage to a Bakwena and hence more prestigious line. See, Okihiro,
"Genealogical Research," pp. 54-61; and H/M/64; H/M/81; H/M/83; H/M/86; H/M/87;
and H/M/93.

[19] H/M/125.

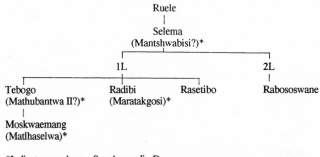

*Indicates *mophato*. See Appendix D.

Table 23. Ga-Sikwa.

Goo-Mabe was created by Sechele for the Boo-Mabe, juniors of the Boo-Kodisa of Ga-Mosima of Kgosing and Goo-Kodisa of Ntlheng-ya Godimo. Within Goo-Mabe were three lineages of Bakwena of Kgabo (*ya molelo*), in order of seniority, the Boo-Mabe, Boo-Digobe, and Boo-Konono. Mabe's genealogy appears in Table 24.[20]

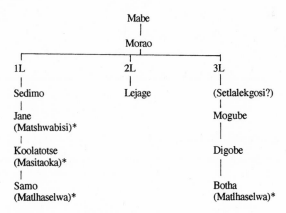

*Indicates *mophato*. See Appendix D.

Table 24. Goo-Mabe.

[20]H/M/58; H/M/79; H/M/83; H/M/87; and H/M/88.

Goo-Meje began as a *kgotla* in Mokgalo. The Boo-Meje were Bakgatla Kgafela who left Kgatleng because of a family conflict and immigrated during the time of Bakwena *kgosi* Sebele (*a* Sechele), who placed them under Kgosidintsi's Mokgalo. When *kgosi* Kealeboga created Goo-Ra-Letlamma for his son, he extracted Goo-Meje from Mokgalo and moved it to Kgosing. Table 25 provides a version of Meje's genealogy.[21]

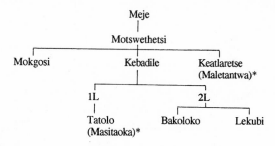

*Indicates *mophato*. See Appendix D.

Table 25. Goo Meje.

Goo-Molale was probably created by Motswasele (*a* Legojane). Its core consisted of Bakubung immigrants who came from the east led by Moeng. The immigrants were scattered throughout the Bakwena capital, but their senior lineage, the Boo-Moeng, were allowed to form their own *kgotla*. Goo-Molale, it was said, received its name from one of its leaders who had a habit of holding his head up when speaking, which became the basis of a popular song composed by women that gave the *kgotla* and its leader a nickname, "Molale," from *go lelala* or "to look upwards." Ketshabile, perhaps the best known of the Boo-Moeng, served Sechele as the *ntona* in charge of Ntlheng-ya Godimo. A genealogy of the Bakubung senior lineage appears in Table 26.[22]

---

[21]H/M/122.
[22]H/M/119.

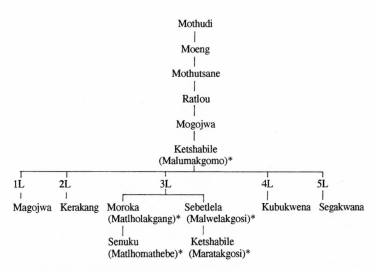

Mothudi
|
Moeng
|
Mothutsane
|
Ratlou
|
Mogojwa
|
Ketshabile
(Malumakgomo)*

1L	2L	3L		4L	5L
Magojwa	Kerakang	Moroka (Matlholakgang)*	Sebetlela (Malwelakgosi)*	Kubukwena	Segakwana
		Senuku (Matlhomathebe)*	Ketshabile (Maratakgosi)*		

*Designates *mophato*. See Appendix D.

Table 26. Goo-Molale.

Goo-Pula was established by Sechele for the Bakwena Mogopa who arrived as a large group fleeing Afrikaner expansion into the Transvaal. The Boo-Pula were particularly sought out by Sechele because they were renowned rainmakers (*baroka ba pula*). A more senior group of Bakwena Mogopa went to the Bakgatla at Mochudi where they constituted the *kgotla* called Tshukudu. As rainmakers, herbalists (*dingaka ya chochwa*), and seers (*dingaka ya marapo*), the Boo-Pula became wealthy and their *kgotla* grew in size. During the Kgari and Sebele dispute, however, Goo-Pula diminished, and a section returned to the Bakwena Mogopa at Phokeng. Immigrants within Goo-Pula included: the Boo-Ra-Modise, Balete who joined during Sechele and who were the seniors of the Boo-Ra-Keetile of Mokgalo; the Boo-Ra-Kgalaeng, Bakgatla Kgafela who immigrated during Kealeboga; and the Boo-Ra-Pantse, Bangwato and recent arrivals from the Goo-Modibedi *kgotla* in Ntlheng-ya Godimo. Table 27 gives the genealogy of the Boo-Pula.[23]

---

[23]H/M/93; H/M/104; H/M/108; and H/M/111.

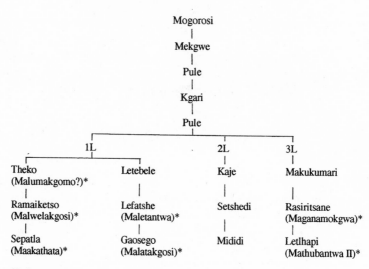

*Indicates *mophato*. See Appendix D.

Table 27. Goo-Pula.

Goo-Ra-Letlamma, comprised of the formerly independent *makgotla* Ga-Mangwato, Goo-Meje, and Goo-Ra-Molefe, disintegrated after the death of *kgosi* Kealeboga's son, Letlamma, for whom the *kgotla* was created and who died without a male heir.[24]

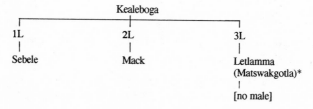

*Designates *mophato*. See Appendix D.

Table 28. Goo-Ra-Letlamma.

---

[24]H/M/122.

Goo-Ra-Mochina was probably created by Sechele who attacked, scattered, and absorbed several of the Bakwena groups that remained in the Transvaal to hunt red buck, the thusly named Baphalane. It appears that the Boo-Ra-Mochina were of a different lineage from the Baphalane of Ga-Maribana who had joined the Bakwena earlier, during the rule of Motswasele (*a* Legojane). During their flight, the Boo-Ra-Mochina sought refuge among the Batlokwa of Gaborone where they received from the Batlokwa *kgosi* the Boo-Ra-Rakgagana who became their *baagedi* (immigrants) and later their relatives through marriage. When the Boo-Ra-Mochina moved to Sechele's capital, likely under Mochina (*a* Taukobong), the Boo-Ra-Rakgagana became members of their *kgotla*. Table 29 lists the line of Boo-Ra-Mochina heads.[25]

Modimosane
|
Motlako
|
Taukobong
|
Mochina
(Mapenapena?)*
|
Sepotlo
(Mantshwabisi)*
|
Sibisibi
(Malwelakgosi)*
|
Mochina
(Maakathata)*

*Designates *mophato*. See Appendix D.

Table 29. Goo-Ra-Mochina.

Goo-Ra-Molefe was formed by Sechele as a reward for Rankuba, a Motlokwa who had distinguished himself in battle. Rankuba's Batlokwa had probably attached themselves to the Boo-Kodisa, Bakwena of Kgabo (*ya molelo*) who fled the Transvaal for Sechele's capital during the *difaqane* upheavals. They

---

[25]H/M/102; H/M/103; and H/M/125.

were accordingly subordinate members of the *kgotla* Goo-Kodisa in Ntlheng-ya Godimo when they first arrived, but moved to their newly created *kgotla* at Kgosing after Rankuba's promotion.   Molefe, Rankuba's son, however, conducted the affairs of the *kgotla* because of his father's advanced age, and thus the *kgotla* was named after him. Later, during Kealeboga's rule, Goo-Ra-Molefe was transferred, along with Ga-Mangwato and Goo-Meje, to Goo-Ra-Letlamma. Rankuba's line appears in Table 30.[26]

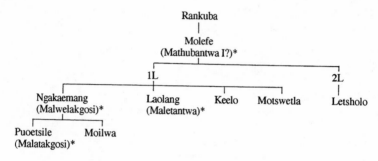

*Indicates *mophato*. See Appendix D.

Table 30. Goo-Ra-Molefe.

Goo-Ra-Molese was created by Sechele for his junior uncle who had refused to relinquish the *bogosi* to him after his release from captivity by the Ndebele. Molese's control over his Bakwena faction ended when his people favored Sechele's return in *c.* 1831.   Intent at first on exiling the rebellious Molese, Sechele instead decided to subordinate the Boo-Ra-Molese to demonstrate that he had vanquished them. Goo-Ra-Molese, thus, became subject to another *kgotla*, Senyadima, instead of being placed directly under the Bakwena *kgosi*. Senyadima was the *kgotla* of Mosimane, a cousin of Sechele and his supporter during his years of exile, who had recommended against exiling Molese. To illustrate the animosity directed at the Boo-Ra-Molese by the *kgosi*, Sechele's son and heir, Sebele, ordered the Boo-Ra-Molese to bring him animal skins through their seniors, the Boo-Ra-Mosimane, in the same way the Bakwena directed their

---

[26]H/M/122.

"Bakgalagadi" servants.   Consequently, Goo-Ra-Molese failed to thrive and grow. Molese's simplified genealogy appears in Table 31.[27]

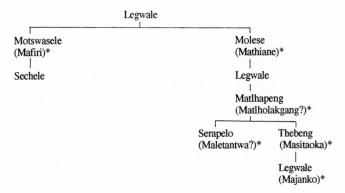

*Indicates *mophato*. See Appendix D.

Table 31. Goo-Ra-Molese.

Kgatleng was formed during Sebele (*a* Kealeboga) for the Boo-Luke, Bakgatla immigrants from Moshupa who left their kin because of a family dispute. They said that they came "seeking peace." Table 32 shows the genealogy of the Boo-Luke.[28]

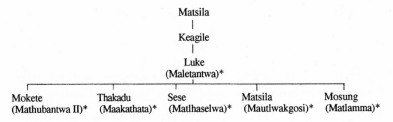

*Indicates *mophato*. See Appendix D.

Table 32. Kgatleng.

---

[27]H/M/105; and H/M/118.
[28]H/M/122.

Masilwana was created before 1852 by Sechele perhaps to connect the Bakwena of Masilo with his Masilonyane line by bringing together immigrant groups under a Masilo head within his section (*motse*). Given the opportunity, Mogotsi left his kin at Ntloedibe and headed Masilwana at Kgosing, that consisted of the Boo-Ra-Tshomane, Balete who had joined Motswasele (*a* Legwale)'s Bakwena following a succession dispute, and probably the Boo-Ra-Mokwatse, Ndebele who had immigrated during Sechele's rule. During the 1852 Afrikaner sacking of Sechele's town at Dimawe, Mogotsi was taken captive and in his absence Tshomane headed Masilwana. Mogotsi regained the *kgotla*'s leadership when he somehow managed to return to the Bakwena, but he lost it permanently after Sechele gave Masilwana to his junior son, Motsatsi.[29] Thereafter, the Boo-Ra-Mogotsi paid tax (*sehuba*) to the Boo-Ra-Motsatsi, their hereditary juniors, which might have been a part of Sechele's plan to absorb and ultimately subjugate the Bakwena of Masilo. During Sebele (*a* Sechele)'s time, the Boo-Ra-Kolane, breakaway Bakwena who left because of the Kgari and Sebele succession dispute, rejoined Sebele's Bakwena and became members of Masilwana, and the Boo-Ra-Mosimanyana who immigrated as a single family of Basikwa were directed to Motsatsi's *kgotla*. The Boo-Ra-Segadimo, Bakgatla Manaana, left Moshupa because of overcrowding and insufficient pastures for their cattle, and joined Masilwana during *kgosi* Kealeboga.[30]

Maulana was formed by Sebele (*a* Sechele) for his junior uncle, Kwenagaeratwe, by assembling immigrant groups, including the Boo-Ra-Dikoko, Boo-Ra-Lelokwane, and Boo-Ra-Molaodi who were taken from Goo-Maoto in Ntlheng-ya Tlhase. After Seabe, Maulana was given over to Kenalekgosi, a son of Kebohula, a junior brother of *kgosi* Kealeboga. A genealogy of Kwenagaeratwe appears in Table 33.[31]

---

[29]Motsatsi probably received his *kgotla* after 1877, the approximate year he was initiated into the Maratakgomo *mophato*.
[30]H/M/88.
[31]H/M/131.

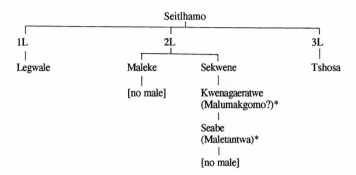

*Indicates *mophato*. See Appendix D.

Table 33. Maulana.

Motonya was constituted by either Sechele or his son, Sebele, for Sekwene, a junior son of Motswasele (*a* Legwale). Like Maulana, the *kgotla* was formed by the *kgosi* for a male member of his royal family by bringing together disparate immigrant lineages. Motonya consisted of Sekwene and his family, and immigrant groups including the Boo-Ra-Mokao, Bakgatla Manaana who joined Sechele as a single man, the Boo-Ra-Sebuo, Balete who were perhaps driven to Sechele because of wars, and the Boo-Ra-Lebelwana, Bakaa whose origins were unclear. Table 34 provides a genealogy of Sekwene and his male descendants.[32]

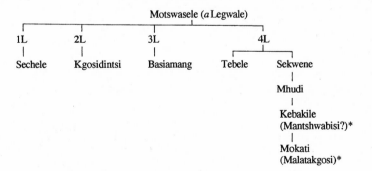

*Indicates *mophato*. See Appendix D.

Table 34. Motonya.

---

[32]H/M/41; H/M/89; H/M/93; and H/M/116.

Senyadima was originally a *kgotla* in Ntlheng-ya Tlhase, along with the other *makgotla* of the *barwa* Motswasele cluster there, perhaps founded by Mothee. During the rule of Motswasele (*a* Legwale), immigrants, the Basikwa of Namaneatau, were placed under the jurisdiction of Senyadima. Mosimane, son of Mothee and Sechele's cousin, had supported the *kgosi* throughout the succession crisis following the assassination of Sechele's father, Motswasele (*a* Legwale). He became a trusted advisor to Sechele, who annexed Senyadima, moving it from Ntlheng-ya Tlhase to Kgosing, and appointed Mosimane to serve as the *ntona* in charge of Mokgalo. At Kgosing, Mosimane created a *kgotla* for his junior brother, Mmutlanyane, saying that the *kgotla* would serve as a pillow for his head. Thus, he named it "Sekamelo," from *go sekama*, meaning to recline or lay down one's head. Immigrants attached to Sekamelo included the Boo-Ra-Gabaitse, Bakwena from Goo-Moloi who married into Sekamelo, and the Boo-Ra-Keabadile, Bakgatla who likewise married into the Boo-Ra-Mmutlanyane. Table 35 reveals the genealogy of Senyadima and Sekamelo.[33]

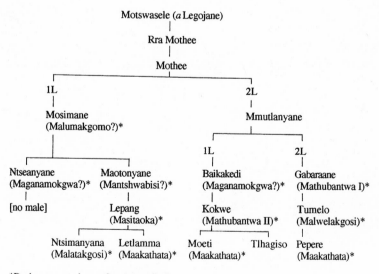

*Designates *mophato*. See Appendix D.

Table 35. Senyadima and Sekamelo.

---

[33]H/M/105. See also, H/M/2 and H/M/118.

Senyadimana was created by Sechele for his son, Tumagole, by extracting Namaneatau's Basikwa from Senyadima, and by adding other immigrants, the Boo-Ra-Modise and Boo-Ra-Sekonopelo, to the *kgotla*. The Boo-Ra-Modise were Bapedi who had likely attached themselves to the Bakwena, called Baphalane, who were attacked and scattered by Sechele. Like the Boo-Ra-Mochina Baphalane, the Boo-Ra-Modise made their way to the Kweneng after Sechele's expansionist attempt to reunite the Bakwena. When Tumagole died, without a male heir, Phetogo, his senior daughter inherited Senyadimana and directed that her male descendants administer the *kgotla*. Chadibe had likewise been placed under Tumagole's direction, and upon his death, Ramakukwana, the son of Namaneatau became Chadibe's head, and after Ramakukwana, the *kgotla* passed to his son, Basimane, and after Basimane, Chadibe passed over to Sekonopelo of the Boo-Ra-Sekonopelo. Besides all originating from Senyadimana, Ramakukwana, Basimane, and Sekonopelo were the chief herders of the Bakwena *kgosi*'s cattle at two outposts in the desert.[34]

Ntlheng-ya Tlhase

The *barwa* Kgabo cluster, comprised of Ramonamane's Maunatlala and Seitlhamo's Goo-Ra-Seitlhamo, settled away from Kgosing at a place called Ntlheng-ya Tlhase or "the lower side" probably during their father's lifetime in the early eighteenth century. About 150 years later, during Sechele's rule, Goo-Ra-Seitlhamo separated into two *makgotla* called Goo-Ra-Monametsana and Goo-Ra-Thipe. A genealogy of the *barwa* Kgabo appears in Table 36.[35]

---

[34]H/M/102; H/M/123; and H/M/125.
[35]H/M/107; H/M/109; H/M/110; and H/M/112.

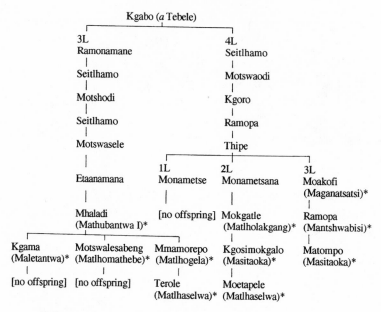

*Indicates *mophato*. See Appendix D.

Table 36. The *barwa* Kgabo.

The *barwa* Kgabo were followed generationally by the *bana ba* Motshodi who settled in Ntlheng-ya Godimo or "the upper side," and after the *bana ba* Motshodi, by the *barwa* Motswasele (*a* Legojane) comprised of Rra Mothee,[36] Kgaimena, Mapaletsa,[37] and Modise, who formed the *makgotla* of Senyadima and Sekamelo, Goo-Ra-Kgaimena, Goo-Ra-Ntsono, and Goo-Ra-Ramabinyana respectively and joined the *barwa* Kgabo in Ntlheng-ya Tlhase.[38] A genealogy of the *barwa* Motswasele (*a* Legojane) appears in Table 37.[39]

---

[36]Not an actual name, as explained page 10, notes 13 and 14.

[37]Cf. Schapera's, *Ditirafalo*, p. 37 and *Praise-Poems*, p. 122, where he incorrectly places Ntsono as the son of Mostwasele (*a* Legojane). Instead, Ntsono was the son of Moikabe and the contemporary of Kgaimena (*a* Motshwane), not Kgaimena (*a* Motswasele). See genealogy of the *barwa* Motswasele (*a* Legojane).

[38]On Senyadima and Sekamelo, see a discussion of them under Kgosing.

[39]H/M/49; H/M/51; H/M/52; H/M/61; H/M/98; H/M/99; H/M/105; and H/M/152.

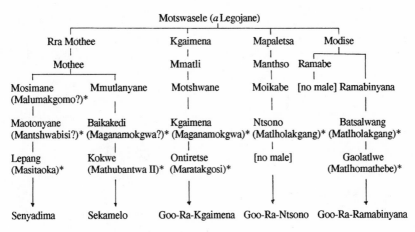

*Indicates *mophato*. See Appendix D.

Table 37. The *barwa* Motswasele (*a* Legojane).

Independent of each other, the *barwa* Kgabo and *barwa* Motswasele conducted their own affairs subject to the hierarchies within each cluster and ultimately to the Bakwena *kgosi* at Kgosing. During the breakup caused by Motswasele (*a* Legwale)'s assassination in *c.*1822, Goo-Moloi, Goo-Moloinyana, and Goo-Moitoi of the *bana ba* Motshodi cluster separated from their kin who had sided with the Boo-Ra-Tshosa faction of Bakwena and joined the *barwa* Kgabo as "immigrants" (*baagedi*). Although genealogically senior to the *barwa* Kgabo, the *bana ba* Motshodi became subordinate to the former because of their move to Ntlheng-ya Tlhase. Bataung immigrants, the Boo-Ra-Mabote, from Goo-Maoto of the *bana ba* Motshodi took refuge among the *barwa* Kgabo and assumed the *kgotla* name, Goo-Maoto, of their former Bakwena heads.[40] Those movements added to the size and influence of the *barwa* Kgabo in relation to their seniors in Ntlheng-ya Tlhase, the *barwa* Motswasele.

Sechele contributed to the decline of the *barwa* Motswasele by taking its senior *kgotla*, Senyadima, and annexing it to Kgosing when he appointed its head, Mosimane, to serve as his counselor (*ntona*). Sechele also removed Ramabinyana from Ntlheng-ya Tlhase and placed the *kgotla* within Kgosidintsi's

---

[40]For a fuller description of the *bana ba* Motshodi, see the discussion of Ntlheng-ya Godimo.

section (*motse*), Mokgalo. As a consequence, Maunatlala, head of the *barwa* Kgabo, assumed preeminence within Ntlheng-ya Tlhase, despite its genealogically inferior standing among several of the *makgotla* of "the lower side." Even though capital, labor, and historical circumstance commonly superceded kinship, descent, and gender as the determinants of privilege and dominance, the head of Maunatlala at the time of my visit in 1975 fabricated and tried to have others affirm genealogies for the *kgotla* that legitimated his lineage's seniority, as defined by kinship and descent, in Ntlheng-ya Tlhase.[41] Of the several possible readings of that attempt to reshape the past by Maunatlala's head, I believe that the colonizers' (and complicit researchers') uses of kinship in distinguishing group membership, determining "legitimacy," and assigning privilege must be among the leading factors prompting that response.

Besides the Bataung of Goo-Maoto, immigrants increased the numbers and diversity of peoples in Ntlheng-ya Tlhase. The Boo-Moloi were joined, during the time of Sechele, by Basikwa, who possessed skills as doctors (*bongaka*).[42] And the Boo-Moitoi brought with them, when they joined Ntlheng-ya Tlhase, "immigrants" like the Boo-Ra-Legakwa who claimed to have been Masilo Bakwena from Ntloedibe and who attached themselves to Goo-Moitoi during Motswasele (*a* Legwale). Legakwa, during Sechele's rule, was apparently so popular that he eclipsed and was sometimes mistakenly referred to as the head of Goo-Moitoi.[43] Bataung, possibly from Ntlheng-ya Godimo's Goo-Thato, were members of Goo-Moitoi perhaps since the time of Sechele, and during Sebele (*a* Sechele)'s reign, the Boo-Tsatsinyana and Boo-Kotwane, Bapedi lineages, joined Goo-Moitoi. These Bapedi were likely once members of Keleketu's Bapedi, who were refugees of Afrikaner expansion into the northern Transvaal and who formed the Kgosing *kgotla*, Bokalaka. Like the Boo-Ra-Legakwa, the Boo-Dijo were Masilo Bakwena, offspring of Ntloedibe's Boo-Ra-Moeng, who moved to Goo-Moitoi and although genealogically senior, subjected themselves to the Bakwena of Masilonyane. Because the Boo-Dijo were the most recent "immigrants" to Goo-Moitoi, having joined the *kgotla* after the Kgari-

---

[41]See my "Unraveling Maunatlala and Ntlheng-ya Tlhase," an unpublished paper in my files.
[42]H/M/127.

Sebele succession dispute, they were the most junior of Goo-Moitoi's immigrants.[44]

Goo-Moitoi was accordingly a complex grouping of *makgotla*. It consisted of the central *kgotla* of Goo-Moitoi (also referred to as Ga-Khunou and Goo-Motlana), surrounded by immigrant *makgotla*, in order of seniority, Goo-Ra Legakwa, Taung, Goo-Tsatsinyana, Goo-Kotwane, and Goo-Dijo. Goo-Moitoi itself was an immigrant *kgotla* in Ntlheng-ya Tlhase, having moved from Ntlheng-ya Godimo and joined the *barwa* Kgabo. Simplified genealogies of Goo-Moitoi's immigrants appear in Table 38.

Boo-Ra-Legakwa	Taung	Boo-Tsatsinyana	Boo-Kotwane	Boo-Dijo
				Tebele
				|
Moratletli	Nchomane			Molomologi
|	|			|
Montsho	Moeng	Tsatsinyana	Molosi	Nthiba
|	|	|	|	|
Legakwa	Dinku	Photonono	Tlhale	Moremong
(Mathubantwa I)*	(Mathubantwa I?)*	(Maganatsatsi)*	(Maganatsatsi?)*	(Maganatsatsi)*
|	|	|	|	|
Gaotlhobogwe	Katane	Daniele	Kgositlhadi	Motlhabane
(Matlhomathebe)*	(Mantshwabisi)*	(Malwelakgosi)*	(Maganamokgwa)*	(Mantshwabisi)*
|	|	|	|	|
Kodinthane	Godisamang	Kenathebe	Molamu	Tshegetsang
(Maakathata)*	(Masitaoka)*		(Mathubantwa II)*	

*Designates *mophato*. See Appendix D.

Table 38. Immigrant *Makgotla* in Goo-Moitoi.

Bobididi and Bokaa were large immigrant *makgotla* in Ntlheng-ya Tlhase that were independent and subject only to Kgosing's Bakwena *kgosi*. Ntlheng-ya Tlhase's Bobididi was an offshoot of Kgosing's Bobididi comprised of the Boo-Ra-Ramasuana. Bokaa arose from immigrants who were originally Barolong, but who became known as the Bakaa, having changed their totem (*sereto*) from the Barolong iron (*tshipi*) to the elephant (*tlou*).[45] The Bakaa joined Motswasele (*a*

---

[43]H/M/140.

[44]H/M/112; H/M/117; H/M/140; and H/M/142.

[45]According to an "informant," the name "Bakaa" came from people who saw their deserted villages and asked, "*ba kae*" (or "where are they")? H/M/112. See also, Wookey, *Ditsho*, p. 82; and Thomas Tlou and Alec Campbell, *History of Botswana* (Gaborone:

Legwale)'s Bakwena, settling at Mopane and working iron from mines at Ntsweng, Thobokwe, and Magokotswane.[46]　The 1822 invasion of Mma Ntatisi's "Mantatees" who later split and a section became Sebetwane's Makololo drove the Bakwena and Bakaa into the Kalahari desert, and when a group of Bakaa returned to the Kweneng in 1849, they found Sechele's Bakwena at Kolobeng.[47] Their numbers increased Sechele's people by about one-third, and thus posed a significant presence. Because of their importance to their hosts as skilled workers of iron, the Bakaa remained intact as a group, even recognized by some as a "nation" (*morafe*) subject only to the Bakwena *kgosi*. Bokaa included immigrants like the Boo-Ra-Masimega who originated from Ga-Tawana and had attached themselves to the Bakaa while the latter were in Ga-Ngwato.[48] Table 39 gives a genealogy of the Bakaa *dikgosi*.[49]

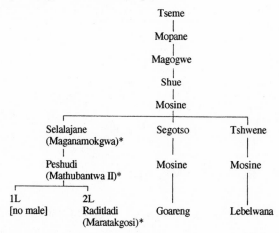

*Indicates *mophato*. See Appendix D.

Table 39. Bokaa.

Macmillan Botswana, 1984), p. 67.

[46]H/M/117. See also, I. Schapera, ed., *David Livingstone Family Letters, 1841-1856*, 2 vols. (London: Chatto & Windus, 1959), 1, p. 214.

[47]Wookey, *Ditsho*, p. 51; I. Schapera, ed., *Livingstone's Missionary Correspondence, 1841-1856* (Berkeley: University of California Press, 1961), p. 127; and Schapera, *Family Letters*, 1, pp. 213-214.

[48]H/M/117.

[49]H/M/112. Wookey's *Ditsho*, p. 82 supplies a different genealogy that extends from Mosine *a* Shue back thirteen generations.

Ntlheng-ya Tlhase, comprised of the *barwa* Kgabo, the *barwa* Motswasele (*a* Legojane), and the breakaway *makgotla* of the *bana ba* Moshodi clusters together with their immigrant *makgotla* and Bobididi and Bokaa, was from the time of Sechele during the mid-nineteenth century to Kgari in the mid-twentieth century simply a location within the Bakwena capital wherein clusters and *makgotla* stood independent of one another and subordinate only to Kgosing's *kgosi*. The genealogically junior Maunatlala, head of the *barwa* Kgabo, gradually grew in size and wealth, leading Kgari to place formally the *barwa* Motswasele (*a* Legojane) and *bana ba* Motshodi *makgotla* and Bobididi, but not Bokaa, under Maunatlala's jurisdiction. Ntlheng-ya Tlhase, thus, was organized into a section (*motse*) -- an administrative unit -- only in about 1950, whereby Maunatlala's head served as Ntlheng-ya Tlhase's *kgosi*, and judicial appeals moved from *kgotla* to cluster to Maunatlala.

Ntlheng-ya Godimo

The *bana ba* Motshodi cluster formed the beginning of Ntlheng-ya Godimo "the upper side," with Maoto and his *kgotla*, Goo-Ra-Maoto, as the most senior men of the cluster, its head. Legojane, the biological progenitor of the cluster and Motshodi, fathered Maoto, Moloi, Tshube, Serojane, and Rra Motshodi. Those sons their sons established the *makgotla* of the *bana ba* Motshodi: Maoto (Goo-Ma Letsholo (Goo-Moloi), Sereto (Goo-Moloinyana), Khunou (Goo-Moitoi, also c Goo-Motlana, named for Khunou's senior brothers who had no heir, and Ga-Khun Moitoinyana (Goo-Moitoinyana), Serojane (Mogogoru), Phatswane (Goo-Molepol and Tlhobosi (Goo-Mosarwa). The genealogy of the *bana ba* Motshodi, in Tabl shows the lineages of those *makgotla*.

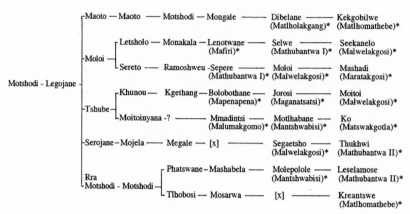

*Indicates *mophato*. See Appendix D.

Table 40. *Makgotla* of the *bana ba* Motshodi.

Before Motshodi's death, a large contingent of Bataung, refugees of war, joined his Bakwena. The *kgosi* placed them in Ntlheng-ya Godimo, but divided them into three groups. The most senior lineage, the Boo-Thato, was permitted to form its own *kgotla* called Goo-Thato under the jurisdiction of Goo-Maoto, a second group, the Boo-Ra-Mabote, were absorbed directly into Goo-Maoto, and a third group was placed under Tshube and his senior son, Moitoi.

During Motswasele (*a* Legojane), Maoto, according to one version, was discredited by jealous uncles, and was forced to go into exile, and in another version, Maoto left when the Bakwena had been scattered by war.[50] Whatever the cause, Maoto settled among the Bangwaketse, but his Bataung, the Boo-Ra-Mabote, remained with the Bakwena and moved from Ntlheng-ya Godimo to Ntlheng-ya Tlhase, where they assumed the *kgotla* name of Goo-Maoto. At Ga-Ngwaketse, Maoto's sons, Dibelane and Sennanyana, struggled over the ownership of their father's substantial *kgotla*, and Sennanyana, although of the second household (*lelwapa*), was born of a Mongwaketse mother and was hence favored over Dibelane whose mother was a Mokwena. Dibelane and his faction of Boo-Maoto returned to the Bakwena after about sixty years of absence, and

---

[50]Schapera, *Ditirafalo*, pp. 38-39; and H/M/65.

became members of Kgakge's Goo-Ra-Tshosa perhaps because Dibelane's mother was the daughter of Pati, Tshosa's brother.[51]

During those intervening years, the *bana ba* Seitlhamo cluster comprised of Tshosa's Goo-Ra-Tshosa, Senese's Matlhalerwa, Mothoabo's Majatsie, and Legojane's Goo-Ra-Mmoopi had joined the *bana ba* Motshodi cluster at Ntlheng-ya Godimo. Goo-Moloi replaced the absent Boo-Maoto as the head of the *bana ba* Motshodi cluster of *makgotla*, and Tshosa's power rose when he served as regent for the young *kgosi*, Motswasele (*a* Legwale). After Motswasele's assassination and the fracturing of the Bakwena in *c.*1822, Ntlheng-ya Godimo's *makgotla* were divided, Goo-Moloi, Goo-Moloinyana, Goo-Moitoi of the *bana ba* Motshodi cluster siding with Segokotlo's faction of Bakwena and leaving the *bana ba* Seitlhamo, but the remaining *bana ba* Motshodi, Goo-Moitoinyana, Mogogoru, Goo-Molepolole, and Goo-Mosarwa, staying with Tshosa's group.

When Kgakge brought the final remnants of the Boo-Ra-Tshosa to join Sechele's Bakwena at Dithubaruba in 1853, his section had evolved into a unitary assemblage of *makgotla* under the leadership of the Goo-Ra-Tshosa *kgosi*. The location of Kgakge's town at Mallakopie, built to the west of Sechele's settlement at Dithubaruba, seemed to underscore its independence, along with Ntloedibe, situated between Mallakopie and Dithubaruba, and Kgosidintsi's town, later called Mokgalo, rising in the valley below Sechele's town. Table 41 shows the descent of the *makgotla* of the *bana ba* Seitlhamo who were the most senior members of Ntlheng-ya Godimo.

---

[51]H/M/65.

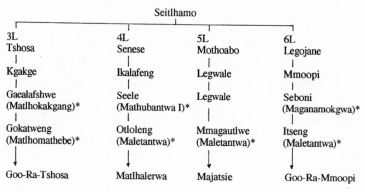

*Indicates *mophato*. See Appendix D.

Table 41. *Makgotla* of the *bana ba* Seitlhamo.

Goo-Ra-Tshosa functioned as the kgosing of Ntlheng-ya Godimo beginning in *c.*1822, and was led successively by Tshosa, Moruakgomo, Bubi, Kgakge, Gaealafshwe, Gokatweng, Barileng, Maothwanong, Samokwati, and Oatlhotse in 1975. The central circle of the *kgotla* included the households of the *kgosi* and his wife/wives and their children, and a few of the *kgosi*'s brothers and uncles and his advisors and servants. Forming a second circle around the *sebeso* were the *makgotla* of junior brothers and uncles together with their immigrants and servants, and the independent immigrant *makgotla*. A genealogy of the Boo-Ra-Tshosa appears in Table 42.

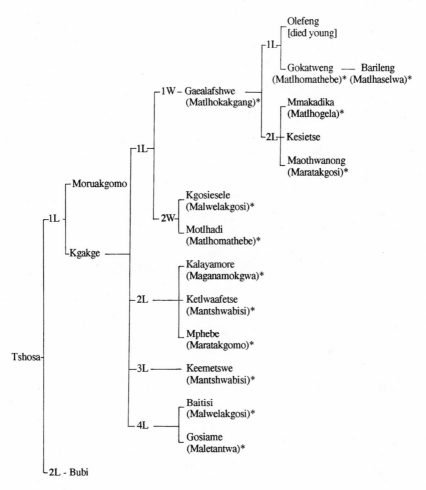

*Designates *mophato*. See Appendix D.

Table 42. Goo-Ra-Tshosa.

Gaealafshwe was *kgosi* of the Boo-Ra-Tshosa from *c.*1881 when his father, Kgakge, died to *c.*1914 when he died. In 1900, Ntlheng-ya Godimo moved from Ntsweng to Borakalalo because of overcrowding. Within Goo-Ra-Tshosa's inner circle at Borakalalo were the households of the *kgosi*, his two wives, and their minor children, Gokatweng, Mmakadika, Kesietse, and Maothwanong. Facing the cattle kraal (*lesaka*) at the circle's center, to

Gaealafshwe's right was the household of his junior brother, Motlhadi, and to his left, those of Kgosiesele and Mphebe. Kgosiesele was Gaealafshwe's *monna kgosi* whose responsibilities included presiding over the affairs of the *kgotla* in the *kgosi*'s absence, serving as principal advisor to the *kgosi*, and installing the *kgosi*'s successor. Kgakge, his father, had placed under Kgosiesele a Balete immigrant group, the Boo-Ra-Tiroakgosi, that had moved from Ga-Morwa at Kgosing to Ntlheng-ya Godimo because of a family dispute. Motlhadi was Gaealafshwe's *mogakolodi* or acting *kgosi*, like the *monna kgosi*, and head of a group of advisors called *ditshotshoma*. Toward the opposite side of the circle were the households of Bathokebafe, a nephew of Gaealafshwe, Baeti, a Mokgatla immigrant who had been designated for Mmakadika when he established his own *kgotla*, Lee, a "Mokgalagadi" servant and the *kgotla*'s fire starter, Ratshiping, a Mokalaka who came with Kgosiesele's wife, Kolojwane, from Ga-Ngwato as a wedding "gift" (*ketleetso*), and Mosarwa, a servant who had accompanied Dibelane's return from Ga-Ngwaketse.[52]

Around Goo-Ra-Tshosa's inner circle were the *makgotla* of the *kgosi*'s junior relations and immigrants (*baagedi*). Kalayamore's *kgotla*, named Dilemana, was situated to the west of his brother Gaealafshwe's Goo-Ra-Tshosa, and consisted of his households and those of the Boo-Ra-Ramonyama, Bakwena originally from another *kgotla* but moved by Sechele to serve as his tax collectors in Dilemana, and the Boo-Ra-Sefako, who were Balete immigrants allocated to Kalayamore by his father, Kgakge.[53] Ketlwaafetse, Kalayamore's junior brother of the same *lelwapa*, did not remain in Dilemana but left the Bakwena with Kgari and his followers and settled among the Bangwato after the Kgari and Sebele succession dispute.[54]

Keemetswe, the only son of Kgakge's third household (*lelwapa*), built his *kgotla* to the east of Goo-Ra-Tshosa with Bakgatla Kgafela immigrants allocated to him by his father. Joining the Bakwena before the time of Kgakge, Keemetswe's Bakgatla Kgafela included the Boo-Ra-Modumwa, the most senior

---

[52]H/M/56; H/M/61; H/M/62; and H/M/104.
[53]H/M/56; H/M/68; and H/M/71.
[54]H/M/56.

and first to immigrate, and the Boo-Ra-Kapo and Boo-Ra-Baori who came as a single group but who separated after having arrived.[55]

Baitisi, the senior son of Kgakge's fourth household (*lelwapa*), and his brother, Gosiame, erected their *kgotla*, Maseka, to the north of Goo-Ra-Tshosa. As people for his *kgotla*, the Boo-Ra-Thebe, Bakaa immigrants who arrived during Kgakge's rule, were given to Baitisi by the *kgosi*. Thebe had three sons, Goetsuetsile, Didimalang, and Mapulana, all of whom built their households (*malwapa*) within Maseka.[56]

Gaealafshwe, Kgakge's senior son and successor, created the *kgotla* Mopotologo for Mokgoko (*a* Mauana), one of his father's advisors (*ditshotshoma*), and placed it to the south of Goo-Ra-Tshosa. His lineage, called the Boo-Ra-Mpe, named for his grandfather, stemmed from the Bataung of the *kgotla* Ga-Khunou (also called Goo-Moitoi) in Ntlheng-ya Tlhase. The Boo-Ra-Mpe apparently moved from Ntlheng-ya Tlhase to Kgosing at the beckoning of Bakwena *kgosi* Seitlhamo, and after Motswasele's assassination, they joined Tshosa's faction and Mpe became one of Tshosa's advisors. At Mopotologo's creation, Gaealafshwe allocated the Boo-Ra-Keaketswe, Boo-Ra-Kuduga, and Boo-Ra-Tsiang to Mokgoko (*a* Mauana). All immigrants, the Boo-Ra-Keaketswe originated from Sekonopelo's people in Senyadimana at Kgosing, but who separated from the Bakwena during the chaotic years following Motswasele's assassination and who eventually joined Kgakge's Boo-Ra-Tshosa. The Boo-Ra-Kuduga were probably among the Bakgatla Mmanaana who fled to Sechele for protection in 1852, joining the Bakwena at Dimawe, and the Boo-Ra-Tsiang were originally servants of the Bangwaketse, joined Mosielele's Bakgatla Mmanaana during the *difaqane*, distinguished themselves in battle and became full-fledged Bakgatla, and accompanied the Bakgatla to Sechele's Bakwena when they were made refugees by the wars. They finally became members of Kgakge's Goo-Ra-Tshosa, and were allocated to Mokgoko (*a* Mauana). A genealogy of the Boo-Ra-Mpe appears in Table 43.[57]

---

[55]H/M/76.

[56]H/M/54; and H/M/68.

[57]H/M/48; H/M/55; and H/M/76.

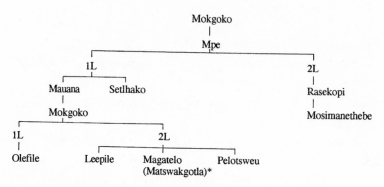

*Designates *mophato*. See Appendix D.

Table 43. Mopotologo.

Between those four *makgotla* that had been positioned at the cardinal points of the compass and along the arc that circled Goo-Ra-Tshosa were the *makgotla* and households of immigrants. The Boo-Ra-Mabokane were Balete from Ramoutswa who left their homes during the *difaqane*, joined the Bakwena, and were separated by Sechele whereby the senior Boo-Ra-Kerang were placed within Mokgalo, the Boo-Ra-Kusi within Kgosing, and Boo-Ra-Mabokane to Kgakge.[58]

Dikgori was formed by Kgakge by merging three immigrant lineages into one *kgotla*, and it was diminished and reconstituted by Gaealafshwe, his son. The most senior lineage were the Boo-Ra-Koosentse, Bangwaketse who were perhaps the first to join the Bakwena, and the Boo-Ra-Dimpe and Boo-Ra-Setilo, Bakgatla Kgafela who were refugees of the *difaqane* and were allocated by Sechele to Kgakge. Gaealafshwe, in creating a new *kgotla* for his junior son Mmakadika, removed Baeti and Kudu of the Boo-Ra-Dimpe and Senwedi of the Boo-Ra-Setilo from Dikgori. Thoisi of the Dimpe line, along with others of the Boo-Ra-Setilo, remained in Dikgori. Thoisi's wife, Mogatsasekgwa, reared her brother, Gofetakgosi, who had been orphaned by the death of their parents when he was about six years old. Masimega, their father, was originally from

---

[58]H.M.55.

Ntloedibe and the son of Morakile, a Masilo Mokwena, but who moved to Masilwana at Kgosing. When Gofetakgosi came of age, Gaealafshwe placed him directly under Goo-Ra-Tshosa, but under Gokatweng, the son and successor of Gaealafshwe, Gofetakgosi received his own *kgotla* called Goo-Morakile, along with Baeti and Kudu taken from Mmakadika and Lepodisi, a Mongwato who had once served Gaealafshwe.[59]

Goo-Ra-Tshosa's internal spatial arrangement was based on general principles that applied to the Ntlheng-ya Godimo section (*motse*) as a whole. As the most senior *kgotla*, Goo-Ra-Tshosa was situated in Ntlheng-ya Godimo's center during the time of Gaealafshwe at Borakalalo, and the other *makgotla* of its cluster, the *bana ba* Seitlhamo, were located at the cardinal points of the compass with Matlhalerwa to its north, Majatsie to the east, and Goo-Ra-Mmoopi to the west. Mogogoru of the *bana ba* Motshodi cluster guarded the south. Like Ntloedibe and unlike Kgosing where kinship was not the basic organizing principle of the section (*motse*), clusters generally formed settlement aggregations. The *makgotla* of the *bana ba* Seitlhamo and *bana ba* Motshodi, accordingly, were grouped together in one area of Ntlheng-ya Godimo, including those of the *bana ba* Kgabo (*ya molelo*) group, comprised of Goo-Kodisa and Goo-Dinti, and the immigrant *makgotla*, Goo-Thato and Goo-Modibedi.

Matlhalerwa was the name of the cattle given by the Bakwena *kgosi* Seitlhamo to his son, Senese, to establish the *kgotla*. Senese had two sons of different households (*malwapa*) Sebekedi and Ikalafeng. Although senior, Sebekedi was passed over for Ikalafeng during the succession possibly because Sebekedi's mother was a Mongwaketse and Ikalafeng's, a Mokwena. The situation appears to have been a mirror image of the succession struggle between Dibelane and Sennanyana, Maoto's sons, at Ga-Ngwaketse. Senese died in battle against the Bangwaketse, and Matlhalerwa's people likely met and voted to install Ikalafeng as his successor. Sechele's return from captivity and the reunion of the Boo-Ra-Tshosa with his Bakwena provided both the new *kgosi* and Sebekedi with an opportunity to even the score against their foes. It seems that Sebekedi told Sechele about the secret location of his father's grave, and the Bakwena *kgosi* passed on the information to the Bangwaketse who unearthed Senese's body parts

---

[59]H/M/54; H/M/56; H/M/62; and H/M/76.

to make medicine (*peku*) against Matlhalerwa's Boo-Ra-Tshosa.[60] Table 44 gives a genealogy of the Boo-Ra-Senese.

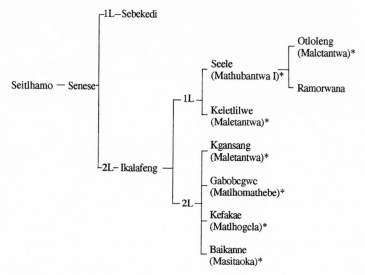

*Indicates *mophato*. See Appendix D.

Table 44. Matlhalerwa.

Immigrants constituted a considerable portion of Matlhalerwa. Those forming *makgotla* included the Boo-Ra-Mongalo, Bakgatla Kgafela, who immigrated during the time of Senese, and the Boo-Ra-Tshwene, Bakgatla Manaana, who joined the Boo-Ra-Tshosa during Ikalafeng's rule. Their *kgotla*, named Ga-Morokgotso, was given by Ikalafeng because, he said, the cattle he set aside to establish Ga-Morokgotso was for the upkeep of the *kgotla*'s orphans. (*Maradu* were cattle given to people for their upkeep.) The Boo-Ra-Motlhakane, originally Bahurutshe but who later adopted the totem (*sereto*) of the Bakgatla, were refugees from the Transvaal Afrikaners arriving during the time of Ikalafeng. The Boo-Ra-Segadimo, perhaps Bapedi, had attached themselves to the Boo-Kodisa and immigrated with their hosts to Sechele's Bakwena about the mid-nineteenth century. When Sechele divided the Boo-Kodisa, a large and highly

---

[60]Okihiro, "Genealogical Research," pp. 53-54.

organized group of Bakwena immigrants, the Boo-Ra-Segadimo were transferred to Matlhalerwa. A family, the Boo-Ra-Molefe, was separated from the Boo-Ra-Segadimo and placed within Matlhalerwa's center (*sebeso*). The Boo-Ra-Seisela, like the Boo-Ra-Segadimo but their seniors, were Bapedi immigrants of the Boo-Kodisa who were given over to Matlhalerwa by Sechele, and the Boo-Ra-Mogapi were the most junior of Matlhalerwa's three Bapedi *makgotla*. The Boo-Ra-Motlhabane, Bakwena Mogopa, joined the Boo-Ra-Tshosa during the time of Senese.

Others of Matlhalerwa's immigrants constituting single households included the Boo-Ra-Molefe, Bapedi subordinates of the Boo-Kodisa like the Boo-Ra-Seisela, Boo-Ra-Segadimo, and Boo-Ra-Mogapi, and the Boo-Ra-Moeng, Balete who immigrated during the time of *kgosi* Sebele (*a* Sechele) because of rinderpest and drought. The Boo-Ra-Leio were Bakgatla Manaana who joined the Boo-Ra-Tshosa with the Boo-Ra-Tshwene, and the Boo-Ra-Serurubele, Bataung who came to Matlhalerwa as a "gift" (*ketleetso*) when Ikalafeng married a daughter of Makgasane, the head of Goo-Thato at the time.[61]

Majatsie followed Goo-Ra-Tshosa and Matlhalerwa in Ntlheng-ya Godimo's order of seniority, and like Matlhalerwa its name derived from the cattle given by Bakwena *kgosi* Seitlhamo to his son, Mothoabo, at the *kgotla*'s establishment. Later, Tselaakwena of the junior line contested Kgwakgwa's leadership of Majatsie, and Goo-Ra-Tshosa's *kgosi* Gokatweng mediated, giving Tselaakwena his own *kgotla*, called Mogochwana, but making it subject to Kgwakgwa's Majatsie. A genealogy of Majatsie appears in Table 45.

---

[61]H/M/80.

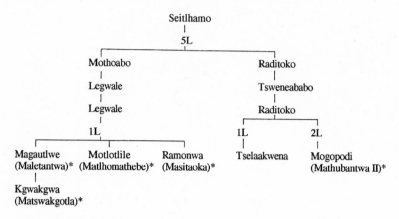

*Indicates *mophato*. See Appendix D.

Table 45. Majatsie.

        Majatsie's immigrants included the Boo-Ra-Gobolang, who were possibly
of the same Bakgalagadi group as the Baphiring in Basimane and Difetlhamolelo
in Kgosing, and who immigrated during the rule of Bakwena *kgosi* Seitlhamo.
The Boo-Ra-Gobolang were led by Mashongwe whose father was Mmutlana and
whose successor was Ditau who had Gobolang (Matlholakgang *mophato*) who
had Phokojwane (Masitaoka *mophato*) who had Ramadia (Maakathata *mophato*).
The Boo-Ra-Sebetlele, Bakgatla Manaana, were war refugees who joined
Mothoabo when Sebetlele's father, Tlhogoame met Mothoabo. Sebetlele served as
advisor to Majatsie's heads, Legwale (*a* Legwale) and Magautlwe. The Boo-Ra-
Seithiketso, Barolong and led by Peloang, attached themselves to Tsweneababo
who had fled to Kudumane after Sechele's defeat of Kgakge.   The Boo-Ra-
Seithiketso became members of Sechele's Bakwena when Tsweneababo rejoined
Kgakge's Boo-Ra-Tshosa at Mallakopie. The Boo-Ra-Molokwe were among the
Babididi who arrived during Sechele's rule, and who were divided between the
makgotla of Bobididi in Kgosing and Ntlheng-ya Tlhase. The Boo-Ra-Molokwe
joined Majatsie during Legwale (*a* Legwale).[62]

―――――――――――――――――

[62]H/M/74; and H/M/75.

Goo-Ra-Mmoopi was the most junior of the *bana ba* Seitlhamo *makgotla*, and it was led by Mmoopi instead of his senior brother Mosimanegape because, it seems, the latter disliked his leadership responsibilities and voluntarily handed over the office to the former. When the Bakwena *kgosi* Kealeboga took a portion of the people with him to Ntsweng after his divorce of Phetogo, Martinus of Seboni's second wife took the opportunity to establish his own *kgotla* by accompanying Kealeboga's faction unlike the majority of the Bakwena, including the people of Ntlheng-ya Godimo who remained at Borakalalo. Table 46 gives a genealogy of the Boo-Ra-Mmoopi.[63]

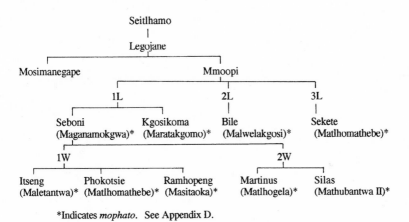

*Indicates *mophato*. See Appendix D.

Table 46. Goo-Ra-Mmoopi.

Ntlheng-ya Godimo's *bana ba* Motshodi were led probably since *c*.1828 by the *kgotla* Mogogoru, because its seniors, Goo-Moloi, Goo-Moloinyana, and Goo-Moitoi had sided with Segokotlo after Motswasele's assassination and joined Ntlheng-ya Tlhase, and because Goo-Maoto had dissolved after Maoto's exile in Ga-Ngwaketse, and even after his son Dibelane's return to the Boo-Ra-Tshosa, the Boo-Maoto became immigrants within the *kgotla* of Goo-Ra-Tshosa and did not reestablish their own *kgotla*. And although the Boo-Moitoinyana had originally remained with the Boo-Ra-Tshosa after Motswasele's death, they subsequently fled for Ga-Tawana and only returned after the Bakwena had been

[63]Okihiro, "Genealogical Research," pp. 48-51.

reunited under Sechele in 1853.   When they rejoined Ntlheng-ya Godimo, Serojane's *kgotla*, Mogogoru, had assumed the leadership of the *bana ba* Motshodi cluster. A genealogy of the Boo-Ra-Serojane appears in Table 47.[64]

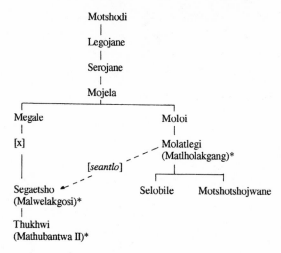

*Designates *mophato*. See Appendix D.

Table 47. Mogogoru.

Mogogoru consisted of an inner circle of Bakwena, that included Serojane's line of Boo-Ra-Segaetsho and Boo-Ra-Molatlegi, along with the Boo-Ra-Segajana, descendants of Moloi, the father of Molatlegi, the Boo-Ra-Mantshima, believed to be Bakwena but without an apparent connection with Serojane, and the Boo-Ra-Molatlo, who were originally from Ntlheng-ya Tlhase and placed in Mogogoru by Sechele to serve as his tax collectors. Megale had no sons, but his brother's son, Molatlegi, with Megale's wife had Segaetsho through a practice called *seantlo*, and Molatlegi served as regent until Segaetsho reached adulthood and again was regent for the young Thukhwi after Segaetsho died. Molatlegi became Sechele's tax collector following the Bakwena *kgosi's* dismissal of Molatlo because of incompetence, and in *c.* 1916, while serving as regent for the minor Thukhwi, Molatlegi broke away from Mogogoru and established his

---

[64]H/M/59; H/M/60; and H/M/68.

own *kgotla*. The Boo-Ra-Molatlo joined the splinter group called the Boo-Ra-Morwang, but Molatlegi's people and *kgotla* remained subordinate to Mogogoru.[65]

Besides the Boo-Ra-Molatlo, there were other immigrant groups within Mogogoru. The Boo-Ra-Molele, Bakubung from Kgosing's Goo-Molale, the Boo-Ra-Mochumisi, Bakaa who first settled among the Bahurutshe of Mankgodi and later joined Segaetsho because of Afrikaner raids, and the Boo-Ra-Molobeng, Balete from Kgosing's Ga-Morwa who became members of Mogogoru after the Kgari and Sebele succession dispute and Kgari's exile. The Boo-Ra-Batlhopang were Bakgatla from Moshupa, and the Boo-Ra-Matlhabaphiri, Bapedi who were related to the Boo-Tsatsinyana and Boo-Kotwane of Goo-Moitoi (also called Ga-Khunou) in Ntlheng-ya Tlhase and the Boo-Keleketu of Kgosing's Bokalaka.[66]

Goo-Molepolole was the next in order of seniority among the *bana ba* Motshodi cluster of *makgotla*. During the time of Bakwena *kgosi* Kgari, the local British commissioner tried to simplify the collection of taxes by merging smaller *makgotla* to create fewer units. As a result, Goo-Molepolole was administratively subsumed under its junior but larger brother, Goo-Mosarwa, allowing the latter to claim seniority over the former.[67] Instead, Goo-Molepolole was often called Mogogorwane, indicating its junior but paired relation with Mogogoru, and unlike its senior and junior *makgotla*, Goo-Molepolole had no immigrants except for one family and was thus numerically small. But Goo-Molepolole was not always small, and it once had many immigrants. Thobega, the brother of the *kgotla*'s founder, Phatswane, my interviewees said, made medicine (*peku*) for himself, rather than for his people, and was suspected of being a witch or wizard (*moloi*). Consequently, people refused to live in Goo-Molepolole.[68]

Goo-Mosarwa, besides challenging Goo-Molepolole's dominance, was internally divided over seniority between two of its lineages. Because Mosarwa died before marriage, Mosarwane headed the *kgotla*. His son, Marokane, and the

---

[65]H/M/71.

[66]H/M/68.

[67]That colonial act and the subsequent claim of the Boo-Mosarwa might have led the anthropologist Isaac Schapera to record uncritically Tlhobosi and Goo-Mosarwa as the seniors of Serojane and Goo-Molepolole. See, Schapera, *Ditirafalo*, p. 37; and Okihiro, "Genealogical Research," p. 52.

woman to whom Mosarwa was engaged before his death produced a son,
Kerantswe, through *seantlo*. When Kerantswe reached adulthood, Mosarwane's
line refused to relinquish control over Goo-Mosarwa having headed it for years,
and to add to their claim, the Boo-Mosarwane were wealthier than Kerantswe's
people. Both sides agreed, however, that by rule (*ka Setswana*), Kerantswe was
the legitimate head of Goo-Mosarwa. Table 48 shows a genealogy of Goo-
Mosarwa.[69]

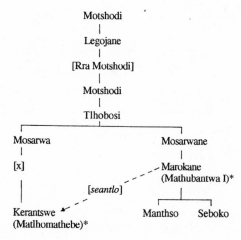

*Indicates *mophato*. See Appendix D.

Table 48. Goo-Mosarwa.

Unlike Goo-Molepolole, Goo-Mosarwa attracted many immigrants. The
Boo-Ra-Rakudu were Bakwena who were descendants of either Motshodi
(Legojane *a* Motshodi) or Mmoopi (Legojane *a* Seitlhamo). Rakudu's parents
died when he was a young boy, and the orphan was taken in and reared by
Marokane. The Boo-Ra-Rahube were Bapedi who, like the Boo-Ra-Modise of
Kgosing's Senyadimana, had attached themselves to the Baphalane, but unlike the
Boo-Ra-Modise who joined the Bakwena after Sechele's attack of them, the Boo-
Ra-Rahube were among the earlier group of Baphalane, like the Boo-Ra-

---

[68]H/M/60; and H/M/74.
[69]H/M/50; H/M/51; H/M/59; and H/M/60.

Magogwe of Kgosing's Ga-Maribana, who joined the Bakwena during Motswasele (a Legojane)'s rule. The Boo-Ra-Rahube were related to the Boo-Ra-Serojane of Mogogoru through marriage and were members of that *kgotla* before joining Goo-Mosarwa. The Boo-Ra-Motlola were Bakaa who perhaps immigrated as refugees of the *difaqane*, and the Boo-Ra-Ramapulana were Bapedi who were noted herbalists (*ngaka e chochwa*) who moved from Masilwana to Goo-Molepolole to Goo-Mosarwa. The Boo-Ra-Ntsilane (or Boo-Ra-Ratsie) were Bakgalagadi servants in Goo-Thato who came to Goo-Mosarwa as a "gift" (*ketleetso*) when a Boo-Thato woman married into Mosarwa's *kgotla*. The Boo-Mosarwa later assimilated the Boo-Ra-Ntsilane as immigrants (*baagedi*) rather than as servants (*batlhanka*), and the Boo-Ra-Ntsilane adopted the totem (*sereto*) of the Bakwena. Similarly, the Boo-Ra-Ramolekwa were Babididi servants in Masilwana who came to Goo-Mosarwa as a "gift" (*ketleetso*) when a Mokwena woman from that *kgotla* married Raborokwe, Marokane's junior brother. A final group, the Bahurutshe Boo-Ra-Ramagano were recent arrivals, during the time of Seboko, who left Manyana because of a family dispute over leadership.[70]

Ntlheng-ya Godimo was comprised of the *makgotla* of the Bakwena clusters, the *bana ba* Seitlhamo and *bana ba* Motshodi and their immigrants, and equally large *makgotla* consisting entirely of immigrants. Clustered to the east of the central Goo-Ra-Tshosa were the *makgotla* of the Bakwena of Kgabo (*ya molelo*), Goo-Kodisa and Goo-Dinti, who joined Sechele's Bakwena when they were at Tshonwane. Fleeing from Afrikaner expansion, the Boo-Kodisa arrived as a large, well-organized group, and many of the young men had been trained as soldiers. After the Afrikaner sacking of Sechele's town at Dimawe, the Boo-Kodisa left the Bakwena and established their own settlement on a hill called Goo-Kodisa near Moshupa. They later moved to Thamaga and rejoined Sechele at Dithubaruba. To break up their power, Sechele divided the Boo-Kodisa into several sections, sending the senior group to Kgakge who in turn subdivided them into Goo-Kodisa and Goo-Dinti, and retaining other sections in Kgosing placing them in Ga-Morwa, Ga-Mosima, and Goo-Mabe. The three major lineages within Ntlheng-ya Godimo were the Boo-Kodisa, Boo-Dinti, and Ba-Diphateletso.[71]

---

[70]H/M/76.
[71]H/M/56; and H/M/58.

To the west of Goo-Ra-Tshosa was a second cluster of immigrant *makgotla* consisting of the Bataung Boo-Thato and the Bangwato Boo-Modibedi. At Ga-Ngwato, Mmakgasane had two sons, Molete and Mokgadi, born of different households (*malwapa*). Molete died without an heir, and Mokgadi served as the *kgotla*'s head until Mathiba, Molete's son produced through a union of his wife and Mokgadi (*seantlo*), came of age. The succession, however, caused a split between followers of Mathiba and those of Mokgadi. Ultimately, Mathiba's people killed Mokgadi and Modibedi, Mokgadi's son, and his faction, including a number of their Bakgalagadi servants, fled to Sechele's Bakwena because Modibedi's mother was a sister of Sechele. The Bakwena *kgosi* handed the Boo-Modibedi to Kgakge in a act described by my Boo-Modibedi "informants" as "cowardly." Sechele, they contended, should have sheltered them at Kgosing instead of subjecting them to the Boo-Ra-Tshosa, the murderers of his and their mother's father. A genealogy of the Boo-Modibedi appears in Table 49.[72]

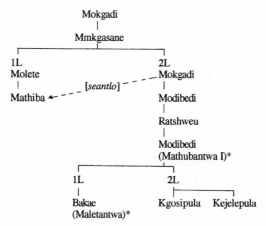

*Indicates *mophato*. See Appendix D.

Table 49. Goo-Modibedi.

----

[72]H/M/85.

Mokgalo

Like Ntloedibe, Mokgalo's core consisted of a single cluster, the *bana ba* Motswasele (*a* Legwale), headed by Kgosidintsi, Sechele's junior brother, and consisting of his *kgotla* Serame and those of his junior brothers Basiamang and Tebele, Moepetlo and Botlhajana, respectively. And like Ntlheng-ya Godimo, Mokgalo could have taken on the characteristics of a section (*motse*) and achieved administrative integrity during the years following Motswasele (*a* Legwale)'s assassination and the scattering of Masilonyane's Bakwena.[73] Mokgalo's name, derived from the *mokgalo* tree whose sturdy trunks and branches were used as fencing for homes, cattle kraals, and meeting places, suggests both the section's (*motse*) purpose and time of founding -- to ward off the enemies brought to the Kweneng by the *difaqane* and Afrikaner expansion.

Serame served as Mokgalo's kgosing, the section's (*motse*) highest court of appeal, and its head was Mokgalo's *kgosi*. Kgosidintsi, from Mokgalo's origin in the 1820s to about the 1890s, led the section (*motse*), and was succeeded by his senior son, Bakwena. Kgosidintsi's male offspring appear in Table 50.[74]

---

[73]H/M/93.
[74]H/M/89; and H/M/91.

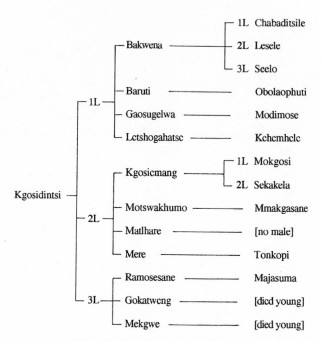

Table 50. Kgosidintsi's Male Offspring.

Bakwena's junior brothers, Baruti, Gaosugelwa, Kgosiemang, and Motswakhumo, formed secondary *makgotla* that, although ostensibly subordinate to Serame, rivalled and surpassed Mokgalo's center. Goo-Ra-Baruti consisted of the households of Baruti, said to have been more popular than Bakwena, his sons, and their immigrants, including the Boo-Ra-Tawana, Boo-Ra-Malekutu, Boo-Ra-Paledi, and Boo-Ra-Dikgang. The Boo-Ra-Tawana were Ndebele[75] who were displaced from the Nokabothete area because of war. Ngwako, their leader, became Sechele's rainmaker (*moroka a pula*) and some of his descendants remained in Kgosing's Difetlhamolelo, but his son, Sedimo, took a faction with him to Mokgalo, where Sedimo served as Kgosidintsi's messenger (*morongwa*) and the Boo-Ra-Tawana, as valued soldiers.[76] They named their *kgotla* Kgakisa.

---

[75]"Ndebele" might refer to any number of non-Batswana groups, and Wookey noted that the Boo-Ra-Tawana's totem (*sereto*), the *phareng* (a small lizard), belonged to the "Bakgalagadi." *Ditsho*, pp. 51-52.

[76]H/M/91.

The Boo-Ra-Malekutu or Boo-Ra-Mothudi were the offspring of the marriage of three Boo-Ra-Tawana daughters to men from Kgosing's Goo-Mabe who moved to settle with their wives' kin within Baruti's *kgotla*. I could not determine the origins of the Boo-Ra-Paledi or Boo-Ra-Radikgageng, except that they constituted a single family group whose totem (*sereto*) was the lion (*tau*), nor was I certain about the Boo-Ra-Dikgang's status as immigrants of Baruti or Gaosugelwa.[77]

Goo-Ra-Gaosugelwa consisted of Gaosugelwa's households along with those of his junior brother, Letshogahatse, and their male offspring. There were no immigrants within Goo-Ra-Gaosugelwa when I visited it in 1975.[78]

Kgosiemang's *kgotla*, called Mhuhutso, included immigrants like the Boo-Ra-Marumoagae, Boo-Ra-Sebeso, Boo-Ra-Molala, and Boo-Ra-Setlhomo. The Boo-Ra-Marumoagae were Bakwena from Tebele's Botlhajana who were placed under Tsotso's Ga-Mosima in Kgosing by Sechele, but who returned to Mokgalo probably after Tsotso's death. Table 51 gives a genealogy of the Boo-Ra-Marumoagae.[79]

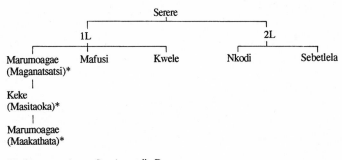

*Indicates *mophato*. See Appendix D.

Table 51. Boo-Ra-Marumoagae.

The Boo-Ra-Sebeso or Boo-Ra-Mosimanegape were perhaps Bapedi from Tlhabala, a place southwest of Serowe. Kgosidintsi, it appears, met and recruited them during the course of his travels, and assigned them to his son, Kgosiemang.

---

[77]H/M/93. It seems that the Boo-Ra-Paledi were originally Motswakhumo's immigrants who subsequently moved to join Baruti.
[78]H/M/93.

The Boo-Ra-Molala were Bakubung from the Kgosing *kgotla* of Goo-Molale, and the Boo-Ra-Setlhomo were "Ndebele."[80]

Although the most junior of Kgosidintsi's four sons who founded *makgotla*, Motswakhumo was the wealthiest and even equaled or exceeded Baruti's fame and influence. Motswakhumo generated his wealth through the Kalahari trade, impressing Bakgalagadi into service to acquire animal skins and trading those, sewn into karosses, for cattle. He moved some of his people to his cattlepost at Lentswe-le-Tau and transformed it into an important settlement in the Kweneng, and with his wealth employed and attracted a large following. Some of the immigrants of Goo-Ra-Motswakhumo included the Boo-Ra-Mareme, Boo-Ra-Mokone, and Boo-Ra-Setloung from Bokalaka, the "Ndebele" Boo-Ra-Obuseng and Boo-Ra-Mokgwaela, the Bahurutshe Boo-Ra-Ditue from Manyana, the Bapedi Boo-Ra-Molaisi, and Boo-Ra-Kebetle.[81] Of Kgosidintsi's sons, Motswakhumo had the most immigrants.

Moepetlo followed Kgosidintsi's *kgotla* Serame in order of seniority. Founded by Basiamang, Moepetlo was simple when compared with Serame. The *kgotla* consists of a single circle of households containing all of Basiamang's sons and their immigrants. A genealogy of Moepetlo appears in Table 52.[82]

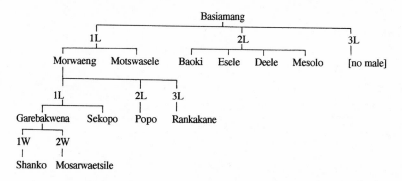

Table 52. Moepetlo.

---

[79]H/M/93; and H/M/150.
[80]See note 75. H/M/93.
[81]H/M/93.
[82]H/M/98.

Moepetlo's immigrants included the Boo-Ra-Mogotsi, Boo-Ra-Mese, Boo-Ra-Pusompe, and Boo-Ra-Mallane. The Boo-Ra-Mogotsi were Balete from Ramoutswa who attached themselves to Basiamang because of family conflict during the time of Sechele. The Boo-Ra-Mese and Boo-Ra-Pusompe immigrated during Sebele (*a* Sechele), the former having arrived as a single family from Swaziland and the latter, Bakaa related to the Boo-Ra-Sekonopelo of Kgosing's Senyadimana, having joined Moepetlo from Ga-Ngwato. The Boo-Ra-Mallane, some say, originated from Kgosing's Ga-Mosima.[83]

Botlhajana was established by Tebele, Mostwasele (*a* Legwale)'s son of his fourth household (*lelwapa*). Tebele's junior brother, Sekwene, was given his *kgotla*, Motonya, by either Sechele or Sebele (*a* Sechele) at Kgosing. Botlhajana, like Moepetlo, was not as large or complex as Kgosidinti's Serame. Table 53 gives a genealogy of Botlhajana.

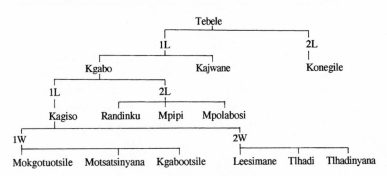

Table 53. Botlhajana.

Goo-Ra-Modise or Ramabinyana was a creation of Sechele, who moved this *kgotla* of the *barwa* Motswasele (*a* Legojane) from Ntlheng-ya Tlhase to Mokgalo. Modise and his people thereby became Kgosidintsi's "immigrants," but they retained their integrity as a *kgotla* subject to Mokgalo's *kgosi*. Goo-Ra-Modise's immigrants included people who accompanied them from Ntlheng-ya Tlhase and those who joined them since having moved to Mokgalo. The Boo-Ra-Magabala, Boo-Ra-Tauyabara, and Boo-Ra-Mokgosi were single families who were absorbed into Goo-Ra-Modise's inner circle (*sebeso*). The Boo-Ra-

---

[83]H/M/98.

Magabala were Basikwa, the Boo-Ra-Tauyabara's totem (*sereto*), like Motswakhumo's immigrants, the Boo-Ra-Setloung and Boo-Ra-Mareme, was the eland (*phofu*) and were said to have come from Bokalaka, and the Boo-Ra-Mokgosi came from Ntlheng-ya Tlhase's Ga-Khunou (or Goo-Moitoi or Goo-Motlana). The Boo-Ra-Kokorwe formed a *kgotla* attached to Goo-Ra-Modise called Maine. Judicial appeals from Maine were taken to Goo-Ra-Modise. The Boo-Ra-Kokorwe were Batshelwana or people whose totem (*sereto*) was the "tshelwana" or in Sekwena, "talabodiba," an insect that walks on water. The Batshelwana were likely dispersed by the *difaqane* or Afrikaner expansion in the Transvaal, some of whom joined the Balete at Ramoutswa and others like the Boo-Ra-Kokorwe moved farther west to Sechele's Bakwena at Dithubaruba. There were at least two lineages of Batshelwana in Maine, the senior Boo-Ra-Kokorwe and the Boo-Ra-Maine.[84]

Rules and Realities

My venture into genealogical research, nudged by my Bakwena teachers, impressed upon me the fundamental fact, almost trite in retrospect, that the realities on the ground were much more interesting and complex than the theoretical representations of those activities by British structural-functionalist anthropologists like Isaac Schapera whom I had long admired. Of course, we have since come a long way from Schapera's foundational studies in the work of Hoyt Alverson and John and Jean Comaroff,[85] and my recitation of genealogies appears positively archaic and regressive in comparison. But it seems to me that we have been engaged in a common project, contemporary ethnographers, cultural critics, and historians -- the location of ourselves as researchers and our responsibilities to our subject matter and our subjects, text and context. And like many others, having the luxury of a grain to go against, I have been more keenly

---

[84]H/M/150.

[85]See, e.g., Hoyt Alverson, *Mind in the Heart of Darkness: Value and Self-Identity Among the Tswana of Southern Africa* (New Haven: Yale University Press, 1978); Comaroff and Roberts, *Rules and Processes*; Jean Comaroff, *Body of Power, Spirit of Resistance: The Culture and History of a South African People* (Chicago: University of Chicago Press, 1985); and Jean and John Comaroff, *Of Revelation and Revolution: Christianity, Colonialism, and Consciousness in South Africa*, vol. 1 (Chicago:

attuned to the interruptions in the pattern, the cracks in the facade, the exceptions that make new rules than to the smooth surface of stability and order.

The Bakwena of Molepolole were not a homogeneous, descent grouping of kinfolk, but a heterogeneous aggregation of ethnically diverse people. Social hierarchies involved blood, gender, and birth order, but also class (including the ownership of capital, labor, and the relation to production, as well as possessing specialized skills) and historical conditions like migration and colonialism. Residential mobility, from one people (*morafe*) to another, from one section (*motse*) to another, from a *kgotla* to another, carried with it hierarchical consequences, and the colonizers' embrace of kinship and codification encouraged historical invention on the part of the colonized.

Structural diversity paralleled the people's ethnic diversity. *Makgotla* composition ranged from ones with only Bakwena to those with Bakwena and immigrants to ones with only immigrants, and they stood alone administratively or were nestled one within another. A *kgotla* might contain other *makgotla* within it, and residential movement might lead to judicial resolutions in one *kgotla* and political and economic responsibilities (like first-fruits and taxed labor) in another. Individual agency and particular moments and forces led to the divergent section (*motse*) forms. Ntloedibe and Mokgalo might be characterized as single cluster with immigrants sections, Kgosing, as an immigrants section, Ntlheng-ya Tlhase, as an unstructured, multiple clusters with immigrants section, and Ntlheng-ya Godimo, as a structured, multiple clusters with immigrants section.

Demographic and institutional changes were aspects of those historical trajectories, but also propelling, at base, that history were the material conditions of Bakwena life. In truth, I understand social relations as the manifestation of the relations of production.

University of Chicago Press, 1991).

3

The Social Formation

When I began my research in 1975, I knew, from my reading of nineteenth-century accounts and twentieth-century ethnographies and histories, that the Bakwena distinguished themselves from their neighbors -- the gathering and hunting San and the mainly pastoral Nguni -- by settling in stable and sprawling, kin-based "villages" and by carrying on a mixed economy of grains cultivation and cattle-keeping. But my surety began to crumble in the dry desert air. I confronted daily accounts supplied by my "informants" that eroded my foundations as quickly as my mind was capable of absorbing and recognizing their implications. Sometimes I was just lucky.

My stumble onto genealogical research was my first big break. When assembled, the genealogies provided me with a means by which to reconstruct Bakwena demographic and social history. The Bakwena didn't always number in the tens of thousands nor were they perpetually an unadulterated kinship group.[1] They began their independent existence as a mere handful, particularly after the Bangwato and Bangwaketse separated from them at the end of the eighteenth century, and the Bakwena, possibly as early as the mid-eighteenth century, absorbed large numbers of immigrants such that by the early nineteenth century they were far more numerous than the original Bakwena. I would later learn that those immigrants not only profoundly altered the size, physical layout, and political and social institutions of the Bakwena capital, but also its relations of production.

Although I knew that demography affected and in turn was affected by the social formation, I hadn't yet fully grasped the economic consequences of those

---

[1]See, W. D. Hammond-Tooke, "Descent Groups, Chiefdoms and South African

population changes.[2]   Once again, I got lucky.   We, a group of Bakwena historians and I, were discussing house-building. I had asked them to tell me about the gendered division of labor in its construction, the amount of labor expended in the project, and the materials used in the structure. They began with the familiar Bakwena *rondavel* built by women and men of mud bricks, wooden posts, and grass thatching. Selebatso Masimega, my translator, asked them again to describe the Bakwena home, but to talk about its construction "a long, long time ago," he said.   The men appeared reluctant, and as they pondered the implications of the question during an awkward moment of silence, one of them blurted out that it would be alright to talk about the *mutibelagatsi* or early home of the Bakwena. I surmised that the men's hesitance had been conditioned by the racist presumptions of Europeans and their perceived representatives like me who denigrated simple forms as "primitive" and "uncivilized."

The *mutibelagatsi*, my "informants" said, consisted of a framework of branches and twigs that was set into the ground and covered over with grass. Later, the *mutibelagatsi* was replaced by the *ntlo ya moraro* ("house of three things") or simply *moraro* ("three"). The name described the three elements of the house, a roof of wooden rafters covered with grass, supported by upright wooden posts, and an intertwined wall of bushes within the circle of roof posts. Eventually, the *moraro* was supplanted by the *ntlo* ("house") that had a wall made of mud bricks smeared with a smooth coating of cowdung, and a roof that used a thicker, more durable variety of grass that was carefully thatched and trimmed. That final refinement, thatching, they said, was introduced by Bahurutshe immigrants about the same time that the plough was brought into the Kweneng.[3]

At long last, I made the connection. What the Bakwena historians were describing, I realized, was not merely the changes in house construction, but also

---

Historiography," *Journal of Southern African Studies* 11:2 (April 1985): pp. 305-19.

[2]At the time, I didn't have the benefit of C. C. Wrigley's, "Population in African History," *Journal of African History* 20:1 (1979): pp. 127-31, which wisely suggested that perhaps the underlying dynamic or motive force in African history were the quiet, ordinary processes of birth and death -- population changes, or of Georges Dupre and Pierre Philippe Rey's, "Reflections on the Relevance of a Theory of the History of Exchange," which challenged Meillassoux's model of a lineage mode of production, and instead argued the centrality of demography in determining the means of production. David Seddon, ed., *Relations of Production: Marxist Approaches to Economic Anthropology* (London: Frank Cass, 1978), pp. 171-205.

the accompanying transformations in their economy. I had put aside, because they contradicted my long held assumptions, their earlier accounts of the centrality of hunting and gathering among the first Bakwena in the Kweneng. Finally it all made sense. House construction, demography, and modes of production came together.

Herding, Gathering, and Hunting, c.1700-1831

Throughout the eighteenth century, it appears, the Bakwena numbered less than a hundred people, who possessed herds of short-horned Setswana cattle and who settled in temporary villages along the fringes of the Kalahari desert, alternating among sites like Mochudi, Shokwane, Molepolole, and Dithejwane. Having come from the better watered Transvaal, the Bakwena probably found the desert to be a barrier at first, but also discovered the Molepolole vicinity, with its perennial streams and pools, its high, defensible hills, and its plains that teemed with a variety of game, to be conducive to their material needs.

Labor was employed principally in herding, gathering, and hunting. Plant cultivation was clearly secondary to those forms of production. Bakwena fields were small and the leading crops, several kinds of beans (*dinawa*) and melons (*marotse*), were both short-season and drought resistant, making them ideal for the nomadic life of hunting, herding, and gathering, and for the semi-arid surroundings. Similarly the *mutibelagatsi* was an economic structure that complemented those requirements of production and environment.

The Bakwena obtained animal protein both from the milk and meat of their cattle and from hunting, which was for the most part a collective effort beyond the capacity of a single household. Requiring about forty men one month to build, the game trap (*gopo*) was a common way of acquiring meat and other products like hides. A trap consisted of a trench varying in size but averaging perhaps twenty meters in length, six meters in width, and seven meters in depth, with two bush fences extending one-and-a-half kilometers in length and spreading to about 750 meters at the entrance that directed animals toward the pit. Set at the bottom of the trench were upright, sharpened stakes, and the hole was camouflaged with

[3]H/M/101.

a cover of twigs and grass. Men, women, and children circled the countryside driving the game toward the *gopo*. Those traps were built in valleys near the saltlicks that were frequented by game animals to the north and south of Molepolole, and although they represented a considerable investment in labor, both in their construction and upkeep, they were used repeatedly and were an efficient way of hunting as long as game remained in the area.[4]

The sudden and large infusion of people into the Kweneng during the early nineteenth century, brought about mainly by the *difaqane* and Afrikaner expansion, was accompanied by a decrease in game and edible fruits and roots around Molepolole, even though David Livingstone reported that the Kolobeng area during the 1840s still had an abundance of game, including buffaloes, and herds of elephants roamed the valleys behind Molepolole.[5] Still, the substantial increase in human population eventually overtaxed the fragile, borderland environment, and drove the game into the less densely peopled Kalahari.

The *difaqane* and Afrikaner expansion also brought raiders into the Kweneng, both African and European, who preyed upon the cattle of the Bakwena and their immigrants. Those declines in hunting and herding were accompanied by increases in the importance of plant cultivation and women's labor, and in the immigration of premier agriculturalists from the Transvaal like the Bahurutshe and Baphalane, who brought with them labor but also skills. I believe that those refugees, especially the iron-workers like the Bakaa and the agriculturalists like the Bahurutshe, lay the foundation for grain cultivation as stressed and practiced by the contemporary Bakwena.

Cultivating and Gender, *c.*1831-1885

Because of the threat of foreign invasions, nineteenth-century Bakwena settlements were generally situated on the summits of rocky, defensible hills, and the agricultural fields lay in the plains below. Field sites were selected on the

---

[4]H/M/12; H/M/18; and H/M/19.

[5]David Livingstone to R. Moffat, Kolobeng, August 13, 1847, LMS-SOAS, Africa Odds, Box 9, Folder 2A; David Livingstone to Benjamin Pyne, Kolobeng, May 28, 1846, LMS-SOAS, Africa, Odds, Box 22; David Livingstone to Agnes Livingstone, Bakwain Country, April 4, 1842, NLS, Ms. 10701; and David Livingstone to Mr. Livingston,

bases of proximity, vegetation, and soil. To reduce effort and travel time, agriculturalists preferred field locations within easy walking distance from their homes. Accordingly, people's fields were generally just beyond their *makgotla* or section (*motse*), producing the familiar Batswana settlement pattern of towns with arable lands encircling it.[6]

But distance wasn't the only criterion that determined one's choice of fields. The kind of vegetation that grew on the land also affected the agriculturalist's decision. Plots on which grew the *motlwa* grass, for instance, were invariably avoided during this period of hoe cultivation because of the tenacious nature of the grass. *Motlwa* was hardy and had a spreading root system that entangled itself with the roots of growing garden plants, making them impossible to weed without uprooting the crop at the same time. If left to grow, *motlwa* absorbed the moisture and nutrients intended for the garden plants, stunting and strangling them. Even cleared fields could be taken over by the grass within three years rendering them unproductive. Only after the introduction of the iron plough was it possible to rid a field of *motlwa* by turning the soil at a sufficient depth to uproot the grass.[7]

Soil type was also factored into a decision on field site.[8] The Bakwena recognized three main varieties of soil suitable for their crops: *seloko*, a black, brown soil found in valleys; *mokata*, a red soil found in open plains; and *chawana*, a sandy mixture of *seloko* and *mokata*. Sorghum (*mabele*) grew best on *seloko*, but beans and other crops like groundnuts (*ditlou*) thrived on *mokata*. And the best overall for most crops was *chawana*.[9]

During the eighteenth century when fields were small, a woman and her husband cleared and prepared the land. Clearing (*go reza*) involved cutting smaller bushes, ringing and burning larger trees, and burning the heaped vegetation on the field, leaving the ashes to serve as fertilizer. When plant

Kuruman, March 15, 1847, NLS, Ms. 10701.

[6]For details on Bakwena cultivation during this period, see William R. Duggan, *An Economic Analysis of Southern African Agriculture* (New York: Praeger, 1986), pp. 69-74.

[7]H/M/12; and H/M/28.

[8]See, David Livingstone, *Missionary Travels and Researches in South Africa* (London: John Murray, 1857), p. 22.

[9]H/M/23.

cultivation increased during the nineteenth century, clearing was accomplished through the collective labor of the women of a *kgotla*. Those labor gangs moved from one field to another, clearing the ground for all of the members in their collective and being fed by the field's owner. As the cost of labor and value of agricultural products grew, and as social stratification became more pronounced and rigid, households organized work days, entered into a contract agreement (*tumalano*) with laborers, or employed the free, bound labor of servants.

A work day or the *malaletsa* system was sponsored by a household that announced it, and slaughtered and divided a cow into even sections that were given as payment to laborers who appeared on the appointed day. The contract or *tumalano* system was simply an agreement between an employer and a worker, whose labor cost depended on the field's size and the varieties and quantities of vegetation to be cleared. Those costs in *c.*1910 were, according to an "informant," one goat for clearing one Sekwena acre or twelve paces square, one sheep for clearing two acres, and a cow for larger areas.[10] Throughout most of the nineteenth century, the servant or *batlhanka* system involved the use of Basarwa (San) and "Bakgalagadi" labor by Bakwena masters who were obliged only for the upkeep of their wards.[11]

Those systems of labor were similarly employed in the planting and cultivating of Bakwena fields. The cultivating season opened after the first rains fell in about mid-October and after the *kgosi* had called for *letsema* (from *tema*, "a piece of cultivated ground") and closed near the end of December. Requiring that all Bakwena households commence their agricultural activities at the same time after *letsema* failed to level the economic playing field because certain households possessed more resources and laborers than others.

A typical day, I was told, began at about *makuku* or the second crowing of the cock when a woman awakened, and by *o dinaka tsa kgomo* or when it was light enough to make out the horns of the cattle, she was out in her field and working. She labored until about *motsegare wa sethobolo* or midday when the

---

[10]H/M/22; and H/M/32.

[11]See, London Missionary Society, *The Masarwa (Bushmen): Report of an Inquiry* (Lovedale: Lovedale Press, 1935), for a discussion of the Bangwato use of San labor, and Gaontatlhe Mautle, "Bakgalagadi-Bakwena Relationship: A Case of Slavery, c.1840-c.1920," *Botswana Notes and Records* 18 (1986): pp. 19-31.

sun was at its hottest. Stopping for a rest, the "average" cultivator, said my "informants," returned home to cook for herself and her household, but the "industrious" woman remained in her field, ate her packed lunch, and quickly resumed working. The "average" worker resumed her labors and continued until *lephirima* or sunset, but the "industrious" laborer quit only after she could not see, around *maabaneane*, and even worked into the night if there was moonlight.[12]

The Sekwena method of hoe cultivation involved tilling the soil and planting the seeds in one operation. The cultivator marked off a rectangular or square area by notching the ground, and thereby delimited a *temanyana* (diminutive of *tema*). A *letlatlana*, a cone-shaped container made of woven grass with a capacity of five liters or more, was filled with a mixture of seeds, mainly sorghum (*mabele*), but also one or two handfuls of beans (*dinawa*), and a handful each of another variety of legume (*letlhodi*), melons (*marotse*), pumpkins (*maputse*), maize (*midi*), and watermelons (*mahapu*). The seeds were thoroughly mixed in the *letlatlana* and broadcast evenly over the marked field (*temanyana*). Using her hoe, the laborer turned the soil, uprooting weeds and covering the seeds at the same time. She repeated the process, marking, seeding, and cultivating other equivalent areas (*temanyana*) until the end of the day. The day's work, in area of ground cultivated, formed a template for subsequent days until the whole field, the *tema*, had been planted, typically about four to six Sekwena acres or about 2-4,000 square meters.[13]

Work teams helped to relieve the loneliness and monotony of solitary labor, taught inexperienced workers new techniques and skills, and was probably more efficient than individual effort. Nkwane Gaealafshwe of Goo-Ra-Tshosa recalled how in 1906, when she was a young girl, her grandmother initiated her into agricultural labor. A wealthy woman, her grandmother employed about ten "Bakgalagadi" to cultivate her field. The "Bakgalagadi" formed a line and Gaealafshwe and her sisters were placed between the experienced workers so they could learn from them. In one day, Gaealafshwe remembered, she and her sisters

---

[12]This distinction between "average" and "industrious" cultivators was made by the women whom I interviewed. An individual's hours of labor need not have depended solely upon that person's "laziness" or "industriousness." Just as economic were other choices made by women workers. H/M/14; and H/M/23.

[13]H/M/23. See also, H/M/11.

acquired valuable skills, and the group completed about two Sekwena acres.[14] "All of them held native hoes," a nineteenth-century European visitor described Bakwena women outside Tshonwane, "and standing in a line, raised their tools, and worked in time, humming a drawling, monotonous song as a guide to their operations. . . ."[15]

The implement used in cultivation was the Sekwena hoe (sechele), consisting of an iron blade about 17 centimeters in breadth set at an acute angle into a wooden handle of about 900 centimeters in length.[16]   Before the Bakaa iron-workers joined them in 1849, the Bakwena probably purchased iron hoe blades from the Balete and Bakgatla with livestock and skins.[17]   But after the arrival of the Bakaa and other metal-workers from the Transvaal, the sechele was produced locally.[18]   The sechele, my "informants" told me, was small and comparatively thin before the arrival of European traders, because iron was neither plentiful nor cheap.   During the second half of the nineteenth century, however, Bakwena metal-workers obtained large pieces of iron from Europeans, resulting in broader, heavier hoes that lasted longer than the earlier version but were also clumsier, especially in weeding, and required greater effort to wield.

Despite having removed most of the weeds in a garden plot during the cultivation phase, soon after the first rains fell weeds invariably sprouted in profusion.   The Sekwena hoe, it seems, could not reach the depth required to uproot certain weeds completely.   Weeding commenced after the sorghum (mabele) had reached a height of about twelve centimeters, about two weeks after germination, when they could be more easily identified and distinguished from

---

[14]H/M/22; and H/M/23.

[15]Henry H. Methuen, Life in the Wilderness (London, 1846), pp. 185-86. See also, Roualeyn Gordon Cumming, Five Years of a Hunter's Life in the Far Interior of South Africa, 1 (London: John Murray, 1850), p. 232.

[16]H/M/20; and H/M/28.

[17]V. Ellenberger, "Di Robaroba Matlhakola -- Tsa Ga Mosodi-a-Mphela," Transactions of the Royal Society of South Africa 25 (1937-38): pp. 36, 44; Cumming, Five Years, 1, p. 232; Methuen, Life in the Wilderness, pp. 142, 145, 182-84; Schapera, Missionary Correspondence, pp. 34-35; and David Chamberlin, ed., Some Letters from Livingstone, 1840-1872 (London, 1940), pp. 41, 81.

[18]Livingstone, Missionary Researches, p. 22; Schapera, Missionary Correspondence, p. 127; I. Schapera, ed., Livingstone's Private Journals, 1851-1853 (Berkeley: University of California Press, 1960), p. 304; Schapera, Family Letters, 1, pp. 213-14; and Schapera, Family Letters, 2, pp. 25, 28, 49, 60.

weeds. The waiting period allowed the crops to take root and the buried weeds to
show themselves. During the weeding season, generally from January to
February, a worker with a hoe was able to weed, on average, about one Sekwena
acre every two days.[19]

Besides weeding, women horticulturalists thinned the seedlings to avoid
their overcrowding. Sorghum was thinned to a distance of about thirty
centimeters between plants, and beans, melons, and pumpkins were thinned so
they were about a meter apart. But if the soil was fertile and the season promised
abundant rain, the plants were left to optimum crowding to maximize their
yields.[20] In that way, the cultivator decided from among several options after
having considered the relevant variables and uncertainties.

Between February and March, with the flowering of the sorghum plants
and fruiting of melons and beans, birds flocked to the fields to feed on the
maturing grain. Mainly younger children drove off the birds, while women
horticulturalists prepared the storage facilities and threshing floor (*segotlho*) made
of cowdung along the borders of the field. A drying rack (*serala*) from which
were hung sorghum and maize was erected next to the threshing floor by the
woman and sometimes her husband.

Beans and melons were harvested and eaten during this time, and by April
all of the beans would have matured, been picked, mixed with ashes and goat
dung, and stored. In April and May, the air changed and a cold, drying wind
from the west caused the grain to ripen. Women cultivators harvested and hanged
on racks the sorghum until about June when the harvest ended. Using sticks,
they threshed the grain dislodging the sorghum seeds from their heads, and spread
the grain over the threshing floor for a final drying. When thoroughly dry, women
carried the sorghum from the fields to their mothers' households (*malwapa*) where
the grain was treated with a mixture of ashes and cowdung and stored in grass
woven granaries (*desigo*) in the home of each cultivator's mother.[21] Grains
supplanted beans and melons as the principal food crops beginning around 1831.

---

[19]H/M/28.

[20]H/M/27.

[21]A *sesigo* was over two meters high and had a capacity of over eight hectoliters. Often,
the basket was mounted on stones and propped up with supporting stakes. Frequently,
children were lifted into the *sesigo* to pass grain out of the storage containers. See, Robert

That dietary change, enabled by the productive activities of women, altered the social relations between men and women. Within the Bakwena gendered division of labor, men controlled most of the products of hunting and the milk and meat derived from and the capital represented by livestock. During the eighteenth century, gathering and cultivation, mainly but not exclusively "women's work," were secondary in the provisioning of Bakwena households. But for most of the nineteenth century, Sechele's political consolidation and state-building was supported in large measure by a stable and expansive agricultural base that was built and maintained primarily by women. At the household level, women's control over grains, underscored by their storage at the home of the cultivator's mother, provided an insurance against abusive husbands and a way to access power. But men still controlled the distribution of land, including arable fields, and the cattle that was the principal currency and means of exchange. In addition, with the introduction of the plough, men exacted claims on women plant cultivators because they owned the oxen employed in pulling the plough.

Under the system of hoe horticulture, women exercised near-exclusive control over the products of their labor, and grains were matrilocally stored.[22] That one-field system was supplanted with a two-field system after the plough's introduction wherein women cultivated a larger field for themselves called *tshimo a mosadi* ("a woman's field") and a smaller plot for her husband called *tshimo a monna* ("a man's field") whose products were stored at the man's home and generally reserved for special occasions. Some women, to gain greater economic independence under the two-field system, used hoes to cultivate their own garden plots in addition to their two ploughed fields. Although requiring additional labor, those gardens generated products that belonged to the cultivator alone.[23]

The gendered division of labor, nonetheless, was neither timeless nor absolute. Men's control over hunting, herding, felling and hauling trees, and mining did not preclude women's labor in hunting, herding, fencing, and erecting

---

Moffat, *Apprenticeship at Kuruman*, ed. I. Schapera (London: Chatto & Windus, 1951), pp. 136-37; Moffat, *Missionary Labours*, p. 399; John Barrow, *A Voyage to Cochin-China* (London: T. Cadell & W. Davies, 1806), p. 392; and John Campbell, *Travels in South Africa*, 2 vols. (London, 1822), 1, p. 244.

[22]See Duggan, *Southern African Agriculture*, pp. 80-85, for details of women's control over grains.

[23]H/M/22; and H/M/23.

rafters and thatching roofs. And men engaged in basketry and weaving producing objects like the granaries (*desigo*), and in sewing skins and pelts into clothing, rugs, and blankets that were traded. Also, "rules" were bent toward practical solutions to economic needs. When women's labor alone could not produce the desired amount of crops, men assisted their wives in the entire process from cultivating to harvesting, and women, besides men, managed the oxen and helped plough the fields.

In addition, changes in the means and relations of production led to technological changes and alterations in the organization of labor. The move from individual to collective labor, occurring generally during the transition to grains cultivation in the nineteenth century, represented a more efficient organization of agricultural labor. The encouragement of others within the work group provided greater incentives for productivity, and skilled cultivators taught less experienced ones improved techniques. The time required to complete certain tasks was often critical because optimal conditions lasted for a limited time. Cultivating and planting, for example, had to be completed between mid-October and December because of the growing time requirements and changes in the weather. The spring rains helped to loosen the ground for cultivation and to germinate the seeds and nurture their growth, and the cool winds of fall dried the maturing and harvested grain before the hail and frosts of June. Work groups tended to be more productive overall than solitary workers, because individuals possessed differential efficiencies for the various tasks involved in agricultural production. An efficient planter, for example, might not be equally adept at harvesting. Her labor in excess of her needs in planting, thus, benefited another member of the collective, while the labor of a proficient harvester from the collective helped to meet her needs in that task.

But the efficiencies gained through the (re)organization of labor had their limits and were dependent each season upon the variables of individuals, the collective group, and the wider social and environmental contexts. As their reliance upon grains cultivation increased, the Bakwena found new sources of labor to raise the level of production. Men, hunting less with the flight of game into the Kalahari, worked alongside women in the fields,[24] and the Bakwena

---

[24]See e.g., David Livingstone to Mr. Livingston, Kuruman, March 15, 1847, NLS, Ms.

exploited "Bakgalagadi" servant labor as in Sechele's large fields at Midie, about thirty kilometers northeast of Molepolole. Groups of possibly Bakgwatheng "Bakgalagadi" servants who lived there permanently cultivated sorghum fields for the Bakwena *kgosi* throughout the second half of the nineteenth century.[25]

New technologies, like the plough, used by the Bakwena about or just after 1885,[26] further increased agricultural production by enabling larger, more productive fields, but they also had other consequences beyond their impact upon gender relations and the division of labor. More extensive fields exhausted greater tracts of land at a faster rate, and required expanding the areas of cultivation far beyond the contiguous perimeter of the capital. Those distances precluded daily commuting between one's home and field, and led to the building of temporary homes out in areas called "the lands."[27] Labor-saving devices like the plough might have also resulted in labor surpluses and temporary unemployment. To cope with that problem, it seems, Kgosidintsi directed a return to the labor intensive method of hoe cultivation.[28]

The plough itself underwent changes in its design and construction. When it was first introduced, the "white plough" (*mogoma wa sekgoa*) was too expensive for the masses of people. The missionary David Livingstone, writing from the Bakwena capital in April 1849, reported that an iron plough cost 20 pounds (sterling), even though ploughs made in the United States could be purchased about two years later at Port Elizabeth, South Africa for 4 pounds (sterling).[29] The traders' markup made the "white plough" prohibitive for most Bakwena. The plough was Africanized by some Bakwena who manufactured two varieties of the "people's plough" (*mogoma wa setswana*); the cheaper version was made entirely of wood, and the more costly model employed an iron share

---

10701.

[25]H/B/1; and H/B/2.

[26]The Bangwato used ploughs as early as 1878, and a 1911 census revealed 767 ploughs in the Kweneng. Duggan, *Southern African Agriculture*, pp. 103-05.

[27]Later, with building population congestion in the capital, increasing numbers of Bakwena have preferred living out at "the lands," resulting in abandoned homes in Molepolole and more substantial dwellings by their fields.

[28]H/M/23.

[29]David Livingstone to Janet Livingston, Kolobeng, April 20, 1849, NLS, Ms. 10701; and H. Helmore to J. J. Freeman, Likatlong, October 30, 1851, LMS-SOAS, South Africa, Incoming Letters, Box 27, Folder 1, Jacket B.

with wooden handles. Although the "people's plough" broke more frequently and could not turn the soil as deep as its European counterpart, it was affordable and represented an advance over the iron hoe. When the price of the "white plough" declined, Bakwena cultivators switched to the import.[30]

Greater numbers and a more efficient (re)organization of laborers, along with new technologies, allowed horticultural production to keep pace with population growth, and yielded surpluses that were traded. During the time of Sebele (*a* Sechele), the Bangwato, Bangwaketse, and Bakgatla exchanged cattle for grain at Molepolole. A one-year-old cow (*mwalolelo*) bought four sacks (each sack had a capacity of about sixty liters) of sorghum, a two-year-old cow (*magatelo*), five sacks of sorghum, and a three-year-old cow (*moroba*), six to six-and-a-half sacks of sorghum.[31] Besides that grains trade with other Batswana, the Bakwena carried on an important trade with the peoples of the Kalahari, and Bakwena women played crucial roles in both the production and exchange of grains.

Bangwaketse women brought a red stone (*letshoko*), rubbed on pottery to give it a reddish color and found in Ga-Ngwaketse, to Molepolole to purchase grain from Bakwena women at a rate of one measure of *letshoko* for four to six equivalent measures of sorghum. In turn, Bakwena women traveled to Manyana with sacks of sorghum to buy large pots made by famous potters like Mma Morobeng, who created a style known as *mmamorobeng* and whose earthenware pots were renown for their strength and fine quality. The price of a pot depended upon its size, generally fetching its capacity in sorghum. Women, through this trade, were able to accumulate fowls, herds of goats, and even cattle for themselves.[32]

Two crops cultivated almost exclusively for trade were tobacco (*motsoko*) and cannabis (*motokwane*). Although both women and men labored in the cultivation of those products, men monopolized the trade and its profits. Tobacco-growing was a completely separate activity from grains cultivation, and became prominent only toward the end of the nineteenth century. Perhaps

---

[30]H/M/3. Cf. Duggan, *Southern African Agriculture*, p. 105.
[31]H/M/31.
[32]H/M/24; and H/M/26.

Bahurutshe immigrants introduced the plants and method of cultivation to the Bakwena.[33] The two varieties of tobacco, the short-leafed (*magonotwane*) and long-leafed (*motsoko wa setswana* or *tsebeditelele*), were grown from seed each year to produce plants with leaves that were rich and strong in flavor. Cultivators planted the seeds in August, and transplanted the seedlings in September or October, usually into plots that had a loose, rich soil called *lerotobolo* or soil that was fertilized with manure (*mosotelo*) located along the banks of a fountain or stream to allow for an easy irrigation of the plants.[34] The tobacco was watered twice daily, ideally in the morning and at sunset, and cultivated through May. As the leaves matured, they were picked, graded, and cured.[35]

For the Kalahari trade, the tobacco leaves were graded into three categories. The top grade leaves were placed in a heap in the sun and covered with a skin, or hung individually inside the home if it rained. After about a week, while the leaves were still pliable, they were rolled into a cylindrical bundle called a *togwa* of two standard sizes: a larger roll of about thirty centimeters in length by eighteen centimeters in diameter, and a smaller roll about half that size. The larger *togwa* was exchanged for a cow (*mwalolelo*), while the smaller roll fetched a goat. The medium grade leaves were crushed with stones while still green and placed in a container to dry. About five teacups of this medium grade purchased a goat. The poorest grade tobacco was simply sold in heaps primarily for small items like chickens, but larger heaps could be exchanged for goats and sheep. Prices, of course, varied, depending upon the quality of the articles of trade, the bargaining ability of the trader, and the times. For instance, during Sechele's reign, a single cup of cannabis bought a cow (*mwalolelo*), but by the time of Kealeboga, Sechele's grandson, a cow (*mwalolelo*) could only be gotten with a large pillowcase of cannabis.[36]

---

[33]The Bahurutshe, according to European travellers, had precedence in first-fruits, and the exclusive right among the Batswana to grow tobacco. See, e.g., Schapera, *Apprenticeship*, p. 187; William J. Burchell, *Travels in the Interior of Southern Africa*, 2 vols. (London, 1822, 1824), 2, p. 321; Campbell, *Travels*, 2, p. 216; Percival R. Kirby, ed., *The Diary of Dr. Andrew Smith*, 2 vols. (Cape Town, 1939, 1940), 1, p. 251; and 2, p. 221-22; Livingstone, *Missionary Researches*, p. 51; and Schapera, *Handbook*, pp. 3-4.
[34]H/M/78.
[35]H/M/9; H/M/11; H/M/23; and H/M/78.
[36]H/M/9; and H/M/11.

Cattle and Class, *c.*1831-1885

Cattle was both a source of animal protein and a valued, scarce resource. It was thus accumulated, appropriated, and (re)distributed within and without the Bakwena social formation. Cattle transfers took place in several ways. In individual households, fathers willed to their children cattle as gifts, called "cattle of the inheritance" (*kgomo ya boswa*), while they were still minors, and the herd and its offspring formally belonged to those children. Sons, as they matured, received from their fathers cattle called "herding cattle" (*dikgomo tsa madisa*, from *go disa*, "to herd"), indicating that the cattle belonged to the father but under the guardianship of his son. This cattle constituted the owner's estate that was, upon his death, distributed by the men of his *kgotla* to his dependents.[37] Husbands gave to their wives cattle (*kgomo ya letsele*) as an outright gift that was jointly managed while the man was still alive, but which became the wife's sole property upon his death.[38] Those transfers redistributed but retained cattle within a family group, except for daughters who married out. Children were exhorted to keep the family's wealth with the proverb, *ngwana wa rrangwane nnyale, kgomo di boele sakeng* ("child of my paternal uncle marry me, so the cattle may return to the cattle fold").[39]

Whether within family groups or the state, concentrations of cattle generally defined the loci of power. But the distribution of cattle also enabled the owners to consolidate and expand their influence and reach. The *mafisa* system, practiced widely throughout the nineteenth century, was a principal means by which cattle-owners sought to dominate the social formation. Owners loaned their cattle to dependents referred to as *kala* ("branch") or *tsala ya me* ("my friend"), who herded and cared for the cattle in exchange for the milk and use of the animal(s). *Mafisa* cattle thereby created and solidified a social relationship, and helped to alleviate envy and conflict over access to the means of production. Bakwena rulers employed the *mafisa* system to attract and ensure the loyalty of

---

[37]H/M/100.
[38]H/M/90.
[39]Schapera, *Handbook*, p. 128.

immigrants, many of whom came to the Kweneng devoid of stock.[40] Further, the system provided owners with essentially free labor, and lessened the risk of disease wiping out their entire herd by having their cattle distributed over a wide area.

Yet the system held dangers for owners, and opportunities for recipients. The terms *mafisa*, from *go fisa* ("to burn"), "cattle which burn," the name of *mafisa* cattle, and "rhinoceros" (*tshukudu*), a dreaded beast, the term for the cattle's owner denotes the delicacy of the arrangement. Despite their obligations, recipients could lose cattle or cause them to deteriorate, they might not report the births of calves, and they had ample opportunity, because of the long distances that frequently separated the owners from their *mafisa* cattle, to hide the cattle's status. Recipients could slaughter the animal and report that it strayed or was killed by wild animals, and keep the offspring of *mafisa* cattle for themselves instead of adding them to the owner's herd. The *mafisa* system, accordingly, was simultaneously a way of control and of resistance.

Bakwena rulers had other means of accumulating wealth and preserving the status quo, by taxing labor and goods. The *kgosi's* perogative to summon a royal hunt (*letshomo*) was particularly important during the period before *c.*1831 when hunting, besides herding, provided the main source of protein. The hunt produced food and skins, some of which he kept for himself and others, distributed to his people.[41] The *kgosi* mobilized age-regiments (*mephato*) for cattle raids on neighboring peoples, the products of which he retained or gave as rewards, and he sent the regiments into the desert to secure its products. Sechele, for instance, ordered the Maganamokgwa *mophato* to Ga-Tawana to collect elephant ivory for him during the late nineteenth century.[42] And Gaealafshwe, *kgosi* of Ntlheng-ya Godimo, organized a hunt (*letshomo*) and sent his men into the desert to get meat and skins for him (*setlhako*) about the turn of the century. Workers called *makata* cultivated the *kgosi's* field in a labor tax that probably gained prominence only after the rise of grains production. The *makata* were

---

[40]See, e.g., O/H/35.
[41]H/M/69.
[42]H/M/12.

usually men, to allow women to cultivate their own fields, and were responsible for the full agricultural cycle, from planting to harvest.[43]

In addition to taxing labor, the *kgosi* taxed goods collectively known as *sehuba*. Although compulsory, *sehuba* did not entail a specific amount, but tax payers had incentives for generosity. A pleased senior might reward the giver with *mafisa* cattle, a political title and office, servants and immigrants, or a *kgotla*.[44] A ruler received cattle, small stock, and other property as *dikatso* at his installation, frequently making him an even wealthier man. Besides the usual occasions for *sehuba* and perhaps because of the taxes levied by individual heads of sections, Sechele devised a systematic way of collecting taxes by installing his collectors in each section of the capital. Gaealafshwe, for example, usually collected his *sehuba* in pelts during the winter when the fur was thick and at its peak. Under the eye of Sechele's man in Ntlheng-ya Godimo, Gaealafshwe counted and selected about ten percent of the taxed pelts and sent them on to Sechele, while keeping the remainder for himself. Gaealafshwe in turn received a fraction of the *sehuba* collected by his juniors.[45]

Perhaps the most important privilege of the ruling class throughout the nineteenth century was its virtual monopoly over the labor of servants (*batlhanka*). This labor system, created by the *kgosi* Moruakgomo and modified by Sechele, provided the rulers with an enormous supply of workers to cultivate their fields, herd their cattle, and bring them *sehuba* in skins, ostrich feathers, and ivory. The *batlhanka* were principally "Bakgalagadi," peoples who inhabited the Kalahari desert, and some San who were conquered or drawn into the orbit of Bakwena authority. They, like cattle outposts, were a part of the territorial properties carved out of the desert for certain members of the elite, and like cattle, were allocated from father to child and from *kgosi* to loyal subject.[46] Toward the end of the nineteenth century, Sebele (*a* Sechele) declared an end to this system of master and servant for the ruling class as a whole, and sought to establish his sole hegemony over the peoples of the Kalahari. He failed in that attempt, but his

---

[43]H/M/61; and H/M/69.
[44]See, e.g., Gofetakgosi's rise in H/M/54; H/M/71; H/M/73; and H/M/106.
[45]H/M/70; H/M/71; and H/M/73.
[46]H/M/71; and H/L/12.

actions influenced a defection of over half of the Bakwena to Kgari, Sebele's junior brother, who led the secessionists into exile.[47] The formal demise of the *batlhanka* system, however, ended the virtual monopoly held over access to the desert and its products by Bakwena *dikgosi* and opened the resources of the Kalahari to all.

Trade and Class, *c.*1885-1920

The Kalahari trade generated an economic expansion, and helped to "democratize" cattle ownership and power among the Bakwena. For the "Bakgalagadi," trade with the Bakwena became possible only after they had been granted property rights by Sebele (*a* Sechele) through his termination of the master and servant relationship. Under the *batlhanka* system, Bakwena masters ordered their servants to hunt fur-bearing animals like the fox (*motlhose*) and jackal (*phokojwe*), usually with dogs, or simply raided and confiscated "Bakgalagadi" stores of ivory, ostrich feathers, furs, and other valuable commodities that were denied to the "Bakgalagadi" under Bakwena law.

Influential in building the Kalahari trade were Europeans who purchased the desert's products from the Bakwena, and who first arrived as itinerant traders on ox wagons and who later settled in the Bakwena capital and opened shops. My interviewees could remember only two European shops during Sechele's time, one owned by Terry Gower and a partner called "Big Man," and another managed by a man simply called "Pete." During the time of Sebele (*a.* Sechele), there were six shops in Molepolole that belonged to "Big Man," a man nicknamed "Majaasuma," M. J. Kablay, R. Khan, and two shops owned by the Hirschfeld brothers. Those stores continued under Kealeboga, Sebele's son, except that "Conoble" took over from "Big Man," and J. C. Fry, "Majaasuma."[48]

Bakwena traders, either singly or in groups, carried sacks of goods into the desert to exchange them for furs, skins, and ostrich feathers. Almost always

---

[47]W. H. Surmon to The Resident Commissioner, Gaberones, September 5, 1896, BNA, RC. 4/4; W. H. Surmon to The Acting Resident Commissioner, Gaberone's, August 8, 1901, BNA, RC. 5/5; and J. Ellenberger to The Acting Resident Commissioner, Gaberone's, August 31, 1900, BNA, RC. 5/12.

[48]H/M/31; and H/M/36.

men, the traders moved in groups for protection and companionship, some employed servants to carry their goods, and the few who owned wagons used them to transport heavy items like grain. They took the produce of their gardens, including grains, tobacco, and cannabis, locally manufactured goods such as iron spears, axes, knives, bracelets, earrings, and wooden bowls and spoons, and European products like buttons, beads, cowrie shells, gunpowder and lead, and cloth. The most sought after objects, for Bakwena traders, were fur pelts in the order of value: fox (*motlhose*), jackal (*phokojwe*), a variety of cat (*lesie*), lynx or red cat (*thwaane*), polecat (*tshipa*), a small cat (*shebalabolokwane*), and another kind of cat (*phage*).[49]

Three main trade routes made their way from Molepolole into the Kalahari: one headed northeast to Lephephe; another went north to Letlhakeng, Mazeaboroko, and through the desert's heart to Ghanzi; and a third branched from Letlhakeng and veered westward to Kang. Each of those destinations required about a month to reach, because a trader stopped at various settlements along the way to buy and sell until he had gotten rid of all of his goods. The process involved careful calculation. Prices were generally cheaper the farther the trader got from the Bakwena capital, but to traverse those distances consumed time, energy, and resources. In addition, the best period for travel in the desert was limited to the winter months of April through July, when the sun wasn't so hot, the furs at their thickest, and the skins less apt to rot, and the markets beyond were unpredictable and there was no way of knowing if other traders had already gathered up the best furs. All along the way, thus, the trader had to risk buying early and paying high prices or holding out for lower prices, but risking the possibility of depleted supplies and returning home with unsold goods and having to wait for the next year's trade season.[50] Although offering the incentive of high returns, the trade involved risks and required physical stamina, acumen, and luck.

Traders further increased their profit margins by producing their own trade goods. Cultivating grains, tobacco, and cannabis expended labor but didn't require much capital, and carving wooden bowls and spoons required skill and labor but the raw materials used in their manufacture were virtually cost-free.

---

[49]H/L/10.
[50]H/M/32; H/M/33; and H/M/34.

Another profit-stretching strategy employed by a trader and woodworker was to sell his wooden products to fellow Bakwena who paid higher prices than "Bakgalagadi" in exchange for their tobacco and cannabis which were lighter and easier to carry and commanded inflated prices in the desert.[51] Wooden bowls and spoons were likely more valuable to the grains producing Bakwena than to the migratory hunting and herding "Bakgalagadi" who preferred skin containers over wooden ones.

About the turn of the century, however, when certain groups of "Bakgalagadi" settled in stable villages and moved increasingly to grains consumption, the appetite for wooden manufactures increased among them and prices rose correspondingly.   Bakwena traders plied that market, taking principally the grain stamping mortar (*kika*), milk pail (*kgamelo*), and bowl (*mogopo*) into the Kalahari.[52] Each item was made from different trees, and required varied amounts of labor. The stamping mortar was made from hardwood trees like the *mosetla* and *monato*, the milk pail, from trees with a softer wood like the *morula*, *mokgalo*, and *mhawa*, and bowls, only from the *morula*. Because of their economic importance, those trees were protected among the Bakwena, and cutting them was limited to the months of January through May. Beginning with a block of wood, carvers required about a day to complete a stamping mortar, two days for a milk pail, and seven to fourteen days for a bowl. The prices of all of those products, despite the labor differentials involved in the making of them, were quite uniform both in the Bakwena capital and in the desert, usually a goat or the object's capacity in sorghum. The stamping mortar's profit margin might be comparatively high, but its sale was quite limited insofar as a family generally needed only one and it lasted for a long time, whereas bowls, although requiring more labor, sold in larger quantities and were always in great demand.[53]

Besides cultivating one's own cash crops and manufacturing wooden products, Kalahari traders sold their labor for cash that was invested in goods for the desert market in the hope of increasing the investment. Bakwena involvement in labor migration preceded the European instigated version. In a system called

---

[51]H/M/45.

[52]H/Mk/2; H/Sh/2; and H/B/2.

[53]H/Mk/2.

majako, especially prevalent during famines, groups of women left their homes for better-watered places where they sold their labor for food and lodging. At the close of the agricultural year, the workers returned home frequently with a portion of the harvest.[54] The Kalahari trade encouraged men's involvement in the European labor market, when the peoples of the desert sought the European products that were sold in Molepolole's stores. White proprietors, though, preferred cattle for their goods, leading some Bakwena to part with their male cattle because they were not as necessary as females in the reproductive process and regeneration of their herds.[55]

Most Bakwena, however, weren't cattle owners or chose not to part with their cattle. To these, the Transvaal diamond and gold mines beckoned with their promise of cash. One such desert trader was Kabelo Kebakae who labored during the time of Sebele (*a* Sechele).[56] Kebakae signed mine labor contracts in Molepolole several times to work for six-month periods in Johannesburg, Kimberley, and Bulawayo. Unskilled workers, he recalled, earned a shilling a day, skilled workers, two shillings per day, and mine policemen, one-half crown daily. Although trade goods were cheaper in Makgoeng ("white man's land"), they were difficult to transport back to Molepolole. Kebakae thus generally returned home with his cash earnings, and bought trade goods in the Bakwena capital.

Kebakae usually left Molepolole for the desert in April because of the cool weather, and he normally travelled in the company of three or four other traders.[57] The men carried their goods in sacks on their backs, and provisioned themselves with sorghum flour, but also relied upon wild berries which they found along the trail and especially on a wild melon (*kgengwe*) that provided both food and water in certain parts of the desert. It took about a day-and-a-half to reach Letlhakeng, a distance of about seventy kilometers, and Kebakae spent several days visiting the scattered settlements that were several kilometers apart, including Mogotlo, Kgesakwe, Letlhakeng river, and Tshwailweng. If he failed to sell all of his

---

[54]H/M/26.
[55]H/M/33.
[56]H/M/4; H/M/32; H/M/33; and H/M/34.
[57]H/M/35.

goods, Kebakae proceeded northward and walked as far as Ghanzi before returning to Molepolole. At Ghanzi, Kebakae reported, a large, European-made blanket fetched a three-year-old cow (*moroba*), whereas in Letlhakeng it only purchased a one-year-old cow (*mwalolelo*), and a pocket knife bought a fox (*motlhose*) or jackal (*phokojwe*) pelt in Letlhakeng, and twice that amount at Ghanzi. Kebakae's profits from his desert trade are shown in Table 54.

Trade Item	Cost in Molepolole	Kalahari Sale Price	Value in Molepolole
axe	10/- to 11/-	3-4 fox pelts	12/- to 20/-
axe	10/- to 11/-	3-4 jackal pelts	12/- to 16/-
beads[58]	2/- to 2/6	1 fox pelt	4/- to 5/-
beads	2/- to 2/6	1 jackal pelt	4/-
large blanket	£2 to £2 10	1 cow	£2 to £3[59]
maseka a maoto[60]	0/6 to 1/-	1 fox pelt	4/- to 5/-
maseka a matsogo[61]	1/-	1 fox pelt	4/- to 5/-
overcoat	£3 to L4	1 cow	£2 to £3
pocket knife	0/6	1 fox pelt	4/- to 5/-
pocket knife	0/6	1 jackal pelt	4/-
suit	£3 to £5	1 cow	£2 to £3

Table 54. Kebakae's Kalahari Trade, *c.*1910.

Not all of the desert's products were sold in their raw state by Bakwena traders to European shopkeepers. Cattle and other livestock were rarely sold, because of their value and their ability to reproduce in excess of the shopkeepers' cash value, and animal pelts were sewn together by traders who were cloak-makers (*basigi*) into a cloak (*kobo*) that fetched up to two cows from the shops and one cow from fellow Bakwena or Batswana.[62] When Kebakae traded,

---

[58]Four to five teaspoonfuls of beads. Each teaspoonful cost 0/6.

[59]A one-year-old cow fetched about £2, a two-year-old, £2 10, and a three-year-old, £3. Although apparently a profit-losing proposition, cows reproduced themselves and thereby increased their net value.

[60]Leglet made by wrapping copper, brass, or iron wire around a ring of wildebeest or cattle hair. About four or five leglets could be made from a roll of wire that cost about 0/6, and four to eight of those leglets were required for a fox pelt.

[61]Bracelet made in the same way as the leglet. A roll of wire, at 0/6, made up to ten bracelets, and twenty of them were required for a fox pelt.

[62]H/M/35.

however, Europeans bought only loose pelts sometimes in exchange for goods referred to as the "goods for" system.

In the "goods for" system, the shopkeeper established the prices of both his goods and the trader's pelts, allowing for exploitation. Once set, however, the Bakwena *kgosi* prohibited prices from fluctuating, although it is conceivable that the *kgosi* might have been less vigilant in return for "gifts" from the shopkeepers. Sechele in particular had a seemingly insatiable appetite for European goods.[63] The shops offered traders a credit sheet on which was recorded the value of the products brought in, usually at winter's end, and the purchases made in that store against the credit throughout the rest of the year. At times, shopkeepers extended loans to traders who had exhausted their savings but who were seen as good credit risks.[64] Called *molato*, the shopkeepers' credit system had an indigenous precedent termed *mosuga*, whereby a person approached another for a loan, the terms of the loan were agreed upon, the loan was given, and it was later collected either in kind or in labor.[65]

Trading during Kealeboga's time, Phutego Mokoka learned his craft from his elder brother, Philippo, who was a trader, woodworker, and cloak-maker. Philippo sold his wood products to Bakwena cultivators for tobacco and cannabis, managing to collect on one occasion a sack of about fifty liters of tobacco and an equal amount of cannabis. He and Phutego carried those loads to Letlhakeng, Mokoma, and Kikawe, about 200 kilometers north of Molepolole. As provisions, they took with them cooked sour porridge (*motogo*) in skin bags (*makuka*) of about ten liters capacity, along with uncooked sorghum flour which served as emergency rations. They travelled for four weeks before reaching Mokoma, all the while trading and resting along the way. With their sack of cannabis, the brothers purchased twelve *ditlhogo*[66] of fox (*motlhose*) pelts, and with their

---

[63]H/M/33; and H/M/36. See also, BNA, HC. 10/53; HC. 15/14; HC. 17/42; HC. 39/32; HC. 80/24; HC. 84/17; HC. 118; HC. 119; HC. 15/1-2; HC. 134/1; HC. 152/4; RC. 4/5; RC. 9/1; S. 290/17; and S. 290/18.

[64]H/M/31; H/M/45; and H/M/46. I don't know if the shopkeepers charged an interest on the loan.

[65]H/M/36.

[66]*Ditlhogo*, *mokhutla*, and *letlhare* are specialized terms of measurement used by cloak-makers. A *tlhogo* refers to a bundle of three pelts, a *mokhutla*, two pelts, and a *letlhare*, one pelt. Thus, a *tlhogo le letlhare* is a bundle of four pelts, *tlhogo le mokhutla*, five

tobacco, obtained five *ditlhogo* of fox (*motlhose*), three *ditlhogo* of polecat (*tshipa*), one *mokhutla* of lynx or red cat (*thwaane*), and one *letlhare* of a small, hyaena-like animal (*thukhwi*), totaling thirty-six pelts.   After returning to Molepolole, Phutego sewed a cloak with thirty-six fox (*motlhose*) pelts, and sold it to a Mokwena for a one-year-old cow (*mwalolelo*).[67]

Like Kebakae, Phutego went to Makgoeng to work in the mines for cash wages that he invested in trade goods like gunpowder, lead, beads, cowrie shells (*dikgopana*), and knives.   At a Kimberley diamond mine, Phutego loaded and unloaded soil from rail carts for about five shillings per day for a contract period of four months.   Skilled workers, he said, earned only 2/6 to 3/- daily.   He was able to average a comparatively higher wage because he was paid by piece-work at 0/6 per load.   Phutego bought a blanket for 14/- and a coat for 10/- at Kimberley, and traded the blanket for a one-year-old cow (*mwalolelo*) and the coat for a mature ewe (*moroba*) in Molepolole.   Most of his Kalahari trade goods, nonetheless, were purchased in Molepolole's shops.   On his next desert expedition, Phutego was accompanied by four "Bakgalagadi" servants who belonged to Disang, the *kgosi* of his *kgotla*.   With his porters, Phutego retraced the route shown him by his brother, Philippo, and traded and sold the items shown in Table 55.

---

pelts, and so on. H/M/9.
[67]H/M/9.

Trade Item	Cost in Molepolole	Kalahari Sale Price	Value in Molepolole
beads	0/6	1 polecat pelt	none[68]
cowrie shells	0/6	2 fox pelts	4/-
flint and steel	1/-	2 fox pelts	4/-
gunpowder	6/-	27 fox pelts	£2 14[69]
lead solder[70]	6/-	6 fox pelts	12/-
packet of firing caps	5/-	24 fox pelts	£2 8
pocket knife	0/6 to 1/-	2 fox pelts	4/-
tobacco[71]	5/-	33 fox pelts	£3 16

Table 55. Phutego's Kalahari Trade, c.1918.

After his second successful trade expedition, Phutego was asked by one of the Hirschfeld brothers, a Molepolole shopkeeper, to trade exclusively for his shop. Hirschfeld offered to supply Phutego with the trade goods, which he would take to the desert for pelts, all of which belonged to the shopkeeper, who would "thank" the trader with gifts of sugar, tea, and other commodities. Its clear exploitative intention notwithstanding, Phutego seized on the offer as a way to avoid having to migrate to Makgoeng for cash and to skim profits because Hirschfeld could not know the actual returns achieved by the trader, varying from place to place and fluctuating with the bargaining skill of the trader. Once, Phutego remembered, Hirschfeld gave him a metal container (*malekane*) worth two shillings and told him that he expected two fox (*motlhose*) pelts for it, but in the desert, Phutego got three fox pelts for the object and thereby earned a pelt in the transaction. Phutego undertook five expeditions for Hirschfeld, and on one of them, he acquired nine *ditlhogo* (twenty-seven pelts) for the shopkeeper, and gained twelve *ditlhogo* (thirty-six pelts) for himself.[72] Despite earning more than his patron, Phutego's net profit from the desert trade fell below his earnings as an independent trader by more than a half. Still, the arrangement allowed Phutego to

---

[68]To the Bakwena, the polecat (*tshipa*) pelt had virtually no value, but they traded them to Mochudi's Bakgatla who retraded it with their eastern neighbors. H/M/35.

[69]By Phutego's time, fox (*motlhose*) pelts had declined in value, a fine pelt fetching 2/-, as compared with the 4/- to 5/- realized by Kebakae.

[70]Lead solder was melted and molded into musket balls. Each solder roll, costing 6/-, made thirty balls, five of which sold for one fox (*motlhose*) pelt in the desert.

[71]Purchased from Bakwena cultivators, a roll of tobacco about twenty-three centimeters in height and ten centimeters in diameter cost Phutego 5/-.

engage in the Kalahari trade while avoiding four months at a stretch of labor in Makgoeng.

The desert commerce supplied the Transvaal migrant labor traffic, and domestically employed traders and others connected with the trade, like the cultivators who grew tobacco and cannabis, woodworkers who produced stamping mortars, milk pails, bowls, and spoons, metal artisans who crafted leglets, bracelets, knives, spears, and hoes, and cloak-makers who sewed the pelts into blankets and cloaks. During the time of Kealeboga, white shopkeepers hired cloak-makers to sew the pelts they acquired in the trade. They paid cloak-makers between £1 and £2 10 for completing a large fox (*motlhose*) cloak, a project that required about a month of solid work, and they paid from 10/- to 15/- for sewing a large duiker (*phuti*) cloak, a task requiring two weeks of intense effort. To help keep the underpaid cloak-makers contented, the shopkeepers occasionally distributed "gifts" of sugar, tea, and other articles from their shops.[73] Bakwena traders oftentimes hired others in their place, to herd their cattle, clear agricultural land, erect homes, and the like, while they were away working in Makgoeng or trading in the desert.

Other consequences flowed from the Kalahari trade. Before it began, cattle was mainly concentrated among the elite class of the original Bakwena, because the masses were comprised of immigrants who generally came to the Kweneng without cattle. The desert trade made possible the acquisition of livestock, and helped introduce and redistribute cattle among more of Molepolole's people. A trader who exchanged his goods for cattle at a place like Ghanzi brought new stock into the Kweneng, while another who sewed a cloak and with it purchased a cow from a Mokwena, usually of the elite class, assisted in the redistribution of wealth within the Kweneng.[74] Another form of redistribution took place when Bakwena traders bought livestock from the "Bakgalagadi," many of whom had acquired their cattle while tending the herds of the Bakwena ruling class. At the same time, the Kalahari trade had the opposite effect in concentrating wealth in the hands of the few, like Motswakhumo,

---

[72]H/M/36; and H/M/37.
[73]H/M/34; and H/M/46.
[74]H/M/9.

Kgosidintsi's junior son, who bought wagons, provisioned them, and dispatched them to trade for pelts and livestock. Motswakhumo thereby employed many laborers, attracted a considerable following, and built and settled a large cattle outpost at Lentswe-le-Tau.[75]

A final result of the desert trade was the Bakwena penetration of lands to the north and west of their capital, and the far-reaching consequences of that incorporation in the lives of the peoples of the Kalahari.

---

[75]H/M/93.

4

The Peoples of the Kalahari

Incorporation

"Bakgalagadi," the term employed by Bakwena to designate the non-San inhabitants of the desert, is both ambiguous and pejorative. Derived from the Sekwena "people of the Kgalagadi" (*batho ba Kgalagadi*), "Bakgalagadi" excludes the original Kalahari peoples, the San, and carries multiple meanings depending upon one's physical and ethnic location. Accordingly, the Barolong of Mafeking, perhaps with a degree of superiority, refer to Molepolole's Bakwena as "Bakgalagadi" because of the latter's closer proximity to the desert, and the Bakwena refer to Bakgatla and Batlhako living in the heart of the Kalahari at Lephephe "Bakgalagadi." Additionally, the appellation, "Bakgalagadi," lumps diverse ethnic groups, mainly Bangologa, Babolaongwe, Bakgwatheng, and Bashaga, within an undifferentiated category. That slighting of ethnic distinctions underscored the lack of respect accorded the so-named peoples by the Bakwena who equated "Bakgalagadi" with "servant" or inferior. Most of the "Bakgalagadi" I interviewed, thus, rejected the term and preferred to be known by the names of their particular ethnic groups.[1]

Despite their different economies and histories, and despite the denial of a common origin and kinship by members of the four principal "Bakgalagadi" groups, anthropologists like D. F. van der Merwe have identified "Shekgalagadi"

---

[1] A minority who self-identified as "Bakgalagadi" argued, with a degree of pride and disdain for the other peoples of the desert, that they were indeed "the people of the Kgalagadi," whereas the San weren't humans and were "only animals" (*pholoholo heri*). Cf. Susan G. Wynne, "The Land Boards of Botswana: A Problem in Institutional Design," Ph.D. diss., Indiana University, 1989, p. 82, who believes the term "Bakgalagadi" has lost its perjorative connotation.

as a single Sotho dialect cluster, independent of Western Sotho, and thereby classify the Bangologa, Babolaongwe, Bakgwatheng, and Bashaga as a distinctive grouping.[2] Although perhaps accurate, van der Merwe's conclusion might have been based upon dubious evidence, having generalized from texts taken from the Bangologa and Babolaongwe, two groups with an acknowledged and demonstrable kinship link, and having collected Shekgwatheng texts from Bakgwatheng who had lived among Bangologa for about 100 years. The likelihood of cross-contamination is high as was shown by my attempt in 1975 to ascertain the linguistic affinities of the "Bakgalagadi." The "Shekgwatheng" I collected at Letlhakeng, vocabulary of the 100-word list, showed a 100 percent correspondence with Sekwena, whereas the "Shekgwatheng" I recorded at more isolated Moshaweng revealed only a 71 percent correspondence.[3]

The Bangologa, Babolaongwe, and Bakgwatheng appear to be segmentary lineages that have forgotten their common ancestry, possibly as a result of time but also because of dispersal and insulation from one another in the desert.[4] The Bashaga, however, seem to be comprised of diverse Barolong and Batlhaping, post-*difaqane* peoples, and form an ethnic or cultural identity rather than a kin-based grouping. In truth, the desert has colored the historical landscape for both "Bakgalagadi" and historians alike. Because of its limited natural resources, especially water, people have tended to settle in small, scattered, and temporary enclaves. As a consequence, their identities have stressed the local, rather than the wider contexts; at the same time, frequent dislocation and movement have put them into contact with other groups and the new alliances formed can distort remembrances of older relationships. Migration and desert expanses also obscure the origins and tracks and of peoples, influencing the acquisition and interpretation of "Bakgalagadi" histories by nineteenth-century travellers and contemporary observers alike, who have brought their own biases and limitations to the project.

---

[2] I. Schapera and D. F. v. d. Merwe, *Notes on the Tribal Groupings, History, and Customs of the Bakgalagadi* (Cape Town: University of Cape Town, 1945), 23-24.

[3] L/L/1; and L/Ms/4. See Gaontatlhe Mautle, "Bakgalagadi-Bakwena Relationship: A Case of Slavery, c.1840-c.1920," *Botswana Notes and Records* 18 (1986): p. 20, for a contrary review of the linguistic evidence.

[4] For a brief account of the Bangologa, see Adam Kuper, "The Kgalagadi in the Nineteenth Century," *Botswana Notes and Records* 2 (1969): pp. 45-51; and of the Babolaongwe, see I. Schapera, "Ethnographical Texts in the Boloongwe Dialect of Sekgalagadi," *Bantu*

Revealing their human and cultural evolutionary assumptions, some writers have depicted the "Bakgalagadi" as "earthmen," "Vaalpens" or "red belly," and "poor Bechuanas" or "Balala," while others, reflecting the nature of the historical evidence, offer disjointed, brief, and less than comprehensive glimpses of the Bangologa, Babolaongwe, Bakgwatheng, and Bashaga past.[5]

Unlike my view of the Bakwena of whom I can write with a degree of confidence, my perception of the "Bakgalagadi" is exceedingly tentative and restrictive. I have only collected oral histories from the Bakgwatheng, Babolaongwe, and Bashaga residing in major settlements in the Kweneng and Kgalagadi district, including Letlhakeng, Moshaweng, Lephephe, Makabanyane, Sojwe, Shadishadi, Boatlaname, Luzwe, Motokwe, Kang, and Hukuntsi, and my principal interest in conducting that research was the relationship between "Bakgalagadi" and Bakwena. My account, consequently, is bounded by those limitations and vantages.[6]

The proto-Tswana likely originated in the high veld of the central Transvaal perhaps *c.*1000. The Barolong (*ba bina tholo*) separated from the proto-Tswana in *c.*1300, and the Bakwena (*ba bina kwena*), in *c.*1400. In *c.*1450, the Bakaa (*ba bina tlou*) broke away from the Barolong, and shortly thereafter the Bakgwatheng (*ba bina tlou*) separated from the Bakaa and moved northwestward utlimately settling in the Molepolole vicinity in *c.*1500.[7] The

---

Studies 12:3 (1938): pp. 157-87.

[5]See, e.g., Campbell, *Travels*, 1816, pp. 204-05; Campbell, *Travels*, I, pp. 148, 190, 194, 198; Moffat, *Missionary Labours*, pp. 8-13; P. -L. Breutz, *The Tribes of Vryburg District* (Pretoria, 1959), pp. 15-27; and P. -L. Breutz, "Ancient People in the Kalahari Desert," *Afrika und Ubersee* 42 (1958): pp. 49-67. Neither Schapera and van der Merwe, *Tribal Groupings*, nor Adam Kuper, *Kalahari Village Politics: An African Democracy* (London: Cambridge University Press, 1970) offer an overall history of the "Bakgalagadi" in the former and Bangologa in the latter. See also, George B. Silberbauer, *Hunter and Habitat in the Central Kalahari Desert* (Cambridge: Cambridge University Press, 1981); and Alan Barnard, *Hunters and Herders of Southern Africa: A Comparative Ethnography of the Khoisan Peoples* (Cambridge: Cambridge University Press, 1992).

[6]For a more extended discussion on methodology, see my "Essay on Sources" at the back.

[7]Precise dates for the "Bakgalagadi" are simply markers and are wildly speculative based as they are on king-lists. Some of my assumptions reveal the tenuousness of those dates. These are: (a) the lists are accurate; (b) each generation averages thirty years; and (c) groups are founded by the first person on the list. The king-lists of the Barolong and Bakaa are taken from Wookey's *Dico*, and those of the Bakwena, Bakgwatheng, Bangologa, and Babolaongwe are from my collection of oral histories. See David P. Henige, *The Quest for a Chimera: The Chronology of Oral Tradition* (Oxford, 1974), for a cautionary critique of king-lists. Cf. Thomas Tlou and Alec Campbell, *History of Botswana*

proto-Babolaongwe/Bangologa left the Barolong in *c*.1550, and followed the Molopo river westward. Near Lekulachuchwa, the group split into two groups, the Babolaongwe (*ba bina nare*) and Bangologa (*ba bina tholo*). The Bangologa moved toward the north and west, but the Babolaongwe remained in the Lekulachuchwa area until *c*.1650 when one group, the *ba bina phiri* section headed northward toward Dithejwane, and the other, the *ba bina nare* section, east toward Lesotho.[8]

The Bakgwatheng at Molepolole built in stone (Bakwena recall stone houses and walls built by the "Banakedi" just below the northern side of Molepolole's Kgosing), and they dug trench mines for *sebilo* and iron.[9] When Kgabo's Bakwena met them at Molepolole in the early eighteenth century, the Bakgwatheng consisted of two sections: the "Banakedi" at Molepolole and a second group at Dithejwane, about ten kilometers west of Molepolole.[10] The Bakwena defeated the Bakgwatheng and occupied their territory until the death of Kgabo when the Bakwena, under Motshodi, returned east to Mochudi, allowing the Bakgwatheng and Babolaongwe, who had joined the Bakgwatheng since *c*.1650, to regroup at Dithejwane. Motswasele (*a* Legojane) settled in the Molepolole area during the latter part of the eighteenth century, while the Bakgwatheng and Babolaongwe remained at Dithejwane. Seitlhamo (*a* Motswasele) fought the Bakgwatheng and Babolaongwe, defeated them, and moved his Bakwena to Dithejwane in the late eighteenth century.

Perhaps sections of Bakgwatheng and Babolaongwe fled from the Bakwena invaders, but others remained and were absorbed by the conquerers. The integration of Bakgwatheng and Babolaongwe, not as servants (*batlhanka*),

---

(Gaborone: Macmillan Botswana, 1984), pp. 58-59, who propose that the proto-Bakgalagadi originated directly from the proto-Tswana in *c*.1000.

[8]My account of "Bakgalagadi" origins are from H/L/1; H/L/2; H/L/3; H/L/12; H/L/14; H/L/17; H/L/18; H/L/24; H/B/1; H/Lu/2; H/Lu/3; H/Mt/1; H/K/1; H/K/2; H/K/3; H/H/1; and H/H/3.

[9]*Sebilo* was used to decorate people's hair and body. I found at least five trench mines in the vicinity of Molepolole. Some of these reached depths of two meters and lengths of over 100 meters. Associated with those mines were stone-walling, "iron molds," and pottery, all of unknown provenance.

[10]It is unclear whether the Bakwena called the Molepolole Bakgwatheng "Banakedi" because they allegedly refused to fight the invaders ("they slinked away like the *nakedi* or 'polecate'"), or because they were deemed the people of Nakedi, a son of Pitsana, a Mokgwatheng *kgoshi*. H/M/5; H/M/8; and H/L/24.

within the mixed settlement was evidenced in the marriage of Seletlo's daughter, a Mobolaongwe, to Motswasele (*a* Legwale). The union produced Kgosidintsi, who became the *kgosi* of Mokgalo and was perhaps the most powerful Mokwena next to Sechele during most of the nineteenth century. Another of Seletlo's daughters married Mosimane (*a* Mothee), who was the head of the Bakwena *kgotla* of Senyadima and *ntona* under Sechele. The Boo-Motlhabi, Boo-Mhiemang, and Boo-Moitlhobo, lineages that were brought together by Sechele to form the *kgotla* of Basimane, were Babolaongwe who were amalgamated by the Bakwena during this period. Other prominent "Bakgalagadi" might have joined the Bakwena later, like the Mobolaongwe Segakisa, head of Difetlhamolelo, and the Mokgwatheng, Sekonopelo, head of Boatlaname in the northeastern Kweneng.[11]

Seitlhamo and Legwale remained at Dithejwane, but Motswasele, Legwale's heir, moved the Bakwena to Shokwane, taking with him assimilated groups of "Bakgalagadi" and leaving behind other groups of Bakgwatheng and Babolaongwe at Dithejwane. Because of the *difaqane*, in *c.*1820, Babolaongwe of the *ba bina nare* section joined the Bakgwatheng and Babolaongwe at Dithejwane, and when Moruakgomo, *kgosi* of the breakaway Boo-Ra-Tshosa Bakwena, moved to Molepolole after the civil war in *c.*1822 and tried to establish his control over Dithejwane's inhabitants, he was successfully repulsed and the defenders were only defeated by Moruakgomo's second expedition. Some of the Babolaongwe, especially those of the *ba bina nare* group, retreated northward into the desert and settled at Letlhakeng. The majority of the Bakgwatheng, however, remained under Moruakgomo when he moved his Bakwena from Molepolole to Dithejwane.

Whether to punish Dithejwane's "Bakgalagadi" for having resisted his rule or to harness the labor of conquered foreigners, it appears that Moruakgomo instituted the *batlhanka* ("servants") system whereby "Bakgalagadi" served Bakwena.[12] Some of my "Bakgalagadi" interviewees suggested that it was the desert's wealth, evidenced in a gift of elephant ivory from the Babolaongwe who had fled Dithejwane for Letlhakeng, that sparked Moruakgomo's interest in the

---

[11]H/Lu/3.

[12]See, Mautle, "Bakgalagadi-Bakwena Relationship," pp. 19-31,who argues that the

Kalahari's products and "Bakgalagadi" labor. Nonetheless, the concept was not new. Juniors were said to have been the *batlhanka* of seniors, denoting a subordinate position but one that was neither perpetual nor hereditary. But Moruakgomo's system applied the idea to certain groups of people based upon ethnicity, rendering the terms "servant" and "Bakgalagadi" synonymous and creating a permanent labor caste.[13] Before having fully established the system, however, Moruakgomo's Bakwena were driven from Dithejwane's fastness and scattered by Sebetwane's Makololo in *c*.1824.

Moruakgomo's labor system, mainly the use of "Bakgalagadi" labor to exploit the desert's resources, prompted the migration of "Bakgalagadi" into the farther reaches of the Kalahari. Among these were the Bashaga, so-named apparently by the Bakgwatheng who had derisively referred to them as "*batho ba sha sha*" or "Bashaga" because they used "sh" for the Shekgwatheng "s." The Bashaga were of diverse origins unconnected by kinship, but all were former members of Transvaal Barolong and Batlhaping groups who had been dispersed by the *difaqane*. The first group of Bashaga were the Baga-Shekgalo, Baga-Motsoto, Baga-Moriti, and Baga-Panyana. These joined the "Bakgalagadi" settlement at Dithejwane before Moruakgomo's second attack, were placed under Bakgwatheng sections, and fled with the Babolaongwe to Letlhakeng after Moruakgomo's conquest. A second group of Bashaga, the Baga-Panyana and Baga-Monyemane, arrived at Dithejwane after the first group's departure but before the Makololo invasion.[14]

Moswaane's Babolaongwe left Letlhakeng and travelled south seeking refuge among the Bangwaketse, the senior group led by Mokwambe headed west to Luzwe, and a third group under Moiabane remained at Letlhakeng. Many

---

"Bakgalagadi" weren't "servants" (*batlhanka*) but "slaves" (*balata*).

[13]The Batlhaping similarly employed the "Balala." See, e.g., Campbell, *Travels*, 1816, pp. 204-04; Campbell, *Travels*, I, pp. 148, 190, 194, 198; and Moffat, *Missionary Labours*, pp. 8-13.

[14]The Baga-Shekgalo, Baga-Motsoto, Baga-Moriti, and Baga-Panyana were once Barolong and as such were *ba bina tholo*. The Baga-Shekgalo, Baga-Motsoto, and Baga-Moriti, having been placed under the Bakgwatheng, adopted their senior's *shirethyo* and became *ba bina tlou*. Bashaga groups, in addition to their "national" totemic identities, maintained a separate clan identity. Accordingly, the Baga-Shekgalo were so-called because they were praised as eaters of *rikgalo* (fruit of the *mokgalo* tree), and the Baga-Panyana were renowned for their dancing (*go panya*). H/L/24; and H/Mt/2. Cf. Kuper, *Kalahari Village*, pp. 21-22, for his definition of *shirethyo*.

Bakgwatheng, having been ordered by Moruakgomo to harvest the Kalahari's products moved from Dithejwane to lands south of Letlhakeng, and a few left the Kweneng for Ga-Ngwaketse. Most of the first contingent of Bashaga followed the setting sun into the desert, and those of the second migration were scattered by the Makololo advance. The Baga-Panyana initially headed southwest to Verda and Mabuashehube, and then north to Chane, Lehututu, Kang, Tsetseng, and Motokwe. The Baga-Monyemane split into two sections; the senior group led by Pule and his brother, Taritapane, moved northward, while the second group, headed by Morikele, Pule's junior brother, sought refuge among Kanye's Bangwaketse. When the Bangwaketse tried to make Morikele's Baga-Monyemane their servants (*batlhanka*), the Bashaga left Ga-Ngwaketse for Mabuashehube, but finding it too dry there, moved back north but in the far reaches of the desert to Chane, Lehututu, and Kang where the pan held surface water year round and plant and animal life, including large elephant herds, abounded.

Like their juniors, Pule's Baga-Monyemane wandered over the Kalahari's expanses seeking a place of settlement. The group first joined Moiabane's Babolaongwe at Letlhakeng, and together they followed the Letlhakeng river's northward flow to Kudumelapsye, Lephephe, and into Ga-Ngwato. Resisting the Bangwato's attempt to make them servants (*batlhanka*), the Baga-Monyemane headed west to Ga-Tawana where they fought pitched battles with the Batawana to preserve their independence. Taritapane employed guerilla tactics to overcome the numerically superior Batawana who sent expeditions as far south as Pehasegwane (Ghanzi) where the Baga-Monyemane had settled. When word of Morikele's discovery of Kang pan reached them, Pule's Baga-Monyemane moved to Kang to rejoin their juniors.[15]

Sebetwane's Makololo were defeated by the Bangwaketse in 1826 at Dithejwane, and retreated into the Kalahari, where they met Mokwambe's Babolaongwe, then under Morimo and Molehele, at Nokeng-ya Botete. The Makololo defeated the Babolaongwe, killed Molehele, and drove Morimo and his

---

[15]Taritapane assumed heroic status in these accounts. He was a swift runner who taunted the Batawana, and led them into Bashaga ambushes. He also escorted Pule and the Baga-Monyemane to safety at Kang, and returned to Pehasegwane to protect the rear against Batawana incursions. H/K/2.

remnants southward, back to the Kweneg, to Tuusi, Luzwe, and Mazeaboroko.[16] Sebetwane's departure allowed Moruakgomo's Bakwena, the Boo-Ra-Tshosa, to return to Dithejwane where Bubi and his successor, Kgakge, resisted amalgamation by Sechele's Bakwena faction in a struggle called the "wars of the stubborn people" (*dintwa ya mokakana*).[17]

The outcome of those "wars" involved both armed conflict and an economic contest that included the ability to attract European missionaries and traders who supplied guns and immigrants who tipped the numerical advantage. Insofar as they produced the goods for the arms traffic, the desert and its peoples were a key to that competition. At Dithejwane, the Boo-Ra-Tshosa commanded the Kalahari's gateway, but the Bakgwatheng, Babolaongwe, and Bashaga resisted incorporation and were scattered over isolated stretches of the desert. At Tshonwane, Sechele's Bakwena stood between the northward trekking Europeans and fleeing refugees and the Boo-Ra-Tshosa, and were thus better placed to attract both groups. Effectively barred from the guns trade, the Boo-Ra-Tshosa's Kgakge tried to cut off Sechele from the desert by intercepting his Kalahari expeditions in 1846, and in retaliation, Sechele attacked Dithejwane and defeated the Boo-Ra-Tshosa. As spoils of war, Sechele's Bakwena assumed control over large numbers of Boo-Ra-Tshosa "Bakgalagadi" servants (*batlhanka*), like the Boo-Morimo, Babolaongwe, who were taken by Sechele, and the Boo-Moipisi, Bakgwatheng, and Baga-Shekgalo, Bashaga, who were absorbed by Kgosidintsi.[18]

For the mostly reunited Bakwena, the Kalahari trade enabled the amassing of personal fortunes, mainly among the elite class, and was essential for the arms used in the defence against Afrikaner incursions. Europeans, both missionaries and traders, provided guns in exchange for the ivory, ostrich feathers, and skins derived from the desert, and the "Bakgalagadi" possessed the knowledge and

---

[16]H/Lu/2.

[17]See, Cumming, *Five Years*, I, pp. 234-35, 277; Livingstone, *Missionary Researches*, p. 41; Chamberlin, *Some Letters*, pp. 45, 52-53; Schapera, *Family Letters*, I, pp. 51-57, 111-13, 123, 138, 170-71; Schapera, *Family Letters*, II, p. 15; Schapera, *Missionary Correspondence*, pp. 15-17, 34, 81, 89-90; Edwin W. Smith, *Great Lion of Bechuanaland* (London, 1957), p. 150; Sillery, *Sechele*, pp. 69, 81, 83-84; and Robert Moffat to J. J. Freeman, Kuruman, July 16, 1850, LMS-SOAS, South Africa, Incoming Letters, Box 25, Folder 1, Jacket D.

skills that were required for hunting in and traversing the Kalahari. Those circumstances and economic needs, throughout most of the nineteenth century, propelled the Bakwena penetration of the desert. The Bakwena would later discover the desert's enormous potential for their cattle, goat, and sheep herds, before but particularly after the onset of drills and boreholes that tapped the waters that lay below the Kalahari's bone dry surface. But the trade initiative first led to the close contact, interaction, and exploitation between Bakwena and "Bakgalagadi."

The *batlhanka* system probably evolved toward greater stringency over time, such that when Sebele formally ended it in *c*.1892, the Bakgwatheng, Babolaongwe, and Bashaga had no property rights in the Kweneng and were required to provide whatever services were demanded by Bakwena masters. Perhaps most pernicious was the lot of domestic servants (*Makgalagadi a lolwapa*) in which husbands, wives, and their children became inherited property and subject to the whim of their masters.[19] Bakwena exploitation, however, wasn't entirely capricious, but was directed at certain economic ends. Accordingly, the Babolaongwe and Bashaga, premier hunters, were pursued, conscripted, and exploited by the Bakwena, while the Bakgwatheng who were primarily cultivators were less susceptible to sting of Bakwena hegemony.

Expulsion and Flight, *c*.1822-50

The soil and annual rainfall, along with the several perennial streams and pools, in the Molepolole area were ideal for the mixed economy of the Bakgwatheng. First building their stone houses and walls on the northern slope of the Molepolole or Moruakgomo hills in *c*.1450, the Bakgwatheng dug *sebilo* and iron a few hundred meters behind their town, and cultivated fields of sorghum (*mabele*), millet (*lebelebele*), melons (*marotse*), and beans (*dinawa*) with iron hoes in the fertile plain below. To supplement their diet, they gathered wild berries and roots. The Bakgwatheng placed a lesser reliance upon hunting and herding than did the Bakwena, especially before the nineteenth century, and they

---

[18]H/L/2; H/L/12; H/L/14; and H/L/17.

[19]Mautle, "Bakgalagadi-Bakwena Relationship," pp. 22-26.

had no cattle but had herds of goats and sheep, and hunted mainly small animals such as springhare and certain varieties of antelopes.[20]

The Bakgwatheng were forced from Molepolole by Kgabo's Bakwena in the early eighteenth century, moved to Dithejwane but abandoned it during the 1820s for their new homes in the Letlhakeng vicinity to escape being made servants (*batlhanka*) by Moruakgomo's Bakwena. Seiso's *motse* at Mokgwelekgwele, situated about ten kilometers south of Letlhakeng, resembled its nineteenth century Bakwena counterpart. Left largely undisturbed by the turbulence swirling around it caused by the *difaqane* and Bakwena civil war, Mokgwelekgwele was built around a central *sebeso*, called Kgosing, that consisted of an animal fold, a meeting place, and a circle of homes. Beyond the *kgosi's kgotla* were the *makgotla* of his junior uncles (*boo-rrangwane*), Goo-Ra-Nakedi and Goo-Ra-Gaorewe. At the beginning of the present century, immigrants from Ga-Tawana, Kgatleng, and Ga-Ngwato joined Mokgwelekgwele's Bakgwatheng, forming the *makgotla* of Goo-Moretele, Goo-Tsie, and Goo-Tseeng.[21]

Despite those similarities, Letlhakeng's drier conditions induced changes among the Bakgwatheng. They settled in low, sandy areas near seasonal streams, and during the dry season, they dug shallow wells in the riverbed. Mokgwelekgwele, unlike the more compact Bakgwatheng towns at Molepolole and Dithejwane, consisted of scattered homesteads, and because of its sandy soil, the people's fields were at greater distances from their homes. Insufficient for robust crops of grains, the rainfall influenced Bakgwatheng cultivators to rely more upon melons and beans than upon sorghum, millet, and maize. Their gardens, nonetheless, still provided the mainstay of their diet, supplemented by their herds of goats and sheep, wild berries and roots, and hunting.[22]

At winter's end and just before the first rains fell, when strong winds whipped across the veld and the fruits on the *motlhopi* and *moretlwa* trees ripened, Bakgwatheng cultivators, both women and men, cleared their fields.

---

[20]When Bakgwatheng interviewees told me they had "no cattle," they might have been speaking in the comparative sense between the past and 1975 when cattle predominated. However, they specifically noted that the first Mokgwatheng to own cattle was Reokwaeng about the turn of the present century. H/L/5; H/L/10; H/L/15; H/L/20; and H/L/23.
[21]H/L/1; H/L/2; and H/L/24.

Using a digging stick (*kepu*),[23] the cultivator uprooted grass and bushes, and felled trees by burning their trunks. In the late afternoon, the tilled plot was seeded. Using their feet, farmers scooped the soil to a depth of about four centimeters, and stamped it down to cover each seed. Melon seeds were spaced about two meters apart, beans, about one meter, and sorghum and millet, about thirty centimeters. In that way, a woman and man cultivated several fields, each measuring over twenty by forty meters, that included a field of melons and sorghum, another of melons and beans, and a third of maize.[24]

Apparently the Bakgwatheng didn't find iron in the Letlhakeng area, and thus came to rely upon eventually the digging stick. When they obtained the Sekwena hoe (*mogoma*) perhaps during the mid-nineteenth century through trade, the Bakgwatheng modified their method of cultivation by, like the Bakwena, planting the seeds before weeding and tilling the ground around the young shoots.[25]

The resemblance of Bakgwatheng to Bakwena allowed them to escape much of the worst abuses of the master and servant relationship; they had little that the Bakwena wanted. But that innate similarity, and sometimes adaptations, have occasioned the contempt of some Babolaongwe and Bashaga who cided the Bakgwatheng for having "assimilated" and taken on the attributes of the despised Bakwena masters. "Majigwana," they called the supposed assimilationists. In truth, the Bakgwatheng were premier cultivators long before the arrival of the Bakwena, and didn't possess the hunting skills or knowledge of the desert that made the Babolaongwe and Bashaga the desired targets for that particular form of Bakwena exploitation.[26]   Rather, the Bakgwatheng were exploited by the Bakwena in another way; Sechele's extensive fields at Midie were likely cultivated by a permanent workforce of Bakgwatheng servants.

---

[22]H/L/2; H/L/7; and H/L/23.

[23]The *kepu* differed from the *mhana* or digging stick used to uproot edible bulbs and roots. The *kepu* was made from a hardwood tree like the *mokala* and *moselesele*, and was about a meter in length, five centimeters in diameter at the handle, and ten centimeters in diameter at the sharpened, digging end. H/L/4; and H/L/6.

[24]H/L/4.

[25]H/L/23.

[26]H/L/7; H/L/23; and H/L/24.

Hunters and herders of goats and sheep, the Babolaongwe found the desert in the Mabuashehube area well-suited to their productive needs. Game was abundant, and their goats and sheep thrived in that environment. But the Babolaongwe, and Bashaga who later joined them in flight, were only driven by the *difaqane* and Bakwena invaders into the far reaches of the Kalahari, where they sought to hide from their tormenters. During those years of wandering, roughly from the time of Moruakgomo to the mid-nineteenth century, the Babolaongwe and Bashaga formed small, isolated, and mobile communities wherein gathering supplanted agriculture as the most reliable and abundant source of plant food.[27]

Their hemispherical houses, built of poles and grass and called *mosimana*, were constructed by men and women, and had a height of about one-and-a-half meters and a floor diameter of two meters. A fence of thornbushes encircled the *mosimana* and enclosed a garden, about nine by fourteen meters, within its confine. The garden's location was incidental to the selection of a settlement site that was based upon the availability of water, game, and edible roots and berries. Both women and men shared the labor of house-building and fencing, and of clearing and cultivating the garden.[28] Working with a digging stick (*kepu*) in the manner of Bakgwatheng cultivators, the Babolaongwe and Bashaga planted mainly melons and beans because they were the most drought resistant of their crops, had the shortest growing season, and when dried could be stored for long periods of time. Beans, mixed with goat dung ashes, lasted for several years, and dried melon strips (*magapa*) kept almost indefinitely. Because they could be stored, garden produce, despite their secondary position to hunting and gathering, helped to insure against periods of drought during which yields from hunting and gathering declined.[29] In contrast, most roots and bulbs were eaten the same day they were collected, and a storable root, that of the *mongone* tree, lasted for only six months.[30]

---

[27]H/L/1; H/L/3; H/L/4; H/L/6; H/L/7; H/L/9; H/L/11; H/L/13; H/L/16; H/L/19; and H/L/22.
[28]H/L/4.
[29]H/L/13.
[30]H/L/9; H/L/11; and H/L/13.

Goats provided milk, meat, and skins, and were the mainstay of the Babolaongwe diet. Better adapted to the desert than cattle or sheep, goats could survive for several months without water, depending instead upon succulents and wild melons. They also multiplied faster; goats bore from one to four kids per birth, while sheep, one to two lambs, and cows, normally one calf.[31] Goat's milk, drunk fresh or curdled and stored inside a skin sack (*lekuka*), and its meat was preferred over that of cattle by the Babolaongwe, and the skins of goats were important for making clothing, carrying and storing sacks, and floor mats. Their fat-tailed sheep, however, were prized for their fat and their skins, especially when sewn into cloaks, carried greater value.[32]

Babolaongwe goat herders watched and regulated the life cycle of their animals. Mating was timed to coincide with the first rains, in about November, when forage was abundant and when the goats were in peak condition. Born in May during the last rains, goat kids were suckled until July when they were weaned. From July until November, the driest and consequently the leanest time of the year, goat milk provided a staple food for the Babolaongwe.[33] Their herds of goats and sheep were finally a means by which the Babolaongwe acquired cattle during a later period when cattle ownership became economically important.

The Babolaongwe were the most sophisticated hunters among the "Bakgalagadi," as was evidenced in the amount of labor they invested in constructing their traps, the complexity of their hunting technology, and the borrowings of Babolaongwe methods by the Bashaga.[34] The Bakgwatheng game trap (*lemena*) employed the labor of a single hunter or household, and consisted of a pit of about three meters in depth capable of holding two or three animals with sharpened stakes from the *moselesele* tree fixed at the bottom and a grass cover over the opening. The *lemena* was a passive trap. Built along an animal trail, the pit awaited its prey. The Babolaongwe, in contrast, employed at least two main types of game traps that required greater amounts of labor. The *shilekeri* was built by a single household or hunting band, and consisted of a pit with four

---

[31]A she-goat bore kids for up to nine seasons, whereas a cow, twelve. H/L/8; H/L/10; and H/L/15.

[32]H/L/10.

[33]H/L/10; and H/L/15.

[34]H/L/7; H/L/21; and H/L/23.

thornbush fences to direct game to the trap that extended for up to one-and-a-half kilometers in length. The fences, placed at each corner of the pit and set at right angles, moved game toward the trap in all four directions. The *biruku* was an elaborate system of multiple pits about 100 meters long dug along an animal trail with thornbush fences at each end that extended, like open arms, from the trap for about 60 meters to the open plain. The *biruku* was a major project that required the labor of an entire village to construct and the effort of beaters and chasers to drive the game toward the fence and line of pits where hunters hid behind mounds of heaped earth. Among the Bakgwatheng, Babolaongwe, and Bashaga, men, women, and children worked in the construction, use, and maintenance of traps.[35]

Women, however, were the principal gatherers. Despite the importance attached to herding, perhaps by my Babolaongwe men interviewees, gathering provided the daily food staple. Gathering tools included a sharpened digging stick (*mhana*), about a meter in length and one-and-a-half centimeters in diameter, and a variety of carrying sacks, such as the *koma* or sewn purse and the larger *lerachana* made of an entire goat, calf, or other animal skin.[36] Edible roots and bulbs were collectively called *digweke*, and melons and berries, *maungo*. Roots, bulbs, and melons were commonly roasted, and berries were dried or eaten fresh. Because most gathered foods were eaten the day they were collected, gathering was a daily activity that required a substantial knowledge of plant life and hours of tedious labor.

Gathering differed during the dry and rainy seasons.[37] Many varieties of edible *digweke* and *maungo* were available and easily found during the rainy season. Although buried, roots and bulbs could be readily spotted by the leafy growth above the sandy soil. But during the dry season, when the leaves wilted, dried, and were blown away by the cold winter winds, very little trace of the roots and bulbs remained for the gatherer to see. The few exceptions were the *mongone* which was a tree identifiable by its trunk and branches, and the *motsia* and *morama* whose leaves wilted but remained on the plants throughout the dry

---

[35]H/L/7.

[36]H/L/6; H/L/11; and H/L/13.

[37]As in hunting, the Bashaga learned much of their gathering skills from the

season. Gathering, thus, during the lean winter months required considerable skill and a sharp eye. Some of the more popularly consumed *digweke* and *maungo* included the following roots and bulbs: the *motsia*, available year round, *mahubala*, gathered from December to June, and *kole*, found from around mid-October with the first rains to June. Melons like the *kgeme* were eaten from April when it ripened to June, and the *makawa*, from February to April. *Moretlwa* berries ripened in December and continued until April, and *ringone* season lasted from December to January.[38]

Besides having to compensate for the unavailability of certain plant foods during the dry season, gatherers were compelled to search wider areas of the desert for equivalent yields from sunup to sundown. Gakenne Tshipa, a Moshaga, described a typical day. A woman awakened before sunrise and began her day's labor when forms could barely be perceived. Normally working alone to keep her finds for herself, the gatherer tried to hide her favorite spots from her neighbors. Water, if available, was carried in an ostrich eggshell container, and if unavailable, the woman relied upon the *lerija*, a watery root found on the desert. At noon, when the sun was at its hottest, the gatherer rested, roasted and ate some of her morning's collection, and later, resumed collecting until about sunset when she returned home to feed her family.[39]

Living as migrants in inaccessible areas of the Kalahari, groups of Babolaongwe and Bashaga avoided repression and exploitation by the Batswana, but the relative abundance of the rainy season was accompanied by the extreme poverty of the dry season when most of one's labor was consumed in food-production. Better watered places beckoned them, but at a price of their freedom. My interviewees told me that Babolaongwe women, despite their subordinate position to men, were among the first to encourage a move to the rivers and pans nearer and exposed to the Bakwena. Perhaps women's provisioning role gave rise to that sentiment; perhaps a particularly harsh winter forced their hand.

By the middle of the nineteenth century, the Bakwena had penetrated and learned about the desert's corners and couldn't be easily eluded. In addition, after 1852, Sechele systematized the control and distribution of "Bakgalagadi"

Babolaongwe. H/L/22.
[38]H/L/6; H/L/9; H/L/11; H/L/13; H/L/16; H/L/19; and H/L/22.

servants. He allocated certain groups of "Bakgalagadi" to the Bakwena elite, and reserved sections of the desert and the peoples thereon to individuals and sections of his town. Kgakge, head of Ntlheng-ya Godimo, retained mastery over the Bashaga Baga-Motsoto, and acquired the Boo-Mpolayakeswe Bakgwatheng. Mokgalo's head, Kgosidintsi, received Bakgwatheng, most of whom lived near Kurwe, and the Baga-Shekgalo group of Bashaga. Sechele kept all of the Babolaongwe (*ba bina nare*), and three Bashaga groups, the Baga-Moriti, Baga-Panyana, and Baga-Monyemane. Apparently, Sechele's reorganization brought stability to the master and servant relationship, and gave less incentive for "Bakgalagadi" flight.[40]

Whatever the cause for migration, whether they were driven or attracted, gradually throughout the second half of the nineteenth century, groups of Babolaongwe and Bashaga left the driest regions of the Kalahari and settled near sources of water.[41] The move led to significant economic changes.

Acculturation, *c.*1850-92

From *c.*1850 to 1892 when the *batlhanka* system formally ended in the Kweneng, Babolaongwe and Bashaga increasingly settled in more stable and larger concentrations in areas of greater rainfall, they invested more labor in house construction, placed a greater emphasis upon cultivation and began to acquire cattle, and they directed their hunting toward the needs of long-distance trade. A Babolaongwe town, during this period of acculturation, came to resemble its Bakgwatheng counterpart, consisting at its core a senior man called the *kgoshi*, his wife and children, and his junior brothers and uncles. Clients, the Basarwa (San), attached themselves to the Babolaongwe especially during times of drought. At first, the attachment was temporary, only during the dry season or years of drought, but later it became a permanent relationship in which labor was exchanged for food, tobacco and cannabis, and other goods.[42]

---

[39]H/L/19.

[40] Wynne, "Land Boards," pp. 90-95.

[41]H/L/19.

[42]H/L/22; and H/Mk/1. For a comparative description of the "Bakgalagadi" and Bakwena *makgotla*, their formation and organization, see Wynne, "Land Boards," pp. 95-126.

The Bashaga generally chose to retain their life of gathering, herding, and hunting longer than the Babolaongwe. Some, like the Bashaga of Katu and Bokgeme who lived in the vicinity of Kang, refused to acknowledge Bakwena supremacy throughout the second half of the nineteenth century, and were punished by Sechele who crushed them with his army.[43] On the whole, the Bashaga were slower to abandon the single family homestead for the aggregations of the Babolaongwe town, although they eventually underwent a similar pattern of acculturation.[44] Changes, such as increased investments in house construction whereby the *mosimana* shelter was supplanted by a more permanent structure of mud and cowdung bricks, pole frames, and grass thatching, occurred mostly among the Babolaongwe before being undergone among the Bashaga.[45]

Indicative of greater permanence, Babolaongwe houses and towns also revealed basic shifts in the modes of production from gathering to a greater reliance on cultivation, and from isolation to external trade. The Babolaongwe and Bashaga obtained the Masubea type of iron hoe (*mogoma*) from trade with people along the Noka-ya Botete, and with that implement they cultivated larger, more productive fields. The Masubea hoe consisted of an iron blade about eighteen centimeters wide set into one end of a wooden shaft that measured about ninety centimeters in length and twelve centimeters in circumference, and was used in a kneeling position and thrust from side to side in a rowing motion.[46] The hoe enabled the cultivation of fields that were over twice the size of former Babolaongwe gardens and were situated at a distance from the homestead and on fertile ground. Babolaongwe and Bashaga cultivators fenced their fields to protect them from domestic and wild animals, and usually placed them within sight of their homes so they could be watched. Their principal crops remained melons and beans.[47]

The later introduction of the Sekwena hoe and ox plough enabled even larger fields that were located at great distances from Babolaongwe and Bashaga settlements, creating the distinction, as in the case of the Bakwena, between the

---

[43]H/K/3.
[44]H/L/14; H/L/17; H/L/22; H/L/24; H/K/2; and H/K/3.
[45]H/L/16.
[46]H/L/20.

home and "lands." In addition, during the first decades of the twentieth century, with the ox plough came a change in staple food crops among the Babolaongwe and Bashaga, from beans and melons to grains. Their production, however, frequently failed to supply their demand; grains, accordingly, were commonly purchased from Molepolole.[48]

Bakwena demands for the desert's products, most notably the pelts of fur-bearing animals, and the opportunity for "Bakgalagadi" gain changed the nature of hunting, mainly among the Babolaongwe. Hunting, during the former period, was essentially for internal consumption and directed at certain species of antelopes. In contrast, Bakwena masters gave hunting dogs to their Babolaongwe servants and directed them to collect fox (*motlhose*), jackal (*phokojwe*), and polecat (*tshipa*) skins. Although exploited, Babolaongwe servants used the system to their advantage.

Babolaongwe hunters trained the dogs, hunted with them, and at the end of the season travelled to Molepolole to deliver their loads to their masters. Babolaongwe were forbidden from keeping a single pelt for themselves, and were only allowed to eat the meat of their quarry. Although comprising an important source of animal protein during the lean and difficult winter months when hunting season was at its peak, the meat of fur-bearing animals was meager compensation for a consuming occupation. Hunting season lasted for three months, from March to May, when pelt quality was at its thickest and finest. Working all day, the hunter and his team of dogs set out before sunrise to locate and track animal spoor that had been imprinted the night before and was still fresh in the damp, morning sand. If found, the prey was usually trapped in groups, enabling the likelihood of several kills with each successful tracking. At noon, when the sun was hottest, the hunter stopped to skin his morning's catch, and resumed hunting in the afternoon until about sunset. With a team of three dogs, a skillful hunter could obtain nine to eleven pelts daily.

The next day, the hunter stretched the previous day's catch, fur side facing down, on the ground with wooden pegs. The pelt was allowed to dry for only two to three hours in the sun, after which water was sprinkled on the skin and it

---

[47]H/L/16; and H/L/19.
[48]H/L/19; and H/L/21.

was scraped using a goat's jawbone to remove the remaining tissues. The hunter then tanned the pelt by rubbing each skin until it was soft and supple. A man was able to finish about three to four pelts per day, and thus one day of successful hunting required about three days of tanning.[49]

Bakwena masters expected all of the season's catch, but only a "fool," said Moloiwa Molale, a Mobolaongwe, took all of his pelts to Molepolole.[50] Molale estimated that servants kept for themselves at least half of their season's labor, much of which was employed in establishing new trade routes with peoples to their north, beyond the Kweneng and away from the Bakwena. In that way, Babolaongwe hunters became traders, some of whom took up the occupation fulltime and comprised a class called *bigwaba*. Some *bigwaba* grew wealthy from trading, retired, and attracted dependents who were retained with gifts in return for services.[51] Clients, particularly Basarwa (San), allowed Babolaongwe traders to carry on tasks such as hunting and trading simultaneously supplying both Bakwena masters and themselves during the winter months that were optimal for both activities. Eventually, the Basarwa shouldered most of the labor required for the acquisition of pelts along with the burden of goods and supplies on Babolaongwe trade expeditions.[52]

The most important trade route, conducted surreptitiously within Bangwato territory, headed north to the peoples along the Noka-ya Botete, including the Bakalaka, Bakhurutse, Banyanza, Basubea, Bakoba, and Batete. Babolaongwe traders took fur skins, leather made from wildebeest skins (*dikgole*), and ostrich feathers, and purchased tobacco, iron hoes, beads, gourds, and cooking and water pots. They returned and retraded their wares for considerable profits. During the first decades of the twentieth century, for instance, Babolaongwe traders bought a block of crushed tobacco of about 2,200 cubic centimeters in volume for one fox (*motlhose*) pelt at Nokeng-ya Botete. In the Kalahari, a mere 8 cubic centimeters of that crushed tobacco purchased a fox

---

[49]H/L/10; and H/L/20.
[50]H/L/10.
[51]H/L/21.
[52]H/L/21; H/L/22; and H/L/24.

skin.[53] Besides accumulating goods in that way for his next expedition, the trader purchased goats and sheep with skins to increase his herds and thereby attract clients.

Two other trade destinations, Bakalaka areas to the west and north of Serowe, the Bangwato capital, held little price or distance advantage over the Nokeng-ya Botete route. Babolaongwe traders took fur skins, *dikgole*, and small goats in exchange for tobacco, cannabis, cooking and water pots, and beads.[54] In turn, "Matabele" traders from the northeast visited the Babolaongwe seeking fur pelts, *dikgole*, goats, and sewn cloaks (*dikobo*), and bringing spears, axes, adzes, bracelets, and copper beads called *khumo*. Two strands of beads, each about thirty centimeters in length, bought one fox (*motlhose*) skin.[55]

The northern trade enhanced class distinctions and led to a redistribution of wealth among the Babolaongwe, it enabled, indeed encouraged, Basarwa clientage and servitude, it introduced new technologies and luxury goods into Babolaongwe households, and it was a means of escape from Bakwena exploitation. The power of Bakwena masters was neither total nor absolute. The Babolaongwe had turned to their advantage a system that had been designed to repress and exploit them. Sebele's abolition of the masters and servants system helped to redirect trade south toward Molepolole. It was good business. Further, abolition in 1892 made the "Bakgalagadi" subject to Bakwena taxes (*sehuba*) which were collected by Bakwena officials who made annual circuits throughout the Kalahari gathering skins, ostrich feathers, and other desert products for the *kgosi*. The taxes were transported to the Bakwena capital by impressed people from whence the goods derived.[56]

Evidence suggests that the system had been crumbling before 1892. Kgosidintsi, son of a Mobolaongwe mother, "felt pity" for the "Bakgalagadi," according to an unnamed "Mokgalagadi," and urged Sechele to "'leave them so that they may own this and that just like us BaKwena.' And through this word of Kgosidintsi the MaKgalagadi became people, they began to buy guns and cattle,

---

[53]H/L/21.
[54]H/L/21.
[55]H/L/13; H/L/16; and H/L/21.
[56]H/Lu/3; and Wynne, "Land Boards," pp. 104-05.

and advanced until they became (civilised) people."[57]   Property rights were conferred upon "Bakgalagadi" in the Kweneng in *c*.1887.[58]

Besides the economics of abolition, politics played an influential role in the decision to end the *batlhanka* labor system.   Sebele, along with his fellow Batswana *dikgosi*, feared Transvaal Afrikaner incorporation and thus had lobbied for a British declaration of a Protectorate.   Batswana treatment of Basarwa and "Bakgalagadi" servants, however, were embarrassments to the Protectorate cause. Abolition was thus good politics.

Dependency, Post-*c*.1892

With the way open, the Babolaongwe took the lead over Bashaga and Bakgwatheng in the trade with Molepolole. They took fur skins, ostrich feathers, *dikgole*, and goats to purchase guns, powder, tobacco, cannabis, cattle, and sorghum and maize.   Bashaga and Babolaongwe women initiated a parallel trade with Bakwena women. At Luzwe, women dug for and gathered a kind of blue colored soil called *thyalanyane* which was used by Bakwena women to decorate their homes.   They molded the *thyalanyane* into brick slabs measuring about thirteen by eight by three centimeters, and traded them at Molepolole where each slab fetched about one basin-full of sorghum.[59] Women traders also took dried desert berries, like *richama*, *rikgose*, *moretlwa*, and *rimmoo*, and fried melon seeds called *richelwa* to trade for sorghum.

Initially, during Sebele's time, cattle held little intrinsic value to the Babolaongwe and Bashaga.   Cattle had a use-value to them, as beasts of burden rather than as capital.[60] The Bashaga and Babolaongwe used pack-oxens to carry their trade goods, and when the plough and wagon were introduced during the latter part of the nineteenth century, cattle was used for pulling ploughs and

---

[57] I. Schapera, "Ethnographical Texts in the Boloongwe Dialect of Sekgalagadi," *Bantu Studies* 12:3 (1938): pp. 162-164.

[58] I. Schapera, *Tribal Innovators: Tswana Chiefs and Social Change, 1795-1940* (New York: Athlone Press, 1970), pp. 90, 255; and Mautle, "Bakgalagadi-Bakwena Relationship," p. 26.

[59] H/L/21.

[60] H/L/5; H/L/8; H/L/10; H/L/15; H/L/20; and H/L/21.

wagons. Cattle thereby helped to expand trade and agriculture by increasing the volume of goods carried and the amount of land cultivated.

The first ox wagon was purchased by a Mobolaongwe shortly after the granting of property rights. He was soon followed by two other Babolaongwe, and later by Bakgwatheng and Bashaga. They bought the wagons from Molepolole's white shopkeepers for eight to ten cattle each. Sometimes cooperatives were launched to purchase wagons. The plan began with a wealthy man who would form a purchasing cooperative by providing the seed money and inviting relatives and neighbors to buy shares in the wagon. The original proposer was the wagon's sole owner and final arbiter of its use, but cooperative members were entitled to have the wagon carry their goods whenever it was used, and they could borrow the wagon but had to provide their own oxen team to pull it.[61]

Besides increasing the volume of trade, wagons helped to reduce the costs of most goods for the peoples of the Kalahari. Bakwena traders sold their wares for inflated prices in the desert. The "Bakgalagadi" reduced those prices by going directly to Molepolole where they bought bulk quantities of sorghum and maize from either Bakwena farmers or white shopkeepers. The prices were fairly uniform in Molepolole, because although the shops were retail outlets with profit margins, they generally bought grains from Bakwena farmers who only sold them during times of financial exigency or when there were large surpluses. In either case, shopkeepers purchased grains when prices were depressed, and their mark ups consequently raised them to roughly the going rate during a normal agricultural year.[62] Sometimes, "Bakgalagadi" shoppers bought excesses in Molepolole and sold them for profits in the desert.

As servants, several groups of Bakgwatheng and Babolaongwe herded cattle for Bakwena masters. Sebele, for instance, sent two *madisa* cattle to his Babolaongwe servants of Goo-Morimo, Kgosidintsi sent enough cattle to constitute a herd to his Bakgwatheng servants of Goo-Moipisi, and the Bakgwatheng of Goo-Ra-Tshosa herded Gaealafshwe's cattle.[63] Bakwena cattle

---

[61]H/L/20; and H/L/21.
[62]H/L/20; and H/M/31.
[63]H/L/5.

were generally delivered to the heads of "Bakgalagadi" groups who distributed them among his people. Mere herders of those *madisa* cattle, "Bakgalagadi" servants could only drink their milk and employ them as beasts of burden, and unlike *mafisa* cattle, the owners did not pay for the labor of the herders.

The area around Lephephe, including Lephephe, Makabanyane, Sojwe, Shadishadi, Toteng-ya Morula, and Boatlaname, was developed as a result of the *madisa* system. Despite its abundance of grass and game, that corner of the Kweneng wasn't settled until about the mid-nineteenth century when Dihatswe and his Babolaongwe moved there from the Letlhakeng vicinity. The Boo-Dihatswe gathered, hunted, and herded their goats and sheep in the area, wandering from pan to pan and depending on rain for their water. On a hunting expedition, upon reaching into a hole burrowed by an antbear, Dihatswe discovered good drinking water just below the surface of the Lephephe pan.[64] His find greatly increased the importance of the area, and the line of wells on the pan formed the boundary between the Kweneng and Ga-Ngwato.

News of Dihatswe's discovery spread to Molepolole to Mmatli, head of Goo-Ra-Kgaimena, Sechele's uncle, and master of the Boo-Dihatswe. Mmatli, Sechele, and other prominent Bakwena sent scores of *madisa* cattle to the area which was able to sustain huge herds with its grass cover and wells on the Lephephe pan. The cattle denuded the area of its grass and vegetation through over-grazing, but the Babolaongwe and Bakgwatheng who served as herders allegedly plucked from the ranks of their masters' herds to increase those of their own and grew wealthy in cattle.[65] *Madisa* cattle, like *mafisa* cattle among the Bakwena, were easily culled because the owners rarely visited the outposts, relying mainly upon periodic reports on the condition of their stock, and because of the number of unpredictable variables that affected the herd's well-being.

The "Bakgalagadi" began and increased their herds also through buying cattle from the Bakwena and others after the end of the *batlhanka* system. Cattle was purchased with fur pelt cloaks, sorghum, and small stock. A cow, its size dependent upon the cloak's quality, could be acquired for one cloak, and likewise, depending upon grain prices at the time of the sale, a cow was bought for two to

---

[64]H/Lp/2; and H/Sh/1.
[65]H/Lp/1; H/Lp/2; H/Lp/3; H/S/1; H/Sh/1; and H/Sh/2.

three sacks of sorghum. The sack was made from the entire skin of a hartebeest (*kgama*), and had a capacity of about thirty-eight liters. Six sheep or nine goats were exchanged for a one-year-old cow (*mwalolelo*), seven sheep or eleven goats, for a two-year-old cow (*magatelo*), and eleven sheep or thirteen goats, for a three-year-old cow (*moroba*). Usually among the small stock exchanged for a cow was a male animal, referred to as *ledalo* or "skin," because it was given to the cattle-seller in thanks and was intended to be eaten and skinned. The mix of female and male animals also helped to insure that the stock could reproduce itself and constitute the nucleus of a herd.[66]

"Bakgalagadi" cattle-owners preferred the Sengologa variety over the Setswana breed. The long-horned Sengologa cattle had been introduced into the Kalahari about the close of the eighteenth century by the Bangologa who had acquired them from the peoples of the Nokeng-ya Botete. They were a sturdier breed than the short-horned Setswana cattle, and were better able to withstand the desert conditions. Bakgwatheng, Babolaongwe, and Bashaga traders thus travelled west to the Bangologa to buy Sengologa cattle which became the dominant variety, even among the Bakwena, during the nineteenth century.[67]

Cattle-herding in the Kalahari varied throughout the year.[68] For most of the year, from December to August, the cattle were kept in their fold (*lesaka*) at night, but during the warm months of September through November, they were allowed to graze freely on the veldt day and night. Cattle were penned at night from December to May to prevent them from destroying the garden crops, and from May to August, to protect them from the cold winter nights. During the three months of free grazing, herders rounded up the cattle each morning, watered them, and released them. The cows usually calved in October, so herders searched the veldt each morning for newly born calves which were taken to a special fold (*lesakana*) where they were kept until weaning. During the rest of the year, herd boys took the cattle to pasture at sunrise and younger boys took the calves to another pasture to graze until about noon when both herds returned to the fold and the cows were milked. In the early afternoon, the cattle were taken out of

---

[66]H/L/10.

[67]H/Sh/2; H/L/5; and H/H/3. See also, Wilmsen, *Land Filled with Flies*, p. 84.

[68]H/L/5; H/L/8; and H/L/10.

pasture again, and were brought back at about sunset. The calves were permitted to suck from their mothers, and after feeding the cows and calves were separated for the night.

As with their other animals, "Bakgalagadi" herders timed the reproductive and hence milking cycle of cattle for optimal conditions. Calving occurred during the warm, rainy season, from October to January, when there was generally an abundance of water and new grass. Mating likewise took place during those favorable times, from January to March, limiting milk production to the months of October through March, but complementing the milk production of goats that extended from July to November.

Cattle-keeping was perhaps the decisive moment for "Bakgalagadi" incorporation. Property rights and the abolition of the *batlhanka* system rendered cattle economic for the peoples of the desert, as beasts of burden and later, as capital -- a desired end and medium of accumulation and exchange. As greater numbers of Babolaongwe and Bashaga abandoned gathering, herding small stock, and hunting for cultivation, trade, and cattle-keeping, they became increasingly dependent upon the Bakwena and white shopkeepers in Molepolole as outlets for their goods and as suppliers of grains, manufactures, and cattle. Some of the very means of resistance, including external trade and cattle-keeping, became enclosures of dependency for the peoples of the Kalahari.

5

Other Contexts

Trade, Missions, and Colonization

For the Bakwena, especially the elites, the peoples of the Kalahari supplied the labor that allowed them to cultivate larger tracts of land, maintain extensive herds of cattle at productive desert outposts, and collect skins and other desert commodities that fueled trade and accumulation. After the abolition of the masters and servants system, the peoples of the Kalahari served as a market for Bakwena grains, livestock, and manufactures and as a continual source of desert products and cheap labor. The counterpart and cause of Bakwena development was "Bakgalagadi" underdevelopment. To the people of the crocodile, the desert and its peoples constituted a well-spring for the regeneration and expansion of their economy, enabling them to survive and compete in the wider context of Botswana and the Transvaal.

During the eighteenth century, long-distance trade on the southern African high veld seemed to have been initiated by metal-working peoples who had settled along seams of iron and copper. Metal-workers sold their hoes, spears, knives, bracelets, and earrings to those who needed them for skins and livestock.

> Mokgosi's people [Bamalete] had no cattle when first they settled a Rabogadi, but they built up a big trade in iron implements, supplying the BaRolong, the BaTlhaping, the BaNgwaketsi, and the BaHurutse with axes, spears, hoes, bracelets, etc., in return for goats and later for cattle. Four hoes purchased a cow, three an ox. The iron implements were loaded on to pack-oxen and taken to the tribes mentioned above, and when they had been disposed of the Ba-ga-Malete returned home with the goats or cattle they had acquired.[1]

---

[1]Vivien Ellenberger, "Di Robaroba Matlhakola -- tsa ga Masodi-a-Mphela," *Transactions*

The fur skins obtained in the trade were likely consumed by the metal-workers, except for skins of the cat family which had little value among the Batswana and were perhaps retraded to Nguni-speakers to their east.[2]

European-made beads, arriving in the Transvaal from Delagoa Bay to the northeast and the Cape to the south, diversified trade during the nineteenth century. Traders from the northeast sought ivory and skins, while those from the south desired mainly cattle. Henry Methuen, upon noticing that Sechele's beads were "not of British manufacture" but of Portuguese origin, asked the *kgosi* where he had obtained them. Sechele replied, wrote Methuen, that "they procured these ornaments . . . [from] some traders, the Maloquane, called also Baquapa from their tatooing the nose . . . that these men trade as far south as the Baquaines; that they are very strong, and bear their ivory away on their shoulders. . . ."[3]

The missionary John Campbell described the "Molloquam" as neighbors of the "Mahalaseela" and "Matleebeylai," who lived near "the Great Water," and his informants confirmed Sechele's account that the "Molloquam" were the people who had brought beads to the Bakwena in exchange for ivory.[4] In 1846, David Livingstone described Transvaal Ndebele traders who visited Sechele at Tshonwane. The men, he wrote, had "leglets of brass manufactured by themselves" which they brought to trade, and "many of them had cloaks of cotton cloth. They have seen the sea & describe all that region as densely populated."[5] The Dighoya, southern neighbors of the Barolong, told of a trade with "the people from the Great Water":

> A people beyond the Gohas, towards the rising sun, had told them of a Great Water, lying beyond their country, out of which travellers come, bringing beads with them, which they deposit in different heaps; after this they retire, and the natives advance to examine the heaps. On those which they wish to purchase, they lay a skin or

of the Royal Society of South Africa 25:1 (1937-38): pp. 36, 44.

[2]See, e.g., Campbell, *Travels*, 2, p. 219.

[3]Methuen, *Life in the Wilderness*, pp. 146, 199. European beads were in eastern Botswana before 1,000 years ago. Wilmsen, *Land Filled with Flies*, p. 68.

[4]Campbell, *Travels*, 1, pp. 239-41.

[5]David Livingstone to Benjamin Pyne, Chonuane, January 1, 1846, NLS, Ms. 10769.

skins according to the supposed value, when they also retire; and the
people from the Great Water return to see what offers have been
made. If satisfied, they take the skins and leave the beads; otherwise
they leave both the skins and the beads in the same state, and again
withdraw; then the natives return, and lay more skins on the heaps;
after which the skins are taken away by the strangers, and the beads
by the natives. In this way they trade.[6]

It appears that eventually the Transvaal Batswana and Delagoa Bay
Portuguese made direct trade contact, by-passing the middlemen. Writing of the
Bakaa who were at the time just south of the Bangwato, Andrew Smith reported:
"During one month the Portuguese traders had been twice to deal with them [the
Bakaa]. . . .   The Portuguese conveyed their goods on pack-oxen and never
approached the kraal but remained in the fields and sent to the people to come. . . .
They preferred teeth between 40 and sixty pounds; those would not take cow
teeth. . . . The Portuguese will not take teeth with broken points."[7] Likewise, the
Transvaal Bakwena, according to Campbell, apparently reached Delagoa Bay
where Whites "sold guns, powder, horses, wagons, clothes, pots, &c., but that
cattle in that country were scarce; that their houses were white; that clothes and
linen for sale were packed high above each other in their houses . . . that the town
stands on the opposite side of a wide water, which they cross on rafts."[8]

The beads trade to the south involved the Batlhaping who retraded beads
to their northern neighbors for cattle.[9]   The Batlhaping tried to protect their
position as middlemen, but they were eventually circumvented by Griqua and
European traders, who sought not only cattle but also ivory, ostrich feathers, and
skins in exchange for beads, guns, clothing, and other products of European

[6]Campbell, *Travels*, 2, p. 351. See also, J. Read to LMS, Lattakoo, March 15, 1817,
LMS-SOAS, South Africa, Incoming Letters, Box 7, Folder 1, Jacket C, in which Read
writes of a nation called "Mokluwe," twelve days' journey northeast of the Batlhaping,
who traded for beads "where the tide flows."

[7]Kirby, *Diary of Dr. Andrew Smith*, 2, pp. 42-43. See also the uncritical account by
Louis Knobel based upon his collection of oral tradtion in "The History of Sechele,"
Botswana Notes and Records 1 (1968): pp. 51-63, which mentions a "Portuguese trader"
who accompanied Mosimane to the Bakwena.

[8]Campbell, *Travels*, 2, pp. 358-59. See also, Alan Smith, "Delagoa Bay and the Trade of
South-Eastern Africa," in *Pre-Colonial African Trade*, ed. Richard Gray and David
Birmingham (London: Oxford University Press, 1970), pp. 284-86; and R. Hamilton,
Kuruman, January 7-December 29, 1821, LMS-SOAS, South Africa, Journals, Box 3.

[9]Gary Y. Okihiro, "Precolonial Economic Change Among the Tlhaping, c.1795-1817,"

manufacture. In the early nineteenth century, the *difaqane* and Afrikaner expansion into the high veld disrupted, but didn't choke off, the traffic, although the destruction of Batswana chiefdoms encouraged the rise of brigandage in which cattle-raiding became a dominant form of economic activity. Still, the search for markets for European goods was carried into the interior by the frontiersmen of the expanding world-system, enhancing the importance of the Batswana who lived along the borders of the desert from whence came the desired ivory, ostrich feathers, and skins.

Sechele's monopoly of the trade contributed to the defeat and absorption of the Boo-Ra-Tshosa faction of Bakwena, and played a role in his defensive preparations against invaders from the Transvaal. "A short time previous to my arrival," observed hunter Gordon Cumming, "a rumor having reached Sichely that he was likely to be attacked by the emigrant Boers, he suddenly resolved to secure his city with a wall of stones, which he at once commenced erecting." By November 1844, the wall at Tshonwane, noted Cumming, had been completed, "entirely surrounding the town, with loopholes at intervals all along through which to play upon the advancing enemy with the muskets which he had resolved to purchase from hunters and trader like myself."[10]

The guns traffic continued unabated despite the Sand River Convention, signed in January 1852 by Britain and the Transvaal, which prohibited the sale of arms to the "native tribes." The trade, carried on by British and Afrikaner alike, yielded handsome profits. Cumming, for example, received ivory from the Bangwato in 1844 that was worth over L30 for a musket that cost him 16/-.[11] Sechele's defensive preparations and arms stockpiling were tested by an Afrikaner commando attack on his capital at Dimawe in 1852, that, although was a defeat for

---

International Journal of African Historical Studies 17:1 (1984): pp. 59-79.

[10]Roualeyn Gordon Cumming, *Five Years of a Hunter's Life in the Far Interior of South Africa*, 2 (London: John Murray, 1850), p. 68. See also, David Livingstone to Robert Moffat, Mabotsa, September 22, 1845, LMS-SOAS, Africa, Odds, Box 21.

[11]Cumming, *Five Years*, 1, p. 330. See also, James Chapman, *Travels in the Interior of South Africa*, 1 (London, 1868), p. 18; Robert Moffat to Wm. Thompson, Kuruman, September 20, 1852, LMS-SOAS, South Africa, Incoming Letters, Box 27, Folder 1, Jacket B; David Livingstone to Mr. Livingston, Banks of the Zouga, October 1851, NLS, Ms. 10701; David Livingstone to Benjamin Pyne, Chonuane, January 1, 1846, NLS, Ms. 10769; and *British Parliamentary Papers*, Further Correspondence Relative to the State of the Orange River Territory, Colonies, Africa (London, 1854), enclosure 2, p. 270.

the Bakwena, demonstrated their resolve and showed that with guns they posed a formidable opposition.[12]

From his new capital at Dithejwane, Sechele sent his army (*mephato*) into the desert and to Lake Ngami for the purpose of collecting skins, ostrich feathers, and ivory that were traded for guns and powder. By September 1857, hunter William Baldwin reported that the Bakwena had "no end of guns," but still wanted more guns, powder, lead, and caps for their trade goods.[13] Sechele also used Dithejwane's terrain to his advantage, surrounding his town, built at the top of a hill, with stone walling and digging numerous pits with sharpened stakes in the valley below to neutralize the advantage that Afrikaner horsemen enjoyed over Bakwena foot soldiers.[14]

Perhaps because of its largely political nature directed at defence and the integrity of the state, trade was controlled and regulated by Sechele throughout most of his rule. As in cattle-raiding, the *kgosi* dispatched his army to search for and confiscate the objects of trade, acquiring ivory in Ga-Tawana and ostrich feathers and skins from the "Bakgalagadi." Besides monopolizing virtually all of the trade goods, Sechele controlled the transactions of visiting traders insofar as he allowed them into the Kweneng and was the first to negotiate with them thereby setting the trade terms and rates. Likely uncharacteristic of the Bakwena, Sechele's regulation of trade was mainly a function of his political office and role in protecting the integrity of the state.[15]

Sechele's defensive strategy, besides collecting arms, included the acquisition of a resident British missionary who provided access to the British

---

[12]Okihiro, "Resistance and Accommodation," pp. 104-16. See also, Schapera, *Family Letters*, 2, p. 50.

[13]William Charles Baldwin, *African Hunting and Adventure* (London: Richard Bentley, 1863), p. 175. See also, Alfred Dolman, *In the Footsteps of Livingstone* (London: John Lane, 1924), pp. 196-99; Sillery, *Sechele*, p. 111; and Holloway Helmore, "Journal of Journey from Kuruman to the Zambesi River for the Purpose of Establishing a Mission Amongst the Makololo," LMS-SOAS, Africa, Personal, Box 1, Document 31, pp. 17-18.

[14]J. P. R. Wallis, ed., *The Matabele Journals of Robert Moffat, 1829-1860*, 1 (London, 1945), pp. 170-71, 344-46, 377; Smith, *Great Lion*, pp. 66-67; and Helmore, "Journal," p. 12.

[15]Cf. Monica Wilson, "Changes in Social Structure in Southern Africa: The Relevance of Kinship Studies to the Historian," in *African Societies in Southern Africa*, ed. Leonard Thompson (New York: Praeger, 1969), pp. 71-85, who sees the control of trade by seniors as characteristic of the Batswana.

government and supplied guns and other European goods. Sechele invited David Livingstone to Tshonwane in 1846, and later told him at Kolobeng, "'I desire to build a house for God, the defender of my town, and that you be at no expense with it whatever.'"[16] Toward that end, the *kgosi* ordered more than 200 laborers to help Livingstone erect a church and dig a watercourse for the mission's garden. Sechele's words echoed the declaration of Mosielele, the Bakgatla *kgosi*, when he told Livingstone three years earlier: "'O, I shall dance for joy if you do; I shall collect all my people to hoe for you a garden, and you will get more sweet reed & corn than myself.'" The missionary, in a candid appraisal of Mosielele's entreaty, commented: "I need scarcely add that his wish, although sincere, does not indicate any love to the doctrines we teach. It is merely a desire for the protection & temporal benefit which missionaries are everywhere supposed to bring."[17]

In truth, the supposed "protection" and "temporal benefit" of mission stations were employed by missionaries as wedges into Batswana society. London Missionary Society missionaries among the Batlhaping first agonized over, then participated in the cattle, ivory, and beads trade, justifying their commercial activities as necessary for the support of the mission. Others, perhaps more alert to the opportunity for personal gain, quit mission work to become fulltime traders, or used gifts as a way to win souls and ensure their mission's success.[18] James Chapman, a self-declared friend of missions, reported that Livingstone had left the impression with Sekeletu and his Makololo that he was "their trader -- who would give them two barrels of powder, a large heap of lead, and sundry other articles for a small tusk of ivory, or mend a dozen broken guns for a paltry remuneration," and he would bring them traders from the west coast who would bring them "all the good things of the white men."[19]

---

[16]Schapera, *Missionary Correspondence*, p. 112.

[17]*Ibid.*, pp. 35-36. See also, David Livingstone to J. J. Freeman, Kolobeng, January 9, 1850, LMS-SOAS, Livingstone Letters, Folder 49; and David Livingstone to Arthur Tidman, Lattakoo, October 30, 1843, LMS-SOAS, Africa, Odds, Box 9, Folder 2A.

[18]W. Anderson to LMS, Clearwater, September 1, 1807, LMS-SOAS, South Africa, Incoming Letters, Box 3, Folder 4, Jacket C; and Moffat, *Missionary Labours*, pp. 215-18. See, Roger B. Beck, "Bibles and Beads: Missionaries as Traders in Southern Africa in the Early Nineteenth Century," *Journal of African History* 30 (1989): pp. 211-25.

[19]Chapman, *Travels*, 1, p. 289.

Sechele held a similar impression of missionaries, when he told Livingstone of his desire "to get a missionary" who would help him in sickness, teach him wisdom, and "mend his gun." Sechele later pointedly declared: "'the English are my friends. I get everything I wish from them.'"[20] The *kgosi*'s boast might have been encouraged by Livingstone, who built him a square house in the European style and gave him sundry gifts, including beads, moleskin trousers, guns, and a plough.[21]

For missionaries and the societies that sent them, mission stations were investments that had to be protected. Thus, when *difaqane* raiders threatened the Kuruman station, missionaries played an active role in the battle of June 1823 that preserved both the mission and its Batlhaping congregation. As it turned out, the missionary presence failed to prevent the Afrikaner sacking of Sechele's Dimawe, and his baptism by Livingstone in 1848 was met with considerable opposition that included those who blamed the missionary and *kgosi* for the drought and famine that followed. It appears that Sechele's penchant for European goods and his desire for "a missionary," his baptism perhaps having been a means to those personal and public ends, nonetheless weakened his legitimacy as the principal rainmaker, and hence the people's provider, and ultimately his authority. The *kgosi*'s power, during Sechele's later years, became vested in Kgosidintsi, his junior brother.[22]

Sechele's consumerism was supported by servant and free labor, taxes, and the resources of the desert, and increased the class divide between ruler and ruled. In 1863, missionary Elizabeth Price noted that "Sechele is in reality poorer in cattle than any great <u>chief</u> in Africa, because he has parted with an immense number for the sake of European goods & valuables wh. he has in abundance. . . ."[23] Just after having paid L300 in ivory and ostrich feathers for the building of

---

[20]Schapera, *Family Letters*, 1, p. 132; and Livingstone, *Missionary Researches*, p. 43.

[21]Schapera, *Family Letters*, 1, pp. 210-13; Schapera, *Family Letters*, 2, pp. 16-17, 40, 89, 91, 104, 107; Chamberlin, *Some Letters*, pp. 122-23; and J. P. R. Wallis, ed., *The Matabele Journals of Robert Moffat, 1829-1860*, 2 (London: Chatto & Windus, 1945), p. 30.

[22]Livingstone, *Missionary Researches*, pp. 19-20, 24-25; Schapera, *Missionary Correspondence*, p. 103; Schapera, *Family Letters*, 1, p. 231; Schapera, *Private Journals*, pp. 299-301; and Okihiro, "Resistance and Accommodation," pp. 107-08.

[23]Una Long, ed., *The Journals of Elizabeth Price* (London: Edward Arnold, 1956), p. 112.

two European-style houses for himself and Sebele, his son, Sechele placed an order for an even larger house from himself, complete with imported furnishings, wallpaper, crystal chandelier, vases, and ornaments. The great house underscored the gap between the *kgosi* and his people. "His chief men," observed Price, "who had been used to come & visit with him in his hut & be quite at ease now trembled to enter this place."[24] Missionary Robert Moffat saw signs of that alienation as early as 1854 when he wrote with undisguised satisfaction about Sechele's "desire for civilization" that compelled the *kgosi* to live apart from his people "in order to keep himself & family more clean than they could otherwise do. . . ."[25]

Other Bakwena less smitten with the bug of conspicuous consumption were more skeptical of the intention of Whites in general and the missionaries and British government in particular. Kgosidintsi expressed some of that skepticism, based upon a growing recognition of racism, to Robert Moffat in November 1854 after the Sand River Convention:

> Is it because we have not white skins that we are to be destroyed like <u>libatana</u> (beasts of prey)? Why do the English assist the Boers? Why do they give them power over lands that are not theirs to give? Why do the English supply them with ammunition, when they know the Boers? Do the English want our country? You have spoken about what the word of God says. Have not the English the word of God, and have not the Boers the word of God? Are we only to obey the word of God because we are black? Are white people not to obey the word of God because they are white?
> We have been told that the English is a strong nation. They have driven their white Bushmen [Afrikaners] into our country to kill us. Is this strength? We are told that the English love all men. They give or sell ammunition, horses and guns to the Boers, who have red teeth, to destroy us, and if we ask to buy powder, we can get none. No, no, no! Black man must have no ammunition: they must serve the white man. Is this their love?[26]

British missionaries, the Bakwena came to know, were not the British government, but British defenders against Afrikaner invaders could easily become

[24]*Ibid.*, pp. 169, 195, 281-83.
[25]Robert Moffat to LMS, Kuruman, February 16, 1854, LMS-SOAS, South Africa, Incoming Letters, Box 29, Folder 1, Jacket A.
[26]Wallis, *Matabele Journals*, 1, pp. 377-79.

British colonizers.[27] Kgosidintsi, thus, in 1863 invited the London Missionary Society to send missionaries to Molepolole, but refused in 1874 to allow them to build a seminary, the Moffat Institution, in the Kweneng. British imperialism, like Afrikaner expansionism, equally threatened Bakwena sovereignty, Kgosidintsi realized from its encroachment to the south. "I believe the real thought that is at the bottom of all this," wrote missionary John Mackenzie to Robert Moffat on Kgosidintsi's opposition to the seminary, "is the political situation in the Batlhaping country, the taking over by the English of the Griqua country, and the expected taking over of the Batlhaping territory also. The people in the interior wish to maintain their right to their own country inviolate; and they think granting a site for a large school would interfere with this."[28]

The Bakwena, nonetheless, depended upon missionaries to supply them with guns and goods, serve as their advocate and intermediary vis-a-vis the British government, and provide them with opportunities for wage labor.[29] Missionaries commonly employed servants on their mission compounds, sent laborers (*babereki*) to work on other mission stations, and wrote letters of identification for migrant laborers who sought work in the Cape and Transvaal. Livingstone, at the start of his mission in 1846, employed a number of Bakwena as servants, paying them in beads, "a variety that costs about 3 shillings per pound," and he hired as many as he could to maximize his purpose of teaching them "civilised ways" and "cleanliness."[30] Later, at Kolobeng, Livingstone hired nine Bakwena men to help him build his house, paying them a heifer for a year's labor, and he paid a calf to a Mokwena to deliver an "express" letter to

---

[27]William Ashton to LMS, Kuruman, May 7, 1854, LMS-SOAS, South Africa, Incoming Letters, Box 29, Folder 1, Jacket A; and Sechele to Robert Moffat, Letubaruba, May 1854, attached to Mary Moffat to William Thompson, Backhouse, Vaal River, January 2, 1855, LMS-SOAS, South Africa, Incoming Letters, Box 29, Folder 3, Jacket A.

[28]John Mackenzie to Robert Moffat, Taung, May 1, 1874, LMS-SOAS, South Africa, Incoming Letters, Box 37, Folder 3, Jacket A. See also, W. H. Surmon to the Resident Commissioner, Gaberones, September 5, 1896, BNA, RC. 4/4.

[29]See, e.g., A. J. Wookey to Administrator, British Bechuanaland, Molepolole, July 12, 1886, BNA, HC. 7/13.

[30]Chamberlin, *Some Letters*, p. 92; and David Livingstone to Charles Whish, Chonuane, October 9, 1846, LMS-SOAS, Africa, Odds, Box 22.

Kuruman.[31] Sechele sold the services of his servants to missionaries at Shoshong, one for a two year period in exchange for a gun.[32]

Missionaries and traders employed Bakwena as guides and carriers, and as early as 1847, Bakwena left for the Cape and Transvaal seeking work from white farmers. At first, labor migration occurred mainly during times of drought and famine only, as during the severe drought of 1847-53, when many Bakwena sought food and labor in Makgoeng, and returned with accumulated wages in cattle.[33] Later, with the opening of the Transvaal gold and diamond mines, labor migration was a way to recoup losses suffered during droughts and hard times and an opening to enter the cash economy to purchase goods for the Kalahari trade. Labor migration was of course a crucial component of capitalist development in South Africa, and impacted significantly upon local production and gender relations.[34]

The resident missionary both infused and drained the Bakwena economy. Bubi and Sechele, in their competitive bid to "get a missionary," provided substantial amounts of their peoples' labor to construct Livingstone's dam, watercourse, house, and church.[35] Sechele's decision to move from Tshonwane, an area where Bakwena gardens thrived, to Kolobeng was influenced by

---

[31]David Livingstone to [?], n.p., 1848, LMS-SOAS, Africa, Odds, Box 18, Folder "15 Fragments"; David Livingstone to Robert Moffat, Kolobeng, January 31, 1849, LMS-SOAS, Africa, Odds, Box 18, Folder 21a; and David Livingstone to Robert Moffat, Kolobeng, April 11, 1849, LMS-SOAS, Africa, Odds, Box 18, Folder 23.

[32]Long, *Journals of Elizabeth Price*, p. 187.

[33]Schapera, *Family Letters*, 2, p. 31; Livingstone, *Missionary Researches*, p. 39; J. P. R. Wallis, ed., *The Matabele Mission* (London: Chatto & Windus, 1945), p. 114; David Livingstone to Robert Moffat, Kolobeng, April 14, 1851, LMS-SOAS, Africa, Odds, Box 18, Folder 33a; and Roger Price to LMS, Molepolole, December 6, 1872, LMS-SOAS, South Africa, Reports, Box 1, Folder 3.

[34]See, e.g., Isaac Schapera, *Migrant Labour and Tribal Life* (London: Oxford University Press, 1947); Norman Levy, *The Foundations of the South African Cheap Labour System* (London: Routledge & Kegan Paul, 1982); Harold Wolpe, "Capitalism and Cheap Labour-Power in South Africa: From Segregation to Apartheid," *Economy and Society* 1:4 (November 1972): pp. 425-56; the *Review of African Political Economy* where, among other places, Wolpe's thesis was debated; Barbara B. Brown, *Women, Migrant Labor and Social Change in Botswana*, African Studies Center Working Papers no. 41 (Boston: African Studies Center, Boston University, 1980); Barbara B. Brown, "The Impact of Male Labour Migration on Women in Botswana," *African Affairs* 82:328 (July 1983): pp. 368-88; and Wendy Izzard, "Migrants and Mothers: Case-studies from Botswana," *Journal of Southern African Studies* 11:2 (April 1985): pp. 258-80.

[35]David Livingstone to Agnes Livingston, Bakwain Country, April 4, 1842, NLS, Ms.

Livingstone's desire for water to irrigate his vegetable plot. The move, like the missionary sponsored move of the Batlhaping from Dithakong to Kuruman, proved disastrous for Batswana cultivators and caused famine and a temporary fragmentation of the people.[36] Church-building required both labor and capital. The Bakwena donated 140 cattle to erect the London Missionary Society church at Ntsweng in Molepolole in 1867, and the completed structure was valued at £500.[37] The overall impact of missions on the Bakwena, though, wasn't confined to an economic balance sheet, but extended to ideology, culture, and social relations broadly. Missionary imperialism ultimately led to British colonialism and the loss of Batswana sovereignty in Botswana.[38]

Intellectual Impositions

When I began this project in 1975, I was not only armed with the tenets of science and the lens of positionality, of "objective" history and "Afro-centrism"; I had, during my graduate years, plunged headlong into the now hoary but then fresh "substantivist" and "formalist" debates in economic anthropology, and was eager to affirm in my study my formalist assumptions with the evidence I was sure to find in the field. I had rejected the ideas of Bronislaw Malinowski, Karl Polanyi, George Dalton, and Marshall Sahlins whose distinction between redistributive and capitalist economies didn't square with my conviction that humans were economic and not social beings at base, although their counter-argument that formalists adhered to an "obsolete market mentality" and were ethnocentric in their universalism resonated with my distaste for Eurocentrism.[39]

10701; and Schapera, *Missionary Correspondence*, pp. 112-13.

[36]Okihiro, "Precolonial Economic Change," pp. 76-77; and Okihiro, "Resistance and Accommodation," pp. 107-08.

[37]Roger Price to LMS, Logagen, December 26, 1867, LMS-SOAS, South Africa, Reports, Box 1, Folder 1. See also, Roger Price to LMS, Molepolole, July 5, 1870, LMS-SOAS, South Africa, Incoming Letters, Box 36, Folder 1, Jacket A; and Roger Price to LMS, Molepolole, November 30, 1870, LMS-SOAS, South Africa, Incoming Letters, Box 36, Folder 3, Jacket C.

[38]Anthony J. Dachs, "Missionary Imperialism -- The Case of Bechuanaland," *Journal of African History* 13:4 (1972): pp. 647-58.

[39]See, e.g., Bronislaw Malinowski, *Argonauts of the Western Pacific* (London: Routledge, 1922); Karl Polanyi, Conrad M. Arensberg, and Harry W. Pearson, eds., *Trade and Market in the Early Empires* (New York: Free Press, 1957); several issues of the

I found compelling Raymond Firth's understanding of economics and his critique of Malinowski, and cheered the anti-racist project of Melville Herskovits who, in his *Economic Anthropology*, stressed the rational choices exercised by peoples in all societies. Edward W. LeClair, Jr. and Harold K. Schneider clarified and reaffirmed my original impulse, and the peerless studies of Polly Hill, a self-described "economist turned economic anthropologist," begged emulation.[40]

I faced fieldwork with other verities. I would show the ingenuity and benign quality of pre-capitalist and peasant producers and the social and environmental dislocations caused by capitalism's grasp based upon my readings on equilibrium theory, ecology, ecosystem, and ecological succession.[41] And I was alert to the social changes wrought by contact and technological innovation.[42] Marxism's excavation of society's materialist base, and its focus upon pre-capitalist societies and the rise and development of capitalism complemented my interests and inclinations, and the modifications of neo-Marxists and their critiques of liberal economics and "neo-Smithian Marxists" alike pointed a way out of the

---

American Anthropologist in which the debate was carried on; George Dalton, ed., *Tribal and Peasant Economies: Readings in Economic Anthropology* (Garden City, New York: Natural History Press, 1967); George Dalton and Paul Bohannan, *Markets in Africa* (Garden City, New York: Anchor Books, 1965); Marshall Sahlins, *Stone Age Economics* (Chicago: Aldine-Atherton, 1972); and A. G. Hopkins, *An Economic History of West Africa* (New York: Columbia University Press, 1973). For a species of the "substantivist" argument from the genre of African development economics, see Montague Yudelman, *Africans on the Land* (Cambridge: Harvard University Press, 1964).

[40]See, e.g., Raymond Firth, *Primitive Polynesian Economy* (London: Routledge, 1939); Melville J. Herskovits, *Economic Anthropology* (New York: Knopf, 1940); Edward E. LeClair, Jr. and Harold K. Schneider, eds., *Economic Anthropology: Readings in Theory and Analysis* (New York: Holt, Rinehart and Winston, 1968); Polly Hill, *Studies in Rural Capitalism in West Africa* (London: Cambridge University Press, 1970); and Harold K. Schneider, *Economic Man: The Anthropology of Economics* (New York: Free Press, 1974).

[41]E.g., Eric R. Wolf, *Sons of the Shaking Earth* (Chicago: University of Chicago Press, 1959); Robert L. Carneiro, "Slash-and-Burn Agriculture: A Closer Look At Its Implications For Settlement Patterns," in *Men and Cultures*, ed. Anthony F. C. Wallace (Philadelphia, 1960); Clifford Geertz, *Agricultural Involution* (Berkeley: University of California Press, 1963); Sherman Roy Krupp, "Equilibrium Theory in Economics and in Functional Analysis as Types of Explanation," in *Functionalism in the Social Sciences*, ed. Don Martindale (Philadelphia: American Academy of Political and Social Science, 1965); and Edward Roux, *Grass: A Story of Frankenwald* (Cape Town: Oxford University Press, 1969).

[42]As in, R. F. Salisbury, *From Stone to Steel* (Victoria: Melbourne University Press, 1962); and Dorothy Shineberg, *They Came for Sandalwood* (Victoria: Melbourne University Press, 1967).

"crisis" in the social sciences during the 1960s and 70s.[43]   The major question posed by Maurice Godelier, Emmanuel Terray, Claude Meillassoux, and Pierre Phillipe Rey, how kinship intersects with pre-capitalist modes of production given their assumption of kinship's dominance in the reproduction of social relations, led to a split between those who favored the study of pre-capitalist formations for their own sake and those for whom their articulation with capitalism and the world-system was paramount.[44]

The influence of those ideas was far-reaching as revealed in the historiography of southern Africa.   Colin Bundy's essay, "The Emergence and Decline of a South African Peasantry" (1972), and Robin Palmer and Neil Parsons' collection, *The Roots of Rural Poverty in Central and Southern Africa* (1977) drew from underdevelopment theory and moved the literature in the direction of imperialism and articulation.   Although pre-capitalist modes of production and ingenious African farmers were essential to their thesis, African producers were clearly secondary to European expansionists.   Afro-centrists like Terence Ranger scored them for their implicit Eurocentrism.[45]   By the 1980s, pre-

---

[43]See, e.g., the British journal *Economy and Society* during this period; Maurice Bloch, *Marxism and Anthropology: The History of a Relationship* (Oxford: Clarendon, 1983); Claude Meillassoux, "From Reproduction to Production: A Marxist Approach to Economic Anthropology," *Economy and Society* 1:1 (February 1972): pp. 93-105; Robert Brenner, "The Origins of Capitalist Development: A Critique of Neo-Smithian Marxism," *New Left Review* 104 (1977): pp. 25-92; and Jean Copans and David Seddon, "Marxism and Anthropology: A Preliminary Survey," in *Relations of Production: Marxist Approaches to Economic Anthropology*, ed. David Seddon (London: Frank Cass, 1978), pp. 1-46.

[44]Karl Marx, *Pre-Capitalist Economic Formations*, ed. E. J. Hobsbawn (New York: International Publishers, 1964); Maurice Godelier, *Rationalite et irrationalitie en economie* (Paris: F. Maspero, 1966); Emmanuel Terray, *Marxism and "Primitive" Societies* (New York: Monthly Review Press, 1972); Claude Meillassoux, *Anthropologie economique des Gouro de la Cote d'Ivoire* (Paris: Mouton, 1964); and Pierre Philippe Rey, *Colonialisme, neo-colonialisme et transition au capitalisme* (Paris: F. Maspero, 1971). See also, Catherine Coquery-Vidrovitch, "Recherches sur un mode de production africain," *La Pensee* 144 (1969): pp. 61-78.

[45]Colin Bundy, "The Emergence and Decline of a South African Peasantry," *African Affairs* 71:285 (October 1972): pp. 369-88; Robin Palmer and Neil Parsons, eds., *The Roots of Rural Poverty in Central and Southern Africa* (Berkeley: University of California Press, 1977); Colin Bundy, *The Rise and Fall of the South African Peasantry* (Berkeley: University of California Press, 1979); Terence Ranger, "Growing from the Roots: Reflections on Peasant Research in Central and Southern Africa," *Journal of Southern African Studies* 5:1 (October 1978): pp. 99-133; and Jack Lewis, "*The Rise and Fall of the South African Peasantry*: A Critique and Reassessment," *Journal of Southern African Studies* 11:1 (October 1984): pp. 1-24.

capitalist modes of production and social history shifted the focus away from macro-processes and structures and toward the details and complexities of African chiefdoms and individual actors to develop what Timothy Keegan has called "a more credible picture of the black rural economy."[46]

Despite that backward glance to what Leonard Thompson has called "the forgotten factor in southern African history" -- African agency -- and despite the works of historians like Shula Marks and J. B. Peires, pre-capitalist modes of production constitute the baseline, but not the pivot for many others like William Beinart, Colin Bundy, Peter Delius, and Stanley Trapido.[47] Their themes of accumulation, dispossession, and resistance, have contributed much to our understanding of peasant and agrarian history, and they have shown us the complexities of capitalism's articulation with indigenous formations. William Beinart and Colin Bundy have charted a new and promising course in positing the proposition that local struggles for autonomy helped shape mass social movements in South Africa.[48]

Of course, most of that excitement over dependency and underdevelopment occurred after my field research in 1975. I didn't have the benefit of that conversation when I planned and carried out the work that resulted in this study. But I too was a product of my times. Like the generation of historians who were influenced in their choice of subject matter and theoretical frames in the 1980s by the epic struggle around them during the final days of apartheid, I had been shaped by my generation's cause, the liberation of Third

---

[46]Timothy Keegan, "Trade, Accumulation and Impoverishment: Mercantile Capital and the Economic Transformation of Lesotho and the Conquered Territory, 1870-1920," *Journal of Southern African Studies* 12:2 (April 1986): p. 196.

[47]Leonard Thompson, *African Societies in Southern Africa* (New York: Praeger, 1969); Shula Marks and Anthony Atmore, eds., *Economy and Society in Pre-Industrial South Africa* (London: Longman, 1980); J. B. Peires, *The House of Phalo: A History of the Xhosa People in the Days of Their Independence* (Berkeley: University of California Press, 1982); Peter Delius, *The Land Belongs To Us: The Pedi Polity, the Boers and the British in the Nineteenth-century Transvaal* (Berkeley: University of California Press, 1984); William Beinart and Colin Bundy, *Hidden Struggles in Rural South Africa: Politics & Popular Movements in the Transkei & Eastern Cape, 1890-1930* (London: James Currey, 1987); William Beinart, Peter Delius, and Stanley Trapido, eds., *Putting a Plough to the Ground: Accumulation and Dispossession in Rural South Africa, 1850-1930* (Johannesburg: Ravan Press, 1986); and J. B. Peires, *The Dead Will Arise: Nongqawuse and the Great Xhosa Cattle-Killing Movement of 1856-7* (Johannesburg: Ravan Press, 1989).

World peoples within and without the U.S. I sought to expose history's efficacy in sustaining the ruling class, and to create a new historical order upon which to build our futures. I determined to position Africans at the center of my narrative, to let them speak for themselves, to inscribe an African history and not the deeds of Europeans in Africa.

But when I sat down to write that history, with my fingers frozen by the cold that seeped through the stone walls of my room in the Orkney Isles, I knew that I was imposing my will upon the vital and vibrant past, doing violence to it and rendering it unrecognizable to those who had lived it and had so generously shared with me its glimmer. Like the alien traders, missionaries, and colonialists who had preceded me, I presumed to represent my subjects and stood to profit from that representation. In addition, although sharing a common humanity, our respective conception of history appeared to me as separate realities, wherein their unruly three-dimensional experience defied discipline and containment within my two-dimensional paper space. But the ethical question, above all, beyond the intellectual conundrums, paralyzed my hand for years. Do we gain sufficient comfort when the "gift" of our invention is presented and "returned" to the people of our study, or are we freed from our responsibility when we insist that we study and write for ourselves only and when we allow that ours is but one version of the past?

To be sure, my understanding of the Bakwena social formation would have been different had I centered the "Bakgalagadi" and marginalized the Bakwena as their "other." And suppose the view was from the San shore, and the "Bakgalagadi" and Bakwena were the intruders?[49] Had I sought to unravel systematically the connections between labor, capital, production, and reproduction in the manner of Margaret Kinsman or Jeff Guy, my account would be less descriptive and offer a more precise explanation of the diversity and unity of economic and social relations.[50] Had I recognized gender relations as the

---

[48]Beinart and Bundy, *Hidden Struggles*.

[49]See, e.g., Wilmsen, *Land Filled with Flies*; and Wynne, "Land Boards," pp. 79-144.

[50]Margaret Kinsman, "Notes on the Southern Tswana Social Formation," in *Africa Seminar: Collected Papers*, no. 2, ed. K. Gottschalk and C. Saunders (Centre for African Studies, University of Cape Town, 1981); and Jeff Guy, "Analysing Pre-Capitalist Societies in Southern Africa," *Journal of Southern African Studies* 14:1 (October 1987): pp. 18-37.

central dynamic of pre-capitalist formations, as argued splendidly by Belinda Bozzoli, Margaret Kinsman, and Jeff Guy, I would have seen as fundamental the domestic sphere and the struggle over the appropriation and control of women's productive and reproductive capacities.[51] And what was the impact of textbooks and other written histories, along with the occasional but increasing intrusions of oral historians, on my collection of oral histories? I have only begun to reflect upon the meanings and contexts of my work.

Somehow, despite my presuppositions and arrogance, I discovered (old news to my tutors) the perhaps now commonplace notion that the Bakwena didn't always live in large towns and carry on a mixed economy of cattle-herding and grains-cultivation, but began as small, mobile groups of herders, gatherers, and hunters.   I learned that the lineage mode of production couldn't have predominated, at least since the late eighteenth century, because kinship wasn't the defining glue that held together the Bakwena social formation.   I came to understand that seniors didn't always dominate juniors, men, women, masters, servants, and I realized that birth, class, gender, and "race" weren't fixed categories but were constantly contested and struggled over, giving history and individual lives their dynamic.   Still, I can now say that my imposition, my version of the Bakwena social formation, seen from the intellectual positions from which I descend, is but a narrow slice indeed of the desert and the vast and variegated past inhabited and shaped by the peoples of the crocodile.

---

[51]Belinda Bozzoli, "Marxism, Feminism and South African Studies," *Journal of Southern African Studies* 9:2 (April 1983): pp. 140-71; Margaret Kinsman, "'Beasts of Burden': The Subordination of Southern Tswana Women, ca.1800-1840," *Journal of Southern African Studies* 10:1 (October 1983): pp. 39-54; and Jeff Guy, "Gender Oppression in Southern Africa's Precapitalist Societies," in *Women and Gender in Southern Africa to 1945,* ed. Cherryl Walker (Cape Town: David Philip, 1990), pp. 33-47.

Appendix A.

Genealogy of Bakwena *Dikgosi*

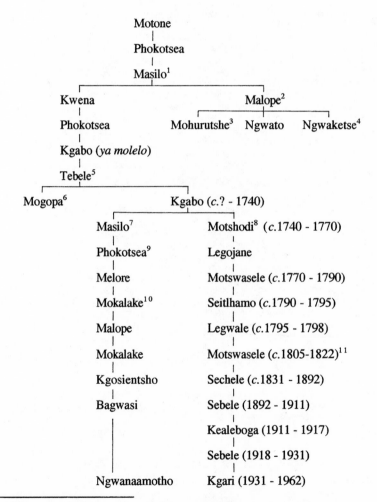

Motone
|
Phokotsea
|
Masilo[1]

Kwena
|
Phokotsea
|
Kgabo (*ya molelo*)
|
Tebele[5]

Malope[2]

Mohurutshe[3]   Ngwato   Ngwaketse[4]

Mogopa[6]   Kgabo (*c.*? - 1740)

Masilo[7]   Motshodi[8] (*c.*1740 - 1770)
| |
Phokotsea[9]   Legojane
| |
Melore   Motswasele (*c.*1770 - 1790)
| |
Mokalake[10]   Seitlhamo (*c.*1790 - 1795)
| |
Malope   Legwale (*c.*1795 - 1798)
| |
Mokalake   Motswasele (*c.*1805-1822)[11]
| |
Kgosientsho   Sechele (*c.*1831 - 1892)
| |
Bagwasi   Sebele (1892 - 1911)
| |
| Kealeboga (1911 - 1917)
| |
| Sebele (1918 - 1931)
| |
Ngwanaamotho   Kgari (1931 - 1962)

---

[1]This sequence, from Masilo to Sebele (*a* Sechele), is taken from Sebele (*a* Sechele)'s recitation as recorded by Wookey, *Dico*, pp. 43-44.

[2]Malope's placement here as Kwena's brother follows the version by Sebele (*a* Sechele) and a Mongwaketse in Wookey's *Dico*. More recent sources place Malope as Kwena's father, as in Schapera's *Ditirafalo*, pp. 33-34.

[3]This placement follows the accounts of Sebele (*a* Sechele) and a Mongwaketse in Wookey, *Dico*, pp. 43-44. A Bahurutshe version, as recorded in Wookey, *Dico*, pp. 38,

42, locates Mohurutshe as the senior brother of Kwena, Ngwato, and Ngwaketse, all born of Malope. The Bakwena claim that originally Kwena, Mohurutshe, Ngwato, and Ngwaketse were Bakwena (*ba bina kwena*), and account for Bahurutshe seniority in the following way. As the senior, Kwena performed the biting of the melons ceremony (*go loma sotse*) to mark the new season, but one year, baboons entered the fields and ate the melons before the ceremony. Kwena, accordingly, refused to eat the melons, because he believed that to follow baboons was an insult to his status. Mohurutshe, however, didn't share Kwena's revulsion and bit the melons, thereby establishing his seniority over Kwena. Thereafter, to signify the event that granted them seniority and independence, the Bahurutshe adopted the baboon as their totem (*ba bina tshwene*).

[4]The genealogies of both the Bangwato and Bangwaketse don't reach back this far. Perhaps Ngwato and Ngwaketse were born of a more recent Malope. Also, their genealogies don't extend back equally far; the Bangwaketse genealogy reaches farther back in time. The Bakwena of Mogopa indicate that Ngwato and Ngwaketse were born of different fathers, Ngwaketse being the son of Ngwato's grandfather. Schapera, *Ditirafalo*, pp. 51, 66.

[5]This sequence, from Kwena to Tebele, varies from the Baga-Mogopa and Baga-Sechele versions as given in Schapera, *Ditirafalo*, pp. 34-35. The Bakwena of Mogopa list them as: Kwena, Mmutle, Kwena, Motswasele (Peegane), Mphela (Phokotsea), Ngwaketse II, Setlhare (Tebele). The Bakwena of Sechele list them as: Kwena, Phokotsea, Malope II, Kgabo, Tebele.

[6]Both the Bakwena of Mogopa and Kgabo agree that the Bakwena Baga-Mogopa are senior to the Bakwena of both Masilo and Masilonyane.

[7]Masilo (*a* Kgabo) has been frequently confused with Masilo (*a* Phokotsea). I have placed Masilo here based upon the genealogy given me by Ngwanaamotho, and the general agreement that the Bakwena Baga-Mogopa and Baga-Kgabo separated after Tebele, and that Masilo's Bakwena are senior to those of Masilonyane (Motshodi).

[8]This line, from Motshodi to Kgari, is known as the Bakwena of Masilonyane. Despite the remembrance of a person named Masilonyane among those I interviewed, I don't believe he existed because of his absence in all of the older genealogical collections. I believe that the term "Masilonyane" derives from the phrase, "the junior brothers of Masilo" or the diminutive of "Masilo," and that recent recitations have given that a literal meaning. A similar situation is that of the Ntlheng-ya Tlhase *makgotla*, Moloi and Moloinyana. In their respective genealogies, there is no person named "Moloinyana"; instead, the name was given to indicate the junior line. H/M/127; H/M/128; and H/M/129.

[9]Phokotsea (*a* Masilo) is a woman. Masilo had no male offspring. Phokotsea was his first-born, and she and her two sisters married Bahurutshe *dikgosi* to continue Masilo's line. H/M/136.

[10]Mokalake (*a* Melore) is my invention, because of a gap in this genealogy and because it is easy to omit a name that repeats. See, H/M/137; and Okihiro, "Genealogical Research," p. 48.

[11]Maleke and Tshosa served as regents during Motswasele's minority, from *c.*1798 to 1805.

Appendix B.

Major[1] *Baagedi Makgotla* in Molepolole, 1975

Motse	Kgotla	Ethnicity	When Formed	Reason[2]
Kgosing	Basimane	Babolaongwe	Sechele	*batlhanka*
	Bobididi	(unknown)	Sechele	*difaqane*
	Bokalaka	Bapedi	Sechele	Afrikaners
	Chadibe	Bangwato	Sechele	rainmakers
	Difetlhamolelo	Babolaongwe	Sechele	*batlhanka*
	Dikoloi	(mixed)	Kealeboga	Afrikaners
	Ga-Mangwato	Bangwato	Kealeboga	friendship
	Ga-Maribana	Baphalane	Sechele	(unknown)
	Ga-Morwa*	(mixed)	Sechele	*difaqane*
	Ga-Mosima	(mixed)	Sechele	*difaqane*
	Ga-Sikwa	Basikwa	Motswasele *a* Legwale	(unknown)
	Goo-Mabe	Bakwena of Kgabo *ya molelo*	Sechele	*difaqane*
	Goo-Meje	Bakgatla Kgafela	Sebele *a* Sechele	internal dispute
	Goo-Molale	Bakubung	Motswasele *a* Legojane	(unknown)
	Goo-Pula	Bakwena Mogopa	Sechele	Afrikaners
	Goo-Ra-Mochina	Baphalane	Sechele	forced to rejoin
	Goo-Ra-Molefe	Batlokwa	Sechele	*difaqane*
	Goo-Ra-Suna	(mixed)	Sechele	*difaqane*
	Kgatleng	Bakgatla Manaana	Sebele *a* Kealeboga	internal dispute
	Masilwana*	(mixed)	Sechele	internal dispute
	Maulana*	(mixed)	Sebele *a* Sechele	(unknown)
	Motonya*	(mixed)	Sechele	Afrikaners

Appendices

	Senyadimana	(mixed)	Motswasele *a* Legwale	internal dispute
Ntloedibe	Goo-Ra-Mathame	Bahurutshe	Motswasele *a* Legwale	wedding "gift"
	Motokwane	Bahurutshe	Motswasele *a* Legwale	wedding "gift"
Mokgalo	(none)			
Ntlheng-ya Godimo	Goo-Dinti	Bakwena of Kgabo ya molelo	Sechele	*difaqane*
	Goo-Kodisa	Bakwena of Kgabo ya molelo	Sechele	*difaqane*
	Goo-Modibedi	Bangwato	Sechele	internal dispute
	Goo-Thato	Bataung	Motshodi	wars
Ntlheng-ya Tlhase	Bobididi	(unknown)	Sechele	*difaqane*
	Bokaa	Bakaa	Sechele	wars
	Ga-Sikwa	Basikwa	Sechele	(unknown)
	Goo-Dijo	Bakwena of Masilo	Sebele *a* Sechele	friendship
	Goo-Kotwane	Basikwa	Sebele *a* Sechele	Afrikaners
	Goo-Tsatsinyana	Basikwa	Sebele *a* Sechele	Afrikaners
	Goo-Ra-Legakwa	(unknown)	Motswasele *a* Legwale	(unknown)
	Taung	Bataung	Motshodi	wars

Summary

Major *baagedi makgotla* in Kgosing	23
Major *baagedi makgotla* in Ntloedibe	2
Major *baagedi makgotla* in Mokgalo	0
Major *baagedi makgotla* in Ntlheng-ya Godimo	4
Major *baagedi makgotla* in Ntlheng-ya Tlhase	8
Number formed before Sechele	7

Number formed during Sechele	22
Number formed after Sechele	8
Emigration because of *difaqane* or Afrikaners	15
Emigration because of internal dispute	5
Emigration because of *batlhanka* or "gift"	4
Emigration because of wars	3
Emigration because of friendship	2
Emigration because of other or unknown causes	8

---

[1]"Major" designates *makgotla* with ten or more households (*malwapa*).
[2]Refers to the causes for emigration. Some, like "rainmakers," were asked by the Bakwena to join them; others, like "*batlhanka*," were forcibly absorbed.
* *Makgotla* headed by Bakwena.

Appendix C.

Major[1] Bakwena [2] *Makgotla* in Molepolole, 1975

Motse	*Kgotla*
Kgosing	Sekamelo
	Senyadima
Ntloedibe	Goo-Ra-Moeng
	Goo-Ra-Mokalake
	Goo-Ra-Moleka
	Mathakala
Mokgalo	Botlhajana
	Moepetlo
	Serame
Ntlheng-ya Godimo	Goo-Mosarwa
	Goo-Ra-Mmoopi
	Goo-Ra-Tshosa
	Majatsie
	Matlhalerwa
	Mogogoru
Ntlheng-ya Tlhase	Goo-Moitoi
	Goo-Moloi
	Goo-Ra-Kgaimena
	Goo-Ra-Monametsana
	Goo-Ra-Thipe
	Maunatlala

---

[1]*Makgotla* with ten or more households (*malwapa*).

[2]Designates *makgotla* founded by the core Bakwena of Molepolole, but in most of which immigrants outnumber Bakwena.

Appendix D.
Bakwena *Mephato*[1]

Mafiri	?
Mapenapena	?
Mathiane	?
Malumakgomo	?
Maganatsatsi	?
Mathubantwa I	*c.*1856
Matlolakgang	*c.*1862
Maganamokgwa	*c.*1867
Mantshwabisi	*c.*1870
Maratakgomo	*c.*1877
Malwelakgosi	*c.*1881
Maletantwa	*c.*1888
Matlhomathebe	*c.*1896
Masitaoka	1901
Matlhogela	1904
Mathubantwa II	1915 or 1916
Maratakgosi	1915 or 1916
Matswakgotla	1917
Malatakgosi	1922
Maakathata	1931
Matlhaselwa	1936
Matlama	
Mautlwakgosi	
Majanko	

---

[1]The *mephato* names and their sequence are taken from, H/M/11; H/M/13; H/M/47; H/M/48; and H/M/59. The dates are from, primarily, Schapera, *Handbook*, p. 312. Cf., H/M/48.

Bibliography

A. Essay on Sources.

B. Oral Sources.

    1. Boatlaname

    2. Hukuntsi

    3. Kang

    4. Lephephe

    5. Letlhakeng

    6. Luzwe

    7. Makabanyane

    8. Molepolole

    9. Moshaweng

    10. Motokwe

    11. Shadishadi

    12. Sojwe

C. Archival Sources.

    1. Botswana National Archives

    2. British Museum

    3. British Museum, Natural History

    4. Church Missionary Society

    5. Hope Department of Zoology (Entomology), University Museum, Oxford

    6. India Office Records

    7. London Missionary Society (Archives of the Council for World Mission)

    8. National Library of Scotland

    9. Rhodes House Library

    10. Royal Geographical Society

    11. Scottish National Memorial to David Livingstone Trust, Blantyre, Glasgow

    12. Wesleyan Methodist Missionary Society

D. Unpublished Sources.

1. Dissertations
2. Manuscripts

E. Published Sources.

A. Essay on Sources.

The initial research for this book was undertaken from September 1974 to February 1976. I spent the first four months of that eighteen-month period combing the archives in Britain, the next twelve months in Botswana collecting mainly oral histories, and the final two months back in the archives and libraries in Britain.

The papers of missionaries, travellers, hunters, and traders constitute the bulk of the contemporary written sources. Missionaries, especially those of the London Missionary Society, lived among the Bakwena and other Batswana almost continuously for over 100 years. Perhaps because of their intimate knowledge of the Batswana, including the Setswana language, missionaries were among the most perceptive observers of Batswana society and the daily lives of people. But missionaries also commonly omitted descriptions of African activities, and tailored their accounts to suit their purposes. Robert Hamilton, for example, a longtime resident missionary to the Batlhaping, wrote very little about Batlhaping society except to mention the people as objects for conversion, and Walter Inglis, in a letter to the Society, described Bahurutshe politics as: "The whole question is an involved mass of native politics -- quite uninteresting to you. . . ," and left the matter at that.[1] And missionaries favored those who showed a desire for European dress and learning, seeing them as "progressive" and "good," while disfavoring those whom they saw as "traditional" and "backward," like the Bakgatla of Mabotsa who were, in the words of Roger Edwards, "pure specimen

---

[1]Walter Inglis to LMS, Bahurutseland, September 26, 1848, LMS-SOAS, South Africa, Incoming, Box 23, Folder 4, Jacket C.

of degraded savageism" and their *kgosi* Mosielele, as "despotic, vain, insatiably covetous & mean."[2]

Missionaries also sought to advance their personal, career interests with their home societies. The conflict between the Kuruman and Klaarwater missionaries certainly affected their contradictory reports on the Waterboer affair, and Livingstone's population estimates were likely affected by his desire for the independence and adventures of the interior.[3] In September 1841, Livingstone, assigned to Kuruman but longing for his own station, wrote to his home society arguing that Moffat and others had inflated Kuruman's population and accordingly its need for missionaries was less than what Moffat had claimed. Compare, he urged, the less than 1,000 inhabitants of Kuruman with the 15,000 to 20,000 Batswana of the interior who longed for the gospel.[4] But once in residence at Mabotsa, Tshonwane, and later, Kolobeng, Livingstone changed his tune, contending that there weren't so many Batswana in the area and that he didn't need anyone else to help him in this corner of the vineyard.[5]

Like the missionaries, more recent observers have both elucidated and obscured and colored our understanding of the Batswana. The anthropologist Isaac Schapera has almost single-handedly affixed the Batswana onto the map of European scholarship. His works are indispensible, richly detailed, and cogently presented.[6] Still, as he candidly described in the preface to the first edition of his landmark *A Handbook of Tswana Law and Custom*, "I spent four months among

---

[2]Roger Edwards to LMS, Mabotsa, August 12, 1849, LMS-SOAS, South Africa, Incoming, Box 24, Folder 1, Jacket B.

[3]See, e.g., LMS-SOAS, South Africa, Incoming, Boxes 16-18.

[4]Moffat had used the English reckoning of five persons per "hut." Not all "huts" were family homes, Livingstone pointed out, many serving as storage facilities and individual, not family residences. David Livingstone to A. Tidman, Kuruman, June 24, 1843, LMS-SOAS, Africa, Odds, Box 9, Folder 2A. See also Inglis' estimates in Walter Inglis to LMS, Griqua Town, September 18, 1844, LMS-SOAS, South Africa, Incoming, Box 20, Folder 1, Jacket B.

[5]David Livingstone to J. J. Freeman, Kuruman, September 23, 1841, LMS-SOAS, Africa, Odds, Box 10, Folder 1, Jacket B; David Livingstone to A. Tidman, Kuruman, June 24, 1843, LMS-SOAS, Africa, Odds, Box 9, Folder 2A; and David Livingstone to D. G. Watt, Bakwain Country, April 14, 1842, LMS-SOAS, Africa, Odds, Box 22. See also, Comaroff and Comaroff, *Of Revelation and Revolution*, I.

[6]See John L. and Jean Comaroff, "On the Founding Fathers, Field Work and Functionalism: A Conversation with Isaac Schapera," *American Ethnologist* 15:3 (1988): pp. 554-65.

the Ngwato . . . and have also paid fleeting visits to the Kwena, Malete, and Tlokwa. I have not yet been able to make any detailed inquiries among these last three tribes, nor have I any first-hand knowledge at all of the Rolong, Ngwaketse, and Tawana."[7] It seems to me that Schapera applied the models derived primarily from his Bakgatla researches onto the Batswana as a whole, resulting in some basic misapprehensions like the significance of immigrants among the Bakwena of Molepolole.

My own researches bear the stamp of my location. Race relations in Botswana and southern Africa in general during the time of my fieldwork was determined by South African apartheid and the paradigm of black and white. To some Bakwena, I was White; to others, perhaps more attuned to subtleties, I was Chinese. The South African labor recruitment compound, the government "camp," and the secondary school and mission hospital were the white enclaves in Molepolole. Many of Molepolole's Whites had closer dealings with fellow Whites in Botswana's capital, Gaborone, a distance of about forty kilometers, than with their Bakwena neighbors.

Although I had lived at the secondary school for three years from 1968 to 1970, during my fieldwork in 1975, my wife Libby and I asked to live in Ntloedibe as the subjects of its head, Ngwanaamotho. We tried to avoid Molepolole's Whites (although we developed a close friendship with a white American, William Duggan, who would complete his doctoral dissertation in African history), and ordered much of our lives around the daily rhythms of fetching water at the tap, shopping at the local butcher shop, and walking rather than driving around the town. I insisted on walking to our interviews, despite the initial protests of my translator Selebatso Masimega, the heat, and the distances that were as far as a mile or two. Of course, the Bakwena weren't fooled into thinking that I was one of them. As a Mokwena told me pointedly, "Who is to receive the credit for this study, and whose information made it possible?" He correctly knew that I was just another outsider -- of the racial other -- who had come to exploit them.

---

[7]Schapera, *Handbook*, p. xxvi. See also, I. Schapera, *Migrant Labour and Tribal Life* (London: Oxford University Press, 1947), p. v; and I. Schapera, *Native Land Tenure in the Bechuanaland Protectorate* (Lovedale: Lovedale Press, 1943), p. vi, for descriptions of the extent of his fieldwork.

Missionaries and Christianity, colonialists and neo-colonialists, South Africa's hegemony that included skin lighteners and hair straighteners, and my racialized, gendered, and classed intrusion invariably affected my collection of oral histories. Some Bakwena were ashamed of their "uncivilized" past, others studiously avoided me, and a few others sought me out as a forum and an arbiter of past conflicts. Immigrants, particularly former servants (*batlhanka*), tried to conceal their origins, and juniors concocted genealogies and histories that legitimized their claims.[8] I know that I appreciate imperfectly the limitations of my research and interpretation, despite my self-conscious reflections, and realize that I have just begun to scratch the surface of the Bakwena past.

Even more humbling was my attempt to collect "Bakgalagadi" oral histories. We chose to begin in Letlhakeng because of its close proximity to Molepolole and because it was the home of the three major groups in the Kweneng, the Bakgwatheng, Babolaongwe, and Bashaga. The decision proved fortuitous, because Letlhakeng's diversity opened my eyes to the complexities on the ground. Wookey classed all Bashaga as Batlhaping and descendants of Morikele, but my interviews among the Bashaga of Letlhakeng revealed that Morikele was the head of only one section of the junior Baga-Monyemane and that groups of Barolong also claimed the "Bashaga" identity.[9] I also learned about the elasticity of ethnicity or ethnic labels, whereby even brothers who shared the same birth father could consider themselves to be members of different ethnic groups. Molaole, who lives in Motokwe, declared himself a Mokgwatheng, while his senior brother, Heri, who lives in Letlhakeng, considered himself a Moshaga.

Mobility, a frequent feature of desert living, added to the complication. Contact and interaction have led to acculturation, including word-borrowings, intermarriages, and fused, consensus histories. Historians intent on tracing lines of descent and excavating the social layers face a challenging, if daunting task made even more demanding by the expanses of the desert and its physical conditions. My modest, impressionistic searches have revealed two features, assuredly neither novel nor unique, but perhaps of some interest.

---

[8] Okihiro, "Genealogical Research."
[9] Wookey, *Dico*, p. 84.

The first is the apparent existence of historical zones wherein groups, even of divergent origins and trajectories, share a common account of the past. Thus, although of different ethnicities and pasts, the Babolaongwe and Bashaga of Letlhakeng show a greater convergence in their historical accounts than do the Babolaongwe of Letlhakeng and the Babolaongwe of Midie who were before c.1822 one people. I suspect at least five historical zones in the "Bakgalagadi" Kweneng: the Moshaweng area; Letlhakeng and vicinity; the area around Boatlaname and Midie; the Lephephe, Shadishadi, and Sojwe vicinity; and the area encircled by Mazeaboroko, Tsetseng, Kang, Motokwe, and Luzwe.

The second, related to and perhaps an aspect of the first, is that the farther I moved away from Molepolole and toward the desert's heart, I found histories with greater time depths and broader compasses. It appears that the more senior "Bakgalagadi" lineages settled as far away as they could from the Bakwena and other Batswana to avoid servitude, while sending their juniors to areas more vulnerable to Bakwena hegemony. Perhaps the junior lineages, by settling under the Bakwena, sought some escape from their seniors. Whatever the cause, the genealogies of lineages in the western Kweneng extend farther back in time and show wider connections among the scattered "Bakgalagadi" groups than those found in the eastern Kweneng. The Babolaongwe of Sojwe, as an example, began their history just three generations past, while those at Letlhakeng traced their origins back six generations, and the Bashaga of Kang maintained a broad sweep of their history, while those of Letlhakeng possessed a history that commenced with their separation from their parent group at Kang.

Despite my attempt at a systematic collection and analysis of oral history, luck and happenstance played pivotal roles in my research. My sketch of "Bakgalagadi" history would have been very different had Libby not convinced me to press on to Hukuntsi or had I not persisted and remained in Luzwe and found the Mobolaongwe historian, Pense Tshaila, who astounded and enlightened me with his ten-generation recitation. Nineteenth-century missionaries and visitors similarly have given us narrow, fleeting glimpses of the Batswana. Marc Bloch, when confronted with similar uncertainties and gaps in writing his great work on French agrarian history, reminded his readers: "It should, after all, be common ground that in a scientific subject every positive statement in simply a hypothesis."[10]

B. Oral Sources.

With few exceptions, all of my interviews were group interviews. I found that method to be more effective than individual sessions, because the interviewees seemed to participate less self-consciously when engaged in a group discussion and the exchange of ideas, even debate, sharpened each member's contribution. On those rare occasions when a dissenting view was noticeably stifled by a dominant member of the group, I approached that person individually after the interview session to get his/her version.

All of the interviews were conducted at the members' *makgotla* or homes. In small settlements like Motokwe and Kang, however, the interviews were held at the central *kgotla*. Every interview was conducted through my interpreter, Selebatso G. Masimega, who was a primary school teacher and a well-known personality in Molepolole. Masimega also worked with Isaac Schapera on his study of marriage and gender relations among the Bakgatla.[11] Although interviewing through an interpreter posed a barrier and raises methodological questions, I needed Masimega's help especially with the vocabularies of specialists. I knew enough Setswana, however, to converse and to catch, on occasion, slips in Masimega's translations and explanations.

I didn't record most of the interviews, because the machine impeded a free flowing discussion and tended to formalize and stiffen my interviewees' responses. Instead, I took notes during the course of the interview, and transcribed them shortly thereafter, usually the night after the session. I found that taking notes as I interviewed kept me more sharply attuned to what was being said, rather than depending upon a recorder for later listening, and it helped me formulate more intelligent follow-up questions.

---

[10]Marc L. Bloch, *French Rural History: An Essay of Its Basic Characteristics*, trans. Janet Sondheimer (Berkeley: University of California Press, 1966), p. xxiv.

[11]Isaac Schapera, *Married Life in an African Tribe* (London: Faber & Faber, 1940).

The interviews are coded by subject, place, and sequence. Thus, H/M/1 indicates a history interview held at Molepolole and the first in a series of such interviews held there, and L/Ms/4 refers to linguistics, Moshaweng, fourth interview. The list below is arranged by town, code, place of interview, date, time, and the names and *mephato* of interviewees.

1. Boatlaname

H/B/1
Ga-Basimane, at the home of Chabai Chuba.
November 8, 1975, 0900 to 1120.
Interviewees: Chabai Chuba (Matlhogela), Motshipa Keimetswe (Matlhogela), Ntlhogo Keborometswe (Matswakgotla), Dao Keborometswe (Maakathata), Masego Golwelwang (Mautlwakgosi), Ranto Thebogo (Matlama), and Gaogilwe Motshipa.

H/B/2
At the primary school.
November 8, 1975, 1415 to 1635.
Interviewees: Kwalona Kgotladintsi (Matswakgotla), Setsowarona Kgotladintsi (Malatakgosi), Lepodisi Ratlhaga (Matlhaselwa), and Thankwane Rakhama (Matlama).

2. Hukuntsi

H/H/1
At the *kgosi*'s office.
November 25, 1975, 0915 to 1115.
Interviewees: Moapare Mosiwa, Olaotse Molathole, Joshua Setshogo, Senatle Mogolele, and Sargeant Kalantle.

H/H/2
At the home of B. M. Moapare.
November 25, 1975, 1500 to 1615.
Interviewees: Namokgotha Moapare, Duhane Mokope, and Mogoke Momakwa.

H/H/3
At the *kgotla*.
November 26, 1975, 0830 to 1100.
Interviewees: Moapare Mosiwa, Joshua Setshogo, Sargeant Kalantle, Senatle Mogolele, Ekenyane Wamotsokwe, Enkopane Mokgwetsi, Rikiti Mokgwetsi, Dikole Baumake, Mabotinyane Baumake, Kebetwani Gakewepe, Monyaise Mogwasi, and Gaditswalele Matibisi.

H/H/4
At the *kgosi*'s office.
November 26, 1975, 1530 to 1630.

Interviewees: Enkopane Mokgwetsi, Ekenyane Wamotsokwe, Sargeant Kalantle, and Senatle Mogolele.

L/H/1
At the *kgosi*'s office.
November 26, 1975.
Interviewee: Sargeant Kalantle.
Language: Sebolaongwe.

3. Kang

H/K/1
At the *kgosi*'s office.
November 22, 1975, 1530 to 1700.
Interviewees: Kereke Seipone (Matlama), Makake Seipone (Matswakgotla), Gaikailwe Seipone (Matlhaselwa), Ngakani Segwape (Maratakgosi), Kgalalero Rithoung (Matlhaselwa), and Pule Tselaabarwa (Mathubantwa II).

H/K/2
At the *kgosi*'s office.
November 23, 1975, 0800 to 1045.
Interviewees: Kereke Seipone, Makake Seipone, Gaikailwe Seipone, Kgalalero Rithoung, Pule Tselaabarwa, Petlu Tselaabarwa (Matswakgotla), Nonyani Motshise (Mathubantwa II), and Adam Phori (Mautlwakgosi).

H/K/3
At the *kgosi*'s office.
November 23, 1975, 1515 to 1700.
Interviewees: Kereke Seipone, Gaikailwa Seipone, Kgalalero Rithoung, Nonyani Montshise, Pule Tselaabarwa, Gakeolope Komoki (Matlama), Sehularo Tlhokwane (Mautlwakgosi), and Sechali Komoki.

4. Lephephe

H/Lp/1
At the *kgotla*.
November 3, 1975, 0750 to 0920.
Interviewees: Mosai Lekapani (Maratakgosi), Mosarwa Molatlegi (Matlhaselwa), Kalala Lebati (Matlhaselwa), Terai Tafi (Matlama), John Mabetwa (Matlama), and Kefitlile Makgai (Majanko).

H/Lp/2
Under a tree adjacent to the *kgotla*.
November 3, 1975, 1430 to 1600.
Interviewees: Mosai Lekapani, Mosarwa Molatlegi, Pelaelo Morwaotsile, Nakedi Maragwana (Maakathata), and Ramogwana Moipolai (Maakathata).

H/Lp/3
Under a tree adjacent to the *kgotla*.
November 4, 1975, 0700 to 0900.

Interviewees: Mosai Lekapani, Mosarwa Molatlegi, Pelaelo Morwaotsile, Nakedi
Maragwana, and Kalala Lebati.

5. Letlhakeng

H/L/1
Kgosing, at the *kgotla*.
October 13, 1975, 1000 to 1100.
Interviewees: Tome Baitsadi (Maratakgosi), Mpolaakeswe Banyatsi
(Matlhaselwa), Moakofi Dinare (Mathubantwa II), Motlhoki Gaoforwe
(Malatakgosi), Lesupi Tshaila (Masitaoka), Motloane Tsietso (Matswakgotla),
Matlho Reokwaeng (Matlhaselwa), Lekate Mokoanele (Maratakgosi), Nkemo
Masono (Matlhaselwa), Moloiwa Molale (Malatakgosi), Somolekae Macheng
(Matlama), Tshipinyane Motseonageng, and Tiro Kgabo (Matlama).

H/L/2
Kgosing, at the *kgotla*.
October 13, 1975, 1445 to 1600.
Interviewees: Matlho Reokwaeng and Nkemo Masono.

H/L/3
Kgosing, at the *kgosi*'s office.
October 14, 1975, 0730 to 0930.
Interviewees: Matlho Reokwaeng, Tiro Kgabo, Somolekae Macheng, Motloane
Tsietso, Moakofi Dinake, Moloiwa Molale, Tshipinyane Motseonageng,
Kooloetswe Sebolao (Malatakgosi), and Gaolefelwe Ratsetshowa
(Matswakgotla).

H/L/4
Goo-Molehele, at the home of Gakenne Tshipa.
October 14, 1975, 1530 to 1645.
Interviewees: Gakenne Tshipa (Masitaoka), Sentlhaga Magono (Mathubantwa
II), Rebolang Lesupi (Masitaoka), Gagonthuse Thebeetsile (Malatakgosi), and
Matsela Nongtsobo (Matlhomathebe).

H/L/5
Kgosing, at the *kgosi*'s old office.
October 15, 1975, 0800 to 0930.
Interviewees: Lesupi Tshaila, Tiro Kgabo, Matlho Reokwaeng, Moakofi Dinare,
Motloane Tsietso, Somolekae Macheng, Moloiwa Molale, and Kooloetswe
Sebolao.

H/L/6
Goo-Molehele, at the home of Gakenne Tshipa.
October 15, 1975, 1020 to 1225.
Interviewees: Gakenne Tshipa, Sentlhaga Magono, Rebolang Lesupi,
Gagonthuse Tebeetsile, and Matsela Nongtsobo.

H/L/7
Kgosing, at the *lgotla*.
October 15, 1975, 1545 to 1700.

Interviewees: Matlho Reokwaeng, Tiro Kgabo, Moloiwa Molale, Motloane Tsietso, Setlhalifinyana Reokwaeng (Maakathata), Ntonya Moretile (Matlhaselwa), and Tlhose Tshekedi (Mathubantwa II).

H/L/8
Kgosing, at the *kgosi*'s old office.
October 16, 1975, 0800 to 0930.
Interviewees: Lesupi Tshaila, Moloiwa Molale, Somolekae Macheng, Kooloetswe Sebolao, and Setlhalifinyana Reokwaeng.

H/L/9
Goo-Molehele, at the home of Gakenne Tshipa.
October 16, 1975, 1020 to 1130.
Interviewees: Gakenne Tshipa, Gakelele Puleng, Rebolang Lesupi, Matsela Nongtsobo, and Gagonthuse Thebeetsile.

H/L/10
Kgosing, at the *kgosi*'s old office.
October 17, 1975, 0800 to 1000.
Interviewees: Lesupi Tshaila, Moloiwa Molale, Somolekae Macheng, Setlhalifinyana Reokwaeng, Kooloetswe Sebolao, and Gaolefelwe Ratsetshowa.

H/L/11
Goo-Molehele, at the home of Gakenne Tshipa.
October 17, 1975, 1045 to 1200,
Interviewees: Gakenne Tshipa, Gakelele Puleng, Rebolang Lesupi, Matsela Nongtsobo, Gagonthuse Thebeetsile, and Sentlhaga Magono.

H/L/12
Kgesakwe, at the home of Koepile Sesinye.
October 18, 1975, 0900 to 1045.
Interviewees: Koepile Sesinye (Matswakgotla), Kobatile Lentswe (Mathubantwa II), Tinye Baikgati (Mathubantwa II), Mpolaekeswe Banyatsi, and Papadi Sesinye (Matlhaselwa).

H/L/13
Goo-Molehele, at the home of Gakenne Tshipa.
October 20, 1975, 0930 to 1100.
Interviewees: Gakenne Tshipa, Gakelele Puleng, Sentlhaga Magono, Gagonthuse Thebeetsile, and Matsela Nongtsobo.

H/L/14
Goo-Baitsadi, at the *kgotla*.
October 20, 1975, 1430 to 1615.
Interviewees: Tome Baitsadi, Moroki Tlhadigorimo (Maratakgosi), Lekake Mokoanele, Athama Setlhako (Matswakgotla), Koboatshwene Boitiro (Matlhaselwa), and Disele Mariba (Malatakgosi).

H/L/15
Kgosing, at the *kgosi*'s old office.
October 21, 1975, 0940 to 1040.

Interviewees: Lesupi Tshaila, Somolekae Macheng, Moloiwa Molale, Pusoetsile Lesupi (Malatakgosi), Obonye Reokwaeng (Maakathata), Tome Baitsadi, and Lekake Mokoanele.

H/L/16
Goo-Molehele, at the home of Gakenne Tshipa.
October 21, 1975, 1125 to 1225.
Interviewees: Gakenne Tshipa, Sentlhaga Magono, Gagonthuse Thebeetsile, and Matsela Nongtsobo.

H/L/17
Goo-Ra-Motsekwe, at the *kgotla*.
October 21, 1975, 1445 to 1600.
Interviewees: Tome Baitsadi, Lekake Mokoanele, Motseganong Magoutswane (Matlhaselwa), and Raphalana Gagoakelwe.

H/L/18
Goo-Mokwele, at the *kgotla*.
October 22, 1975, 0815 to 0915.
Interviewees: Seepa Lekgela (Matlhaselwa), Ramontsho Lekgela (Matlhaselwa), Nkumisang Radimpa (Matlama), Kebonyemotho Moselesele (Matlama), Kebabitse Motlhaping (Masitaoka), and Sagae Lekgela (Malatakgosi).

H/L/19
Goo-Molehele, at the home of Gakenne Tshipa.
October 22, 1975, 1030 to 1145.
Interviewees: Gakenne Tshipa, Gakelele Puleng, Matsela Nongtsobo, Sentlhaga Magono, and Gagonthuse Thebeetsile.

H/L/20
Kgosing, at the *kgosi*'s old office.
October 22, 1975, 1430 to 1630.
Interviewees: Moloiwa Molale, Somolekae Macheng, Gaolefelwe Ratsetshowa, Tome Baitsadi, and Lekake Mokoanele.

H/L/21
Kgosing, at the *kgosi*'s old office.
October 23, 1975, 0845 to 1040.
Interviewees: Lesupi Tshaila, Somolekae Macheng, Moloiwa Molale, Gaolefelwe Ratsetshowa, Pusoetsile Lesupi, Tome Baitsadi, and Lekake Mokoanele.

H/L/22
Goo-Ra-Motsekwe, at the home of Gakelinyatse Mogibidu.
October 23, 1975, 1430 to 1600.
Interviewees: Sechwano Mongologa (Matlhaselwa), Tuelo Merule (Matlama), Gakelinyatse Mogibidu (Matlhaselwa), and Kelebeng Ponego (Matswakgotla).

H/L/23
Kgosing, at the *kgosi*'s old office.
October 24, 1975, 0740 to 0815.
Interviewee: Setlhalifinyana Reokwaeng.

H/L/24
Kgosing, at the *kgosi*'s old office.
October 24, 1975, 0820 to 1110.
Interviewees: Setlhalifinyana Reokwaeng, Lesupi Tshaila, Pusoetsile Lesupi,
Moloiwa Molale, Somolekae Macheng, Gaolefelwe Ratsetshowa, and Lekake
Mokoanele.

L/L/1
Kgosing, at the *kgosi*'s old office.
October 24, 1975, 1415 to 1630.
Interviewee: Setlhalifinyana Reokwaeng.
Language: Sekgwatheng.

L/L/2
Kgosing, at the *kgosi*'s old office.
October 24, 1975, 1415 to 1630.
Interviewee: Moloiwa Molale.
Language: Sebolaongwe.

L/L/3
Kgosing, at the *kgosi*'s old office.
October 24, 1975, 1415 to 1630.
Interviewee: Sechwano Mongologa.
Language: Sheshaga.

6. Luzwe

H/Lu/1
Kgosing, at the *kgotla*.
November 19, 1975, 0800 to 0830.
Interviewees: Lebamodimo Puleng (Mautlwakgosi), Mosuge Senkgakane
(Maakathata), Makwene Mokuduane (Maakathata), and Gawelelwe Katimanang
(Masitaoka).

H/Lu/2
Goo-Molehele, at the home of Pense Tshaila.
November 19, 1975, 1000 to 1130.
Interviewees: Pense Tshaila (Masitaoka), Motule Tshekedi (Malatakgosi), and
Mosuge Senkgakane.

H/Lu/3
Goo-Molehele, at the home of Pense Tshaila.
November 19, 1975, 1430 to 1630.
Interviewees: Pense Tshaila and Motule Tshekedi.

7. Makabanyane

H/Mk/1
At the *kgotla*.
November 4, 1975, 1800 to 1830.
Interviewees: Keheletswe, Mamosweu, and Gabankitse.

H/Mk/2
At the *kgotla*.
November 5, 1975, 0845 to 1025.
Interviewees: Titomore Kefurile (Matlama), Ranko Kefurile (Majanko), Baichoki Ipolokeng (Malatakgosi), Koosentse Gabanakgosi (Mautlwakgosi), and Mosai Lekapane [of Lephephe].

8. Molepolole

H/M/1
Kgosing, at the *kgosi*'s *lelwapa*.
February 12, 1975, 1000 to 1045.
Interviewee: Timpa Mosarwa.

H/M/2
Kgosing, at the *kgosi*'s *lelwapa*.
February 13, 1975, 1100 to 1230.
Interviewees: Ratlou Ketshabile, Koama Motlhale, and Pepere Gabaraane.

H/M/3
Kgosing, at the *kgotla*.
February 12, 1975, 1445 to 1715.
Interviewees: Timpa Mosarwa, Koama Motlhale, Mack K. Sechele II, Pepere Gabaraane, and Kgafela Motswasele.

H/M/4
Ga-Morwa, at the home of Kabelo Kebakae.
February 18, 1975, 0930 to 1100.
Interviewees: Kabelo Kebakae (Masitaoka), Gaetwesepe Rasebe (Mathubantwa II), and Gagonthone Kgari.

H/M/5
Kgosing, at the *kgosi*'s *lelwapa*.
February 10, 1975, 0930 to 1100.
Interviewees: Mathwane Bolote, Mosimanegape Matlhoko, Timpa Mosarwa, Koama Motlhale, and Kebelaetse Wamoku.

H/M/6
Kgosing, at the *kgosi*'s *lelwapa*.
February 11, 1975, 0910 to 1130.
Interviewees: Timpa Mosarwa, Koama Motlhale, Kebelaetse Wamoku, and Pepere Gabaraane.

H/M/7
Goo-Ra-Tshosa, at the *kgotla*.
February 17, 1975, 0900 to 1130.
Interviewees: Thukhwi Segaetsho, Maothwanong Gaealafshwe, Serare Mathong, Magatelo Mokgoko, and Oatlhotse Kgakge.

H/M/8
Goo-Ra-Tshosa, at the home of Timothy Gaealafshwe.

February 18, 1975, 1445 to 1630.
Interviewees: Thukhwi Segaetsho, Maothwanong Gaealafshwe, Serare Mathong, and Magatelo Mokgoko.

H/M/9
Goo-Ra-Tshosa, at the home of Timothy Gaealafshwe.
February 19, 1975, 0830 to 1230.
Interviewees: Thukhwi Segaetsho, Maothwanong Gaealafshwe, Serare Mathong, Magatelo Mokgoko, and Phutego Mokoka.

H/M/10
Ga-Morwa, at the home of Kabelo Kebakae.
February 20, 1975, 0830 to 1130.
Interviewees: Kabelo Kebakae and Gaetwesepe Rasebe.

H/M/11
Goo-Ra-Tshosa, at the home of Timothy Gaealafshwe.
February 20, 1975, 1430 to 1830.
Interviewees: Thukhwi Segaetsho, Phutego Mokoka, Maothwanong Gaealafshwe, Serare Mathong, and Magatelo Mokgoko.

H/M/12
Goo-Ra-Tshosa, at the home of Timothy Gaealafshwe.
February 21, 1975, 0830 to 1100.
Interviewees: Thukhwi Segaetsho, Maothwanong Gaealafshwe, Serare Mathong, and Magatelo Mokgoko.

H/M/13
Maunatlala, at the home of M. Mhaladi.
February 25, 1975, 1500 to 1700.
Interviewees: Semetsataola Maselesele (Masitaoka), Kokwe Segaetsho (Matswakgotla), and Motseotsile Molefe (Matlhaselwa).

H/M/14
Maunatlala, at the home of M. Mhaladi.
February 26, 1975, 0830 to 1030.
Interviewees: Semetsataola Maselesele, Kokwe Segaetsho, Sepotoka Mafuri (Matswakgotla), Ramotoko Nonyane (Matswakgotla), Matome Mpusang (Matswakgotla), and Moagi Sebomo (Mathubantwa II).

H/M/15
Maunatlala, at the home of M. Mhaladi.
February 27, 1975, 0845 to 1100.
Interviewees: Semetsataola Maselesele, Kokwe Segaetsho, Sepotoka Mafuri, Ramotoko Nonyane, and Modisakgomo Thipe.

H/M/16
Maunatlala, at the home of Semetsataola Maselesele.
February 28, 1975, 0900 to 1030.
Interviewee: Semetsataola Maselesele.

H/M/17
Maunatlala, at the home of Sepotoka Mafuri.
February 28, 1975, 1600 to 1800.
Interviewee: Sepotoka Mafuri.

H/M/18
Masilwana, at the *kgotla*.
March 10, 1975, 1530 to 1700.
Interviewees: Kabelo Serole (Maratakgosi), Keikanetswe Sebolao (Maratakgosi), Kebopeleng Tshomane (Maakathata), Phutego Kotonyane (Maakathata), Baikalafi Makwatse (Maakathata), and Setlhaku Tawana (Matlhaselwa).

H/M/19
Masilwana, at the *kgotla*.
March 11, 1975, 0845 to 1230.
Interviewees: Kabelo Serole, Kebopeleng Tshomane, Phutego Kotonyane, and Baikalafi Makwatse.

H/M/20
Masilwana, at the home of Kebopeleng Tshomane.
March 16, 1975, 0930 to 1200.
Interviewees: Kabelo Serole, Kebopeleng Tshomane, and Phutego Kotonyane.

H/M/21
Goo-Ra-Tshosa, at the home of Selebatso G. Masimega.
March 19, 1975, 0900 to 1000.
Interviewee: Sepotoka Mafuri.

H/M/22
Kgosing, at the *kgosi*'s *lelwapa*.
March 19, 1975, 1500 to 1630.
Interviewees: Keakele Sechele II (Malatakgosi), Nkwane Gaealafshwe (Matlhogela), Ditloung Kusi (Mathubantwa II), and Tshitshawenyane Tebele (Matlhogela).

H/M/23
Kgosing, at the *kgosi*'s *lelwapa*.
March 20, 1975, 0945 to 1200.
Interviewees: Keakele Sechele II, Nkwane Gaealafshwe, Ditloung Kusi, and Tshitshawenyane Tebele.

H/M/24
Kgosing, at the *kgosi*'s *lelwapa*.
March 21, 1975, 1000 to 1115.
Interviewees: Keakele Sechele II, Nkwane Gaealafshwe, Ditloung Kusi, and Tshitshawenyane Tebele.

H/M/25
At the home of J. Jansen.
March 22, 1975, 1600 to 1630.
Interviewee: J. Jansen.

H/M/26
Kgosing, at the *kgosi's lelwapa.*
March 26, 1975, 0930 to 1100.
Interviewees: Keakele Sechele II, Nkwane Gaealafshwe, Ditloung Kusi, and
Tshitshawenyane Tebele.

H/M/27
Kgosing, at the *kgosi's lelwapa.*
April 1, 1975, 0945 to 1145.
Interviewees: Keakele Sechele II, Nkwane Gaealafshwe, Ditloung Kusi, and
Tshitshawenyane Tebele.

H/M/28
Kgosing, at the *kgosi's lelwapa.*
April 2, 1975, 1515 to 1715.
Interviewees: Keakele Sechele II, Nkwane Gaealafshwe, Ditloung Kusi, and
Tshitshawenyane Tebele.

H/M/29
Goo-Molale, at the home of Ratlou Ketshabile.
April 4, 1975, 1545 to 1645.
Interviewees: Ratlou Ketshabile and Sepotoka Mafuri.

H/M/30
Ga-Morwa, at the home of Kabelo Kebakae.
April 9, 1975, 0830 to 1030.
Interviewees: Kabelo Kebakae and Gagonthone Kgari.

H/M/31
Ga-Morwa, at the home of Kabelo Kebakae.
April 10, 1975, 0830 to 1000.
Interviewees: Kabelo Kebakae and Gagonthone Kgari.

H/M/32
Ga-Morwa, at the home of Kabelo Kebakae.
April 11, 1975, 0830 to 1000.
Interviewees: Kabelo Kebakae and Gagonthone Kgari.

H/M/33
Ga-Morwa, at the home of Kabelo Kebakae.
April 14, 1975, 0900 to 1130.
Interviewees: Kabelo Kebakae, Gagonthone Kgari, and Gaetwesepe Rasebe.

H/M/34
Ga-Morwa, at the home of Kabelo Kebakae.
April 15, 1975, 1015 to 1130.
Interviewees: Kabelo Kebakae, Gagonthone Kgari, and Gaetwesepe Rasebe.

H/M/35
Ga-Morwa, at the *kgotla.*

April 16, 1975, 0900 to 1200.
Interviewees: Gagonthone Kgari and Phutego Mokoka.

H/M/36
Ga-Morwa, at the *kgotla*.
April 17, 1975, 0830 to 1100.
Interviewees: Gagonthone Kgari and Phutego Mokoka.

H/M/37
Ga-Morwa, at the *kgotla*.
April 18, 1975, 1045 to 1300.
Interviewees: Gagonthone Kgari and Phutego Mokoka.

H/M/38
Kgosing, at the *kgotla*.
April 21, 1975, 0945 to 1045.
Interviewees: [Not an interview but a recording of the deliberations of several *dingaka* investigating two cases of suspected witchcraft.]

H/M/39
Ga-Morwa, at the *kgotla*.
April 21, 1975, 1145 to 1245.
Interviewee: Barakanyo Direlang.

H/M/40
Senyadimana, at the home of Koama Motlhale.
April 22, 1975, 1500 to 1630.
Interviewees: Koama Motlhale and Kebelaetse Wamoku.

H/M/41
Botlhajana, at the home of Mokgotuotsile Kgabo.
April 22, 1975, 1700 to 1800.
Interviewee: Mokgotuotsile Kgabo.

H/M/42
Goo-Ra-Tshosa, at the home of Harry Kgakge.
April 23, 1975, 0830 to 1030.
Interviewees: Harry Kgakge and Magatelo Mokgoko.

H/M/43
Goo-Ra-Tshosa, at the home of Nkwane Gaealafshwe.
Arpil 25, 1975, 0830 to 1030.
Interviewees: Phutego Mokoka, Magatelo Mokgoko, Ranjahu Kobe, and Nkwane Gaealafshwe.

H/M/44
Mogochwana, at the home of Mogopudi Raditoko.
April 27, 1975, 1100 to 1200.
Interviewee: Mogopudi Raditoko.

H/M/45

Goo-Ra-Tshosa, at the home of Nkwane Gaealafshwe.
April 28, 1975, 1100 to 1200.
Interviewees: Phutego Mokoka, Magatelo Mokgoko, Ranjahu Kobe, and
Nkwane Gaealafshwe.

H/M/46
Matlhalerwa, at the *kgotla*.
April 29, 1975, 0915 to 1115.
Interviewees: Phutego Mokoka, Magatelo Mokgoko, Nkwane Gaealafshwe,
Ramasunyana Ikalafeng (Matlhalerwa), and Rame Ramosarwana.

H/M/47
Goo-Ra-Tshosa, at the home of Nkwane Gaealafshwe.
April 30, 1975, 0900 to 1115.
Interviewees: Phutego Mokoka, Magatelo Mokgoko, and Nkwane Gaealafshwe.

H/M/48
Goo-Ra-Tshosa, at the home of Nkwane Gaealafshwe.
May 1, 1975, 0830 to 1030.
Interviewees: Phutego Mokoka, Magatelo Mokgoko, and Nkwane Gaealafshwe.

H/M/49
Goo-Ra-Kgaimena, at the *kgotla*.
June 2, 1975, 1430 to 1530.
Interviewees: Galekgatlhane Motshwane (Mathubantwa II), Inakale Baitlhaki
(Maratakgosi), and Banabakgori Motshwane (Matswakgotla).

H/M/50
Goo-Ra-Tshosa, at the home of Nkwane Gaealafshwe.
June 6, 1975, 1000 to 1200.
Interviewees: Magatelo Mokgoko, Samokwati Kgakge, Gabofilwe Raborokwe,
and Nkwane Gaealafshwe.

H/M/51
Goo-Ra-Tshosa, at the home of Nkwane Gaealafshwe.
June 9, 1975, 1145 to 1315.
Interviewees: Magatelo Mokgoko, Samokwati Kgakge, Gabofilwe Raborokwe,
Nkwane Gaealafshwe, and Rakudu Keakilwe (Mathubantwa II).

H/M/52
Goo-Ra-Kgaimena, at the *kgotla*.
June 10, 1975, 1500 to 1615.
Interviewees: Inakale Baitlhaki, Banabakgori Motshwane, Nonyetsetse
Motshwane (Maakathata), Tiroyafalo Kgotlana (Matswakgotla), and
Molelowakgotla Kgotlana (Matlhaselwa).

H/M/53
Difetlhamolelo, at the home of Letsatsi Mhiko.
June 11, 1975, 0945 to 1100.
Interviewee: Letsatsi Mhiko (Matlhomathebe).

H/M/54
Goo-Ra-Tshosa.
June 13, 1975, 1500 to 1630.
Interviewees: Samokwati Kgakge and Selebatso G. Masimega.

H/M/55
Goo-Ra-Tshosa, at the home of Nkwane Gaealafshwe.
June 18, 1975, 1020 to 1230.
Interviewees: Magatelo Mokgoko, Nkwane Gaealafshwe, Mapote Keaketswe
(Malatakgosi), and Keemhitletse Makwati (Matlama).

H/M/56
Goo-Ra-Tshosa, at the home of Nkwane Gaealafshwe.
June 19, 1975, 1030 to 1200.
Interviewees: Magatelo Mokgoko, Nkwane Gaealafshwe, Mapote Keaketswe,
Ratlhaga Kareng (Matlhogela), and Kesentswe Kareng (Maratakgosi).

H/M/57
Goo-Ra-Tshosa, at the home of Nkwane Gaealafshwe.
June 20, 1975, 0930 to 1000.
Interviewee: Nkwane Gaealafshwe.

H/M/58
Goo-Kodisa, at the *kgotla*.
June 23, 1975, 1030 to 1200.
Interviewees: Malanse Bodigelo (Matswakgotla), Lehubitsa Keetile (Maakathata),
Monametse Gabaki (Malatakgosi), and Sekee Mogapi (Malatakgosi).

H/M/59
Goo-Ra-Tshosa, at the home of Nkwane Gaealafshwe.
June 24, 1975, 1000 to 1130.
Interviewees: Magatelo Mokgoko, Nkwane Gaealafshwe, and Thukhwi
Segaetsho.

H/M/60
Goo-Ra-Tshosa, at the home of Nkwane Gaealafshwe.
June 25, 1975, 0930 to 1130.
Interviewees: Magatelo Mokgoko, Nkwane Gaealafshwe, Thukhwi Segaetsho,
Mapote Keaketswe, Gabofilwe Raborokwe, Motlhanka Morewang
(Matswakgotla), and Simane Molepolole (Matlhaselwa).

H/M/61
Goo-Ra-Tshosa, at the home of Nkwane Gaealafshwe.
June 26, 1975, 0945 to 1045.
Interviewees: Magatelo Mokgoko, Nkwane Gaealafshwe, and Mapote
Keaketswe.

H/M/62
Goo-Ra-Tshosa, at the home of Nkwane Gaealafshwe.
June 26, 1975, 1430 to 1615.

Interviewees: Magatelo Mokgoko, Nkwane Gaealafshwe, Mapote Keaketswe, and Keemhitletse Makwati.

H/M/63
Goo-Ra-Tshosa, at the home of Nkwane Gaealafshwe.
June 27, 1975, 0930 to 1130.
Interviewees: Magatelo Mokgoko, Nkwane Gaealafshwe, Mapote Keaketswe, and Keemhitletse Makwati.

H/M/64
Goo-Ra-Suna, at the *kgotla*.
June 27, 1975, 1445 to 1545.
Interviewees: Magatelo Mokgoko, Lebang Ntloakhumo (Maakathata), Molefe Ngwanang (Maakathata), and Wilfred Ngwanang (Mautlwakgosi).

H/M/65
Goo-Ra-Tshosa, at the home of Nkwane Gaealafshwe.
June 30, 1975, 1030 to 1200.
Interviewees: Magatelo Mokgoko, Nkwane Gaealafshwe, Samokwati Kgakge, and Mokaiwa Kefiletletse (Matlama).

H/M/66
Goo-Ra-Tshosa, at the home of Nkwane Gaealafshwe.
June 30, 1975, 1430 to 1600.
Interviewees: Magatelo Mokgoko, Nkwane Gaealafshwe, Samokwati Kgakge, Mokaiwa Kefiletletse, Keemhitletse Makwati, and Motlhanka Morewang.

H/M/67
Goo-Ra-Tshosa, at the *kgotla*.
July 1, 1975, 0900 to 0930.
Interviewee: Selebatso G. Masimega.

H/M/68
Goo-Ra-Tshosa, at the home of Nkwane Gaealafshwe.
July 1, 1975, 1445 to 1600.
Interviewees: Magatelo Mokgoko, Nkwane Gaealafshwe, Samokwati Kgakge, Thukhwi Segaetsho, Keemhitletse Makwati, and Motlhanka Morewang.

H/M/69
Goo-Ra-Tshosa, at the home of Nkwane Gaealafshwe.
July 2, 1975, 0930 to 1100.
Interviewees: Magatelo Mokgoko, Nkwane Gaealafshwe, Samokwati Kgakge, Thukhwi Segaetsho, and Keemhitletse Makwati.

H/M/70
Goo-Ra-Tshosa, at the home of Nkwane Gaealafshwe.
July 2, 1975, 1445 to 1600.
Interviewees: Magatelo Mokgoko, Nkwane Gaealafshwe, Samokwati Kgakge, Thukhwi Segaetsho, Keemhitletse Makwati, and Motlhanka Morewang.

H/M/71

Goo-Ra-Tshosa, at the home of Nkwane Gaealafshwe.
July 3, 1975, 0945 to 1200.
Interviewees: Magatelo Mokgoko, Nkwane Gaealafshwe, Samokwati Kgakge, Thukhwi Segaetsho, and Mapote Keaketswe.

H/M/72
Goo-Ra-Tshosa, at the home of Nkwane Gaealafshwe.
July 4, 1975, 0930 to 1100.
Interviewees: Magatelo Mokgoko, Nkwane Gaealafshwe, Samokwati Kgakge, Thukhwi Segaetsho, and Mapote Keaketswe.

H/M/73
Goo-Ra-Tshosa, at the home of Nkwane Gaealafshwe.
July 7, 1975, 1415 to 1615.
Interviewees: Magatelo Mokgoko, Nkwane Gaealafshwe, Mapote Keaketswe, Thukhwi Segaetsho, and Motlhanka Morewang.

H/M/74
Goo-Ra-Tshosa, at the home of Nkwane Gaealafshwe.
July 8, 1975, 0930 to 1130.
Interviewees: Magatelo Mokgoko, Nkwane Gaealafshwe, Mapote Keaketswe, Thukhwi Segaetsho, and Ranjahu Kobe.

H/M/75
Mogochwana, at the home of Mogopudi Raditoko.
July 8, 1975, 1430 to 1630.
Interviewees: Mogopudi Raditoko, Thukhwi Segaetsho, and Ranjahu Kobe.

H/M/76
Goo-Ra-Tshosa, at the home of Nkwane Gaealafshwe.
July 9, 1975, 1030 to 1230.
Interviewees: Magatelo Mokgoko, Nkwane Gaealafshwe, Mapote Keaketswe, Thukhwi Segaetsho, and Keemhitletse Makwati.

H/M/77
Goo-Ra-Tshosa, at the home of Selebatso G. Masimega.
July 9, 1975, 1445 to 1545.
Interviewee: Keemhitletse Makwati.

H/M/78
Masilwana, at the home of Motlhatsi Baakang.
July 10, 1975, 1130 to 1200.
Interviewee: Motlhatsi Baakang (Matlhogela).

H/M/79
Goo-Mabe, at the home of Konono Phokojwe.
July 10, 1975, 1230 to 1345.
Interviewee: Konono Phokojwe (Masitaoka).

H/M/80
Goo-Ra-Tshosa, at the home of Nkwane Gaealafshwe.

July 11, 1975, 1100 to 1230.
Interviewees: Magatelo Mokgoko, Nkwane Gaealafshwe, Mapote Keaketswe, Thukhwi Segaetsho, Ramasunyana Ikalafeng, and Shanko Moeng (Matlama).

H/M/81
Goo-Ra-Suna, at the home of Diatla Ngwanang.
July 14, 1975, 1130 to 1400.
Interviewees: Diatla Ngwanang (Matlhaselwa) and Dithibane Seabelo.

H/M/82
Goo-Ra-Tshosa, at the home of Nkwane Gaealafshwe.
July 14, 1975, 1545 to 1700.
Interviewees: Magatelo Mokgoko, Nkwane Gaealafshwe, Mapote Keaketswe, Thukhwi Segaetsho, Keemhitletse Makwati, and Ko Motlhabane (Matswakgotla).

H/M/83
Goo-Mabe, at the home of Konono Phokojwe.
July 15, 1975, 0930 to 1100.
Interviewees: Konono Phokojwe, Samo Koolatotse (Matlhaselwa), and Botha Digobe (Matlhaselwa).

H/M/84
Masilwana, at the home of Kebopeleng Tshomane.
July 15, 1975, 1130 to 1300.
Interviewees: Kebopeleng Tshomane, Phutego Kotonyane, Ramaselesele Mogotsi (Matswakgotla), and Motlhatsi Baakang.

H/M/85
Goo-Ra-Modibedi, at the *kgotla*.
July 15, 1975, 1530 to 1630.
Interviewees: Sengwato Kobwaatshwene (Maratakgosi), Mogatsamothosana Modibedi (Matswakgotla), Okana Modibedi (Mautlwakgosi), Magatelo Mokgoko, and Mapote Keaketswe.

H/M/86
Goo-Ra-Suna, at the home of Diatla Ngwanang.
July 16, 1975, 0945 to 1100.
Interviewees: Diatla Ngwanang, Wilfred Ngwanang, Lebang Ntloakhumo, Magatelo Mokgoko, and Mapote Keaketswe.

H/M/87
Goo-Ra-Tshosa, at the home of Nkwane Gaealafshwe.
July 16, 1975, 1445 to 1630.
Interviewees: Magatelo Mokgoko, Nkwane Gaealafshwe, Mapote Keaketswe, and Nkone Ntshuke (Maakathata).

H/M/88
Masilwana, at the home of Kebopeleng Tshomane.
July 17, 1975, 1030 to 1200.
Interviewees: Kebopeleng Tshomane, Phutego Kotonyane, Ramaselesele Mogotsi, and Motlhatsi Baakang.

H/M/89
Serame, at the home of Bakwena Gananthuso.
July 21, 1975, 0945 to 1100.
Interviewees: Keeng Rabeng (Matswakgotla), Motlhogelwa Tshweu
(Maakathata), and Shanko Morwaeng (Matlhaselwa).

H/M/90
Goo-Ra-Tshosa, at the home of Nkwane Gaealafshwe.
July 21, 1975, 1500 to 1630.
Interviewees: Magatelo Mokgoko, Nkwane Gaealafshwe, Mapote Keaketswe,
and Keemhitletse Makwati.

H/M/91
Serame, at the *kgotla.*
July 22, 1975, 0930 to 1130.
Interviewees: Shanko Morwaeng, Ditloung Kusi, Motlhogelwa Tshweu,
Marumoagae Keke (Maakathata), Antherea Gaesugelwa (Matlhaselwa), and
Pelontle Sebela (Mathubantwa II).

H/M/92
Goo-Ra-Tshosa, at the home of Nkwane Gaealafshwe.
July 22, 1975, 1430 to 1630.
Interviewees: Magatelo Mokgoko, Nkwane Gaealafshwe, Mapote Keaketswe,
Keemhitletse Makwati, and Kebelaetse Wamoku.

H/M/93
Serame, at the *kgotla.*
July 23, 1975, 0930 to 1130.
Interviewees: Shanko Morwaeng, Ditloung Kusi, Motlhogelwa Tshweu, and
Pelontle Sebela.

H/M/94
Goo-Ra-Tshosa, at the home of Nkwane Gaealafshwe.
July 23, 1975, 1415 to 1615.
Interviewees: Magatelo Mokgoko, Nkwane Gaealafshwe, Mapote Keaketswe,
Keemhitletse Makwati, and Kebelaetse Wamoku.

H/M/95
Serame, at the *kgotla.*
July 24, 1975, 0930 to 1100.
Interviewees: Shanko Morwaeng, Ditloung Kusi, Motlhogelwa Tshweu, and
Pelontle Sebela.

H/M/96
Goo-Ra-Tshosa, at the home of Nkwane Gaealafshwe.
July 24, 1975, 1500 to 1630.
Interviewees: Magatelo Mokgoko, Nkwane Gaealafshwe, Mapote Keaketswe,
Keemhitletse Makwati, and Thukhwi Segaetsho.

H/M/97

Goo-Ra-Tshosa, at the home of Nkwane Gaealafshwe.
July 25, 1975, 1500 to 1630.
Interviewees: Magatelo Mokgoko, Nkwane Gaealafshwe, Mapote Keaketswe,
Thukhwi Segaetsho, Kebelaetse Wamoku, Koama Motlhale, and Mosai Lekapana
(Maratakgosi).

H/M/98
Basiamang, at the home of Shanko Morwaeng.
July 28, 1975, 1445 to 1645.
Interviewees: Shanko Morwaeng, Autlwetsi Retsakgosi (Masitaoka), Ramabe
Batsalelwang (Malatakgosi), Magatelo Mokgoko, and Mapote Keaketswe.

H/M/99
Goo-Ra-Tshosa, at the home of Nkwane Gaealafshwe.
July 29, 1975, 1445 to 1645.
Interviewees: Magatelo Mokgoko, Nkwane Gaealafshwe, Mapote Keaketswe,
Thukhwi Segaetsho, Shanko Morwaeng, and Ramabe Batsalelwang.

H/M/100
Goo-Ra-Tshosa, at the home of Nkwane Gaealafshwe.
July 30, 1975, 0915 to 1130.
Interviewees: Magatelo Mokgoko, Nkwane Gaealafshwe, Mapote Keaketswe,
and Thukhwi Segaetsho.

H/M/101
Goo-Ra-Tshosa, at the home of Nkwane Gaealafshwe.
July 31, 1975, 1030 to 1200.
Interviewees: Magatelo Mokgoko, Nkwane Gaealafshwe, Thukhwi Segaetsho,
and Keemhitletse Makwati.

H/M/102
Kgosing, at the *kgosi*'s *lelwapa*.
August 7, 1975, 1520 to 1630.
Interviewees: Magatelo Mokgoko, Mapote Keaketswe, Kebelaetse Wamoku, and
Koama Motlhale.

H/M/103
Kgosing, at the *kgosi*'s *lelwapa*.
August 8, 1975, 1000 to 1200.
Interviewees: Magatelo Mokgoko, Mapote Keaketswe, Matome Mpusang,
Labobedi Ntloakhumo (Matswakgotla), and Mochina Sepotlo (Maakathata).

H/M/104
Kgosing, at the *kgosi*'s *lelwapa*.
August 11, 1975, 1015 to 1200.
Interviewees: Tumisang Ntloyamodimo (Mathubantwa II), Matome Mpusang,
Labobedi Ntloakhumo, Magatelo Mokgoko, and Mapote Keaketswe.

H/M/105
Kgosing, at the *kgosi*'s *lelwapa*.
August 12, 1975, 1000 to 1115.

Interviewees: Tumisang Ntloyamodimo, Pepere Gabaraane, and Tsitoeng Mere (Maakathata).

H/M/106
Goo-Ra-Tshosa, at the home of Nkwane Gaealafshwe.
August 12, 1975, 1430 to 1600.
Interviewees: Magatelo Mokgoko, Nkwane Gaealafshwe, Mapote Keaketswe, Samokwati Kgakge, Oatlhotse Kgakge, and Lori Modiakgotla.

H/M/107
Maunatlala, at the home of Mmamorepo Mhaladi.
August 14, 1975, 1030 to 1130.
Interviewees: Mmamorepo Mhaladi (Matlhogela) and Tumisang Ntloyamodimo.

H/M/108
Goo-Pula, at the *kgotla*.
August 14, 1975, 1500 to 1530.
Interviewees: Tumisang Ntloyamodimo, Pepere Gabaraane, Tsotlego Ramaiketso (Matlhaselwa), Gaosego Lefatshe (Malatakgosi), Batsimako Bogatsu (Matswakgotla), and Kedirwang Tsheko (Matlhaselwa).

H/M/109
Maunatlala, at the home of Mmamorepo Mhaladi.
August 17, 1975, 1000 to 1130.
Interviewees: Mmamorepo Mhaladi, Sekopo Moremong (Maratakgosi), Rabasima Moakofi (Malatakgosi), Galekgatlane Motshwane, Moagi Sebomo, and Garetshogi Garefani (Mathubantwa II).

H/M/110
Maunatlala, at the home of Mmamorepo Mhaladi.
August 18, 1975, 1000 to 1200.
Interviewees: Mmamorepo Mhaladi, Sekopo Moremong, Moagi Sebomo, Garetshogi Garefani, and Rabasima Moakofi.

H/M/111
Goo-Pula, at the *kgotla*.
August 18, 1975, 1500 to 1630.
Interviewees: Gaosego Lefatshe, Batsimako Bogatsu, Kedirwang Tsheko, and Pepere Gabaraane.

H/M/112
Maunatlala, at the *kgotla*.
August 19, 1975, 0945 to 1145.
Interviewees: Mmamorepo Mhaladi, Galekgatlane Motshwane, Pepere Gabaraane, Garetshogi Garefani, Rabasima Moakofi, Moagi Sebomo, Sekopo Moremong, and Matome Mpusang.

H/M/113
Basimane (*baga* Motlhabi).
August 22, 1975, 0900 to 1000.
Interviewees: Pepere Gabaraane and Matome Mpusang.

H/M/114
Basimane (*baga* Mhiemang).
August 23, 1975, 0900 to 1030.
Interviewees: Rampole Moreri (Maakathata) and Lehubitsa Moreri (Matlama).

H/M/115
Dikoloi, at the home of Morubisi Motsamaya.
August 25, 1975, 1030 to 1100.
Interviewees: Morubisi Motsamaya (Matswakgotla) and Ketlhapilwe Kobe
(Matlama).

H/M/116
Motonya, at the home of Lekgalemo Sefako.
August 25, 1975, 1115 to 1145.
Interviewee: Lekgalemo Sefako (Maakathata).

H/M/117
Goo-Moitoi, at the *kgotla*.
August 25, 1975, 1510 to 1700.
Interviewees: Sekopo Moremong, Kenathebe Daniele (Malatakgosi), Kefakae
Keetsile (Majanko), and Matome Mpusang.

H/M/118
Goo-Ra-Molese, at the home of Baitseng Thebeng.
August 26, 1975, 1030 to 1130.
Interviewees: Baitseng Thebeng (Matswakgotla), Ratlou Ketshabile, and Pepere
Gabaraane.

H/M/119
Goo-Molale, at the home of Ratlou Ketshabile.
August 26, 1975, 1400 to 1500.
Interviewee: Ratlou Ketshabile.

H/M/120
Difetlhamolelo (Goo-Ra-Nkane).
August 26, 1975, 1600 to 1700.
Interviewee: Koogotsitse Ramerafe (Masitaoka).

H/M/121
Basimane (*baga* Motlhabi).
August 27, 1975, 0830 to 1000.
Interviewees: Ntsane Matlhokwe (Maratakgosi) and Rampole Moreri.

H/M/122
Goo-Meje, at the home of Ponatsego Letlamma.
August 27, 1975, 1030 to 1215.
Interviewees: Ponatsego Letlamma (Matswakgotla), Masotho Laolang
(Matlhaselwa), Sekaname Setemere (Maratakgosi), Marumwane Keatlaretsi
(Maratakgosi), and Dorothea Luke (Maratakgosi).

H/M/123
Chadibe, at the *kgotla.*
August 27, 1975, 1430 to 1600.
Interviewees: Bale Makepe (Mautlwakgosi), Tichara Keabile (Matlama),
Motlhankana Kaang (Maakathata), Mipi Ntsima (Mautlwakgosi), and Motai
Sekgwa (Matswakgotla).

H/M/124
Bokalaka, at the *kgotla.*
August 28, 1975, 0900 to 0930.
Interviewees: Mpopi Keleketu (Matlama) and Monnaemang Sebase (Matlama).

H/M/125
Ga-Maribana, at the *kgotla.*
August 28, 1975, 1510 to 1700.
Interviewees: Lekgamelo Sefako, Ramaselesele Difele (Maakathata), Matshego
Mojakwate (Matlama), and Mosarwa Serurubele (Malatakgosi).

H/M/126
Ga-Morwa, at the *kgotla.*
August 29, 1975, 0930 to 1045.
Interviewees: Gaetwasepe Rasebe and Gagonthone Kgari.

H/M/127
Goo-Moloi, at the home of Drake Selwe.
September 1, 1975, 1400 to 1445.
Interviewees: Drake Selwe and Sepotoka Mafuri.

H/M/128
Goo-Moloinyana, at the home of Seforabatho Shatera.
September 2, 1975, 0930 to 1000.
Interviewees: Seforabatho Shatera (Mathubantwa II) and Keinyatsegile Sereto
(Maakathata).

H/M/129
Goo-Moloinyana, at the home of Seforabatho Shatera.
September 3, 1975, 0900 to 1000.
Interviewees: Seforabatho Shatera, Baakane Moloi (Maakathata), and Rakabea
Shatera (Maakathata).

H/M/130
Goo-Ra-Mokalake, at the *kgotla.*
September 9, 1975, 0900 to 1030.
Interviewees: Shabaku Mogapi (Matswakgotla), Baochudi Tshwene
(Maratakgosi), Keatshabe Balosang (Malatakgosi), and Masuntla Ntloedibe
(Matlhaselwa).

H/M/131
Goo-Ra-Tshosa, at the home of Serare Mathong.
September 9, 1975, 1500 to 1600.

Interviewees: Serare Mathong, Magatelo Mokgoko, Samokwati Kgakge, and Maothwanong Gaealafshwe.

H/M/132
Goo-Ra-Mokalake, at the *kgotla*.
September 10, 1975, 0900 to 0930.
Interviewees: Ditiro Mogapi (Matlhaselwa), Kaejo Mathame (Matswakgotla), and Baochudi Tshwene.

H/M/133
Goo-Ra-Moeng, at the home of Lefela Setlhako.
September 10, 1975, 1000 to 1030.
Interviewees: Lefela Setlhako (Matswakgotla) and Kwealelwa Baruti (Matlhogela).

H/M/134
Goo-Ra-Tshosa, at the home of Nkwane Gaealafshwe.
September 10, 1975, 1500 to 1600.
Interviewees: Magatelo Mokgoko, Nkwane Gaealafshwe, Samokwati Kgakge, Serare Mathong, and Maothwanong Gaealafshwe.

H/M/135
Kgosing, at the *kgotla*.
September 10, 1975, 1100 to 1130.
Interviewee: Gagonthone Kgari.

H/M/136
Goo-Ra-Moeng, at the home of Majaasuma Motlhabane.
September 11, 1975, 0920 to 1000.
Interviewee: Majaasuma Motlhabane (Matswakgotla).

H/M/137
Goo-Ra-Mokalake, at the *kgotla*.
September 11, 1975, 1030 to 1100.
Interviewee: N. B. Kgosientsho (Majanko).

H/M/138
Goo-Ra-Tshosa, at the home of Nkwane Gaealafshwe.
September 11, 1975, 1445 to 1600.
Interviewees: Magatelo Mokgoko, Nkwane Gaealafshwe, Samokwati Kgakge, Serare Mathong, Mapote Keaketswe, Maothwanong Gaealafshwe, and Kegosele Motlhabane (Mathubantwa II).

H/M/139
Kgosing, at the *kgotla*.
September 15, 1975, 1100 to 1130.
Interviewee: Matome Mpusang.

H/M/140
Ga-Khunou, at the *kgotla*.
September 16, 1975, 1000 to 1200.

Interviewees: Sekopo Moremong, Ntsuru Moagi (Mathubantwa II), and Keetsile Moitoi.

H/M/141
Goo-Ra-Tshosa, at the home of Nkwane Gaealafshwe.
September 16, 1975, 1500 to 1615.
Interviewees: Magatelo Mokgoko, Nkwane Gaealafshwe, Samokwati Kgakge, Serare Mathong, and Mapote Keaketswe.

H/M/142
Goo-Ra-Moeng, at the home of Majaasuma Motlhabane.
September 17, 1975, 0900 to 0930.
Interviewee: Majaasuma Motlhabane.

H/M/143
Mathakala, at the home of Keatshabe Balosang.
September 17, 1975, 1015 to 1130.
Interviewees: Keatshabe Balosang, Baochudi Tshwene, and Kaijo Mathame.

H/M/144
Goo-Ra-Tshosa, at the home of Nkwane Gaealafshwe.
September 17, 1975, 1500 to 1630.
Interviewees: Magatelo Mokgoko, Nkwane Gaealafshwe, Samokwati Kgakge, Serare Mathong, Maothwanong Gaealafshwe, Mapote Keaketswe, and Majaasuma Motlhabane.

H/M/145
Mathakala, at the home of Keatshabe Balosang.
September 18, 1975, 0900 to 1030.
Interviewees: Keatshabe Balosang, Baochudi Tshwene, and Masuntla Ntloedibe.

H/M/146
Goo-Ra-Tshosa, at the home of Nkwane Gaealafshwe.
September 18, 1975, 1500 to 1630.
Interviewees: Magatelo Mokgoko, Nkwane Gaealafshwe, Samokwati Kgakge, Serare Mathong, and Mapote Keaketswe.

H/M/147
Ntloedibe.
September 19, 1975, 0900 to 1100.
Interviewee: Majaasuma Motlhabane.

H/M/148
Goo-Ra-Mokalake, at the home of Shabaku Mogapi.
September 19, 1975, 1100 to 1130.
Interviewees: Majaasuma Motlhabane and Shabaku Mogapi.

H/M/149
Difetlhamolelo (Goo-Ra-Kgalaeng).
September 23, 1975, 0930 to 1100.

Interviewees: Kgosinkwe Kgalaeng (Matlama), Tshweu Kgalaeng (Matswakgotla), and Pepere Gabaraane.

H/M/150
Goo-Ra-Kokorwe, at the home of Ramala Maine.
September 24, 1975, 1000 to 1045.
Interviewees: Ramala Maine (Matlama), Thamaga Tsimama (Matlhaselwa), and Ramabe Batsalelwang.

H/M/151
Mokgalo, at the home of Ditloung Kusi.
September 24, 1975, 1430 to 1600.
Interviewee: Ditloung Kusi.

H/M/152
Kgosing, at the *kgotla.*
September 25, 1975, 0900 to 0930.
Interviewee: Pepere Gabaraane.

9. Moshaweng

H/Ms/1
Kgosing, at the *kgotla.*
October 27, 1975, 0915 to 1100.
Interviewees: Ramosesane Mere (Matswakgotla), Manka Lenkemetse (Malatakgosi), Letshapa Kaile (Malatakgosi), Rasega Dikole (Maakathata), Shianyane Kwaai (Maakathata), Botshelo Makuke (Matlama), Keithaetse Ramooi (Matlama), and Kebitsamang Sethakala (Matlama).

H/Ms/2
Goo-Molaodi, at the home of Lesole Segwape.
October 27, 1975, 1430 to 1530.
Interviewees: Lesole Segwape (Masitaoka) and Montshiwa Lesole (Matlhaselwa).

H/Ms/3
Kgosing, at the *kgotla.*
October 28, 1975, 0800 to 1030.
Interviewees: Ramosesane Mere, Manka Lenkemetse, Rasega Dikole, Shianyane Kwaai, Botshelo Makuke, Keithaetse Ramooi, Kebitsamang Sethakala, and Manthukhwi Teme (Matswakgotla).

L/Ms/1
At the home of Lesole Segwape.
October 28, 1975, 1100 to 1200.
Interviewee: Lesole Segwape.
Language: Sekgwatheng.

10. Motokwe
H/Mt/1
Kgosing, at the *kgotla.*
November 20, 1975, 1440 to 1615.

Interviewees: Keleketu Puleng (Maratakgosi), Gaobope Mochache (Matswakgotla), Tsotlane Bileo (Matswakgotla), Gagosejwe Kgalaeng (Maakathata), Tsiamisi Baelechi (Maakathata), Kelebeng Gaogose (Mathubantwa II), Poloko Moeng (Matswakgotla), Rimpanyane Kgolwe (Matswakgotla), Molaole Mochomabe (Matswakgotla), Tshilo Kobo (Matswakgotla), and Mokolele Lekoberi (Mathubantwa II).

H/Mt/2
At the church.
November 21, 1975, 0630 to 0830.
Interviewees: Keleketu Puleng, Mokolele Lekoberi, Rimpanyane Kgolwe, and Motupi Mankoi (Mathubantwa II).

11. Shadishadi

H/Sh/1
Under a tree near the borehole.
November 6, 1975, 1400 to 1600.
Interviewees: Rakgetsi Ngwako (Matswakgotla), Moroka Sekojane (Matlhaselwa), Ontusitse Suuping (Matlhaselwa), Mathulatshipi Mereki (Matlhaselwa), Molede Lesole (Maakathata), and Ranko Kelefetswe (Majanko).

H/Sh/2
Goo-Ra-Lemasi.
November 7, 1975, 0745 to 0915.
Interviewees: Rakgetsi Ngwako, Moroka Sekojane, Molede Lesole, Ranko Kelefetswe, Masogo Lemasi (Maakathata), Nthole Lemasi (Matlama), Ketlogetse Koohositse (Matlhaselwa), and Ramatota Ngwako (Malatakgosi).

12. Sojwe

H/S/1
Kgosing, at the *kgotla.*
November 6, 1975, 0730 to 1000.
Interviewees: Hube Mooalehi (Matlhaselwa), Kakgamatso Mooalehi (Mautlwakgosi), Rakhumo Moipolai (Matlhaselwa), Mosonyi Setlalekgosi (Maratakgosi), and Seboko Kwetsi (Matlhogela).

C. Archival Sources.

1. Botswana National Archives.

HC 5/42 Carrington to S. G. A. Shippard, Molepolole, May 12, 1886.
7/13 Administrator's Office, British Bechuanaland to High Commissioner at Cape Town, Mafeking, July 15, 1886 (enclosing a letter from A. J. Wookey on behalf of Sechele, Molepolole, July 12, 1886).
10/53 W. Bodle to Acting Adjudant, B. B. Police, Mafeking, December 27, 1886.

14/2   A Report, H. Goold-Adams to Fred Carrington, Mafeking, April
        15, 1887.
15/14   Sidney Shippard to Governor at Cape Town, Vryburg, August 12,
        1887 (enclosing a mining concession given to David R. Hume by
        Sechele).
16/7   Roger Price to Sidney Shippard, Kuruman, September 28, 1887.
17/42   J. Moffat to Deputy Commissioner at Vryburg, Molepolole,
        October 19, 1887.
18/13   F. H. Lucy to Administrator, Mafeking, January 19, 1887.
23/32   A. J. Wookey to Sidney Shippard, Molepolole, October 1, 1888.
23/33   A. J. Wookey to Sidney Shippard, Molepolole, October 18, 1888.
24/7   Sidney Shippard to Governor and High Commissioner at Cape
        Town, Mochudi, August 11, 1888.
26/33   J. S. Moffat to Sidney Shippard, Molepolole, March 15, 1889.
34/29   Parker Gilmore to Colonial Office, March 11, 1885 (enclosed in a
        letter from Lord Derby to Hercules Robinson, March 19, 1885).
39/32   Regarding Sechele's concession to Boyne.
80/24   Regarding Sechele's concession to Sidney Morris.
84/17   Regarding the Secheleland Concession Syndicate.
114/3   "Minutes of Enquiry held by William Henry Surmon . . . at
        Molepolole on the 27th, 28th, and 29th of July 1893."
118   Regarding Sechele's concessions to the Secheleland Concession
        Syndicate; and *The British Bechuanaland Government Gazette*,
        February 3, 1893.
119   Regarding allowances paid by the British South Africa Company
        to Sebele and other Batswana *dikgosi*.
134/1   Regarding Sebele's concession to Riesle and Nicolls of the
        Secheleland Concession Syndicate.
152/4   Regarding the Secheleland Concession Syndicate.
153/1   J. S. Moffat to Administrator, British Bechuanaland, Taung, April
        16, 1887; A. J. Wookey to Administrator, British Bechuanaland,
        Molepolole, June 21, 1887; Sidney Shippard to Governor and
        High Commissioner at Cape Town, Vryburg, July 21, 1887; and
        Henry Holland to Hercules Robinson, Downing Street, September
        29, 1887.
154/5   Deposition of Mahamad Ahamad, Gaberones, March 18, 1892.
182/1   Regarding "hut tax" and the raising of revenues in Botswana.
RC   4/4   W. H. Surmon to Resident Commissioner, Gaberones, September
        5, 1896.
     4/5   Regarding mining concessions in the Kweneng.
     5/5   W. H. Surmon to Acting Resident Commissioner, Gaberone's,
        August 8, 1901.
     5/12   J. Ellenberger to Acting Resident Commissioner, Gaberone's,
        August 31, 1900; and J. Ellenberger to Acting Resident
        Commissioner, Gaberone's, September 5, 1900.
     6/4   Ralph Williams to Acting Resident Commissioner, Mafeking,
        December 18, 1901.
     9/1   Regarding mining concessions in the Kweneng.
S   3/1   "History of the Bakwena Tribe, Notes From Information Given to
        Captain Stigand. . ."
     23/3   Regarding the death of Kealeboga, and the appointment of Sebele.

24/8   Kealeboga vs. Baruti, the divorce of Phetogo, and the move from
        Borakalalo.
25/10   S 24/8, cont.
38/2   Petition signed by Sechele, Sebele, and the Bakwena, addressed to
        the British King, Molepolole, August 16, 1910.
232/2   Resident Magistrate to Resident Commissioner at Mafeking,
        Kanye, June 20, 1931.
290/17 "Bakwena Reserve Mineral Concession Supllementary [sic]
        Grant," 1933; and "Bakwena Mineral Concession," 1933.
300/12 "Bakwena Affairs: Request for Ba-Phalane people to remove from
        Vleischfontein (Zeerust Dist.) into Bakwena Reserve."
352/17 "Notes on the Condition of the European Artisan Community at
        Molepolole," 1939.
406/16 "Dessication and Consequent Decrease of Population in the
        Kgalagadi District," a report by A. N. W. Matthews to
        Government Secretary, Tshabong, May 30, 1937.
447/6   Report by Germond to Resident Magistrate at Gaberones,
        Molepolole, November 30, 1935.
471/3   "Brief Report of the Investigations Carried Out Under the
        Bakwena Re the Administrative Structure of the Bakwena-Tribe,"
        by B. J. van Niekerk; "Additional Report. . . ," by B. J. van
        Niekerk; and "Die Administratiewe Struktuur van die Bakwena-
        Stam van die Betsjoeanalandse Protektoraat," by B. J. van
        Niekerk, M.A. thesis, University of Stellenbosch, 1961.

2. British Museum.

Add. 31356   Gordon Papers (Bell Collection), Maps of Livingstone's Travels,
        1849-1864.
Add. 35300   Aberdeen Papers, Barrow Bequest, vol. i.

3. British Museum, Natural History.

L/O.C.63 Owen Collection, Home Mss Etc., nos. 64-67, five letters from
        Andrew Smith, superintendent of the South African Museum, Cape
        Town, to Everard Home, president of the Royal Society.

4. Church Missionary Society.

Papers of the South Africa Mission, 1836-43.
CA4/M1   Mission Book, 1836-43.
CA4/O2   Newspapers, various.
CA4/O4-6   Letters and papers of individual missionaries.

5. Hope Department of Zoology (Entomology), University Museum, Oxford.

The uncatalogued letters of William J. Burchell.
The diaries of William J. Burchell, May 1812 to September 2, 1812.

6. India Office Records.

Factory Records: Cape of Good Hope.
G/9/1   Correspondence, 1773-1809.
G/9/23 Correspondence, 1821-26.
G/9/24 Correspondence, 1826-36.

7. London Missionary Society (Archives of the Council for World Mission).

Africa: Odds, Boxes 1-12, 17-22, and 40.
Africa: Personal, Boxes 1-6.
South Africa: Incoming Letters, Boxes 1-38.
South Africa: Journals, Boxes 1-4.
South Africa: Reports, Boxes 1-2.

8. National Library of Scotland.

The Letters of David Livingstone. Ms. 10701; Ms. 10707; Ms. 10708; Ms. 10709; Ms. 10710; Ms. 10711; Ms. 10736; Ms. 10768; and Ms. 10769.

9. Rhodes House Library.

Bechuanaland. 353. Mss. Afr. s. 1198 (1).
Bechuanaland. 353. Mss. Afr. s. 1198 (2).
Bechuanaland. 353. Mss. Afr. s. 1198 (3).
Bechuanaland. 785. Mss. Afr. s. 1020.
Bechuanaland. 786. Mss. Afr. s. 424.
10. Royal Geographical Society
Map Room. Africa. S/Div. 47.
Map Room. Africa. S/Div. 53.

11. Scottish National Memorial to David Livingstone Trust, Blantyre, Glasgow.

Analysis of the Language of the Bechuanas, by David Livingstone.

12. Wesleyan Methodist Missionary Society,

Biographical. South Africa. Boxes 1-4.
Correspondence (Incoming). South Africa. Boxes XVII-XVIII, and XXV-XXVII.

D. Unpublished Sources.

1. Dissertations.

Bailey, Charles. "Keeping Cattle and the Development of Water Resources in Eastern Botswana." Ph.D. diss., Cornell University, 1981.
Denbow, James R. "Iron Age Economics: Herding, Wealth, and Politics Along the Fringes of the Kalahari Desert During the Early Iron Age." Ph.D. diss., Indiana University, 1983.
Gailey, Harry Alfred, Jr. "The London Missionary Society and the Cape Government, 1799-1828." Ph.D. diss., University of California, Los Angeles, 1957.
Henderson, Willie. "Letlhakeng: A Study of Accumulation in a Kalahari Village." Ph.D. diss., University of Sussex, 1980.
Legassick, Martin Chatfield. "The Griqua, the Sotho-Tswana, and the Missionaries, 1780-1840: The Politics of a Frontier Zone." Ph.D. diss., University of California, Los Angeles, 1969.
Lye, William Frank. "The Sotho Wars in the Interior of South Africa, 1822-1837." Ph.D. diss., University of California, Los Angeles, 1969.
Peters, Pauline E. "Cattlemen, Borehole Syndicates and Privatization in the Kgatleng District of Botswana: An Anthropological History of the Transformation of a Commons." Ph.D. diss., Boston University, 1983.
Silitshena, R. M. K. "Changing Settlement Patterns in Botswana: The Case of the Eastern Kweneng." Ph.D. diss., University of Sussex, 1979.
Smith, Alan Kent. "The Struggle for Control of Southern Mocambique, 1720-1835." Ph.D. diss., University of California, Los Angeles, 1970.
Solway, Jacqueline. "Commercialization and Social Differentiation in a Kalahari Village, Botswana." Ph.D. diss., University of Toronto, 1986.
Truschel, Louis W. "Accommodation Under Imperial Rule: The Tswana of the Bechuanaland Protectorate, 1895-1920." Ph.D. diss., Northwestern University, 1970.
Wynne, Susan G. "The Land Boards of Botswana: A Problem in Institutional Design." Ph.D. diss., Indiana University, 1989.

2. Manuscripts.

Ellenberger, J. (A critique of Edwin W. Smith's chapter on Sebetwane in his *Great Lion of Bechuanaland*). Bechuanaland. 353. Mss. Afr. s. 1198 (1). Rhodes House Library.
_____. "A Few Notes Relative to Sebetwane's Wanderings in Africa. . . ." Bechuanaland. Mss. Afr. s. 1198 (2). Rhodes House Library.

_____. (Notes on the Bahurutshe *baga* Thobega, Boo-Manyana). Bechuanaland. Mss. Afr. s. 1198 (2). Rhodes House Library.

_____. "Notes taken at interview with Gaborone. . . ." Bechuanaland. Mss. Afr. s. 1198 (2). Rhodes House Library.

_____. "The Last Journey of the Batlokwa Who Had Joined the Conqueror Sebetwane," April 1938. Bechuanaland. 353. Mss. Afr. s. 1198 (1). Rhodes House Library.

Kemmonye. "Information given by KEMMONYE at Kolobeng, in 1936." Bechuanaland. 353. Mss. Afr. s. 1198 (1). Rhodes House Library.

Leech, J. F. "Places of Historical Interest in Botswana." Bechuanaland. 785. Mss. Afr. s. 1020. Rhodes House Library.

Mokone, N. G. (Oral history of the Batlokwa of Lichtenburg district). Bechuanaland. 353. Mss. Afr. s. 1198 (1). Rhodes House Library.

Ratshosa, Simon. "My book on Bechuanaland Protectorate native custom etc." Botswana National Archives.

E. Published Sources.

Allan, William. *The African Husbandman.* New York: Barnes & Noble, 1965.

Alpers, Edward A. "Re-thinking African Economic History: A Contribution to the Discussion of the Roots of Under-Development." *Ufahamu* 3:3 (Winter 1973): 97-129.

Alverson, Hoyt. *Mind in the Heart of Darkness: Value and Self-identity among the Tswana of Southern Africa.* New Haven: Yale University Press, 1978.

Amin, Samir. "Modes of Production and Social Formations." *Ufahamu* 4:3 (Winter 1974): 57-85.

Anderson, Andrew A. *Twenty-Five Years in a Waggon.* 1. London, 1887. Reprint. Cape Town: C. Struik, 1974.

Andersson, Charles John. *Lake Ngami: Or, Explorations and Discoveries, During Four Years' Wanderings in the Wilds of South-Western Africa.* London, 1856. Reprint. Cape Town: C. Struik, 1967.

_____. *The Okavango River: A Narrative of Travel, Exploration and Adventure.* London: John Murray, 1861. Reprint. Cape Town: C. Struik, 1968.

Arbousset, Thomas. *Voyage d'exploration aux Montagnes Bleues.* Paris, 1933.

Baldwin, William Charles. *African Hunting and Adventure.* London: Richard Bentley, 1863.

Barnard, Alan. *Hunters and Herders of Southern Africa: A Comparative Ethnography of the Khoisan Peoples.* Cambridge: Cambridge University Press, 1992.

Barrow, John. *A Voyage to Cochin-China.* London: T. Cadell & W. Davies, 1806.

Beaumont, Peter B. "The Ancient Pigment Mines of Southern Africa." *South African Journal of Science* 69:5 (May 1973): 140-46.

Beck, Roger B. "Bibles and Beads: Missionaries as Traders in Southern Africa in the Early Nineteenth Century." *Journal of African History* 30 (1989): 211-25.

Beinart, William. *The Political Economy of Pondoland, 1860 to 1930.* Johannesburg: Ravan Press, 1982.

Beinart, William and Colin Bundy. *Hidden Struggles in Rural South Africa, Politics and Popular Movements in the Transkei and Eastern Cape, 1890-1930*. London: James Currey, 1987.

Beinart, William, Peter Delius, and Stanley Trapido, eds. *Putting a Plough to the Ground: Accumulation and Dispossession in Rural South Africa, 1850-1930*. Johannesburg: Ravan Press, 1986.

Biebuyck, Daniel, ed. *African Agrarian Systems: Studies Presented and Discussed*. London: Oxford University Press, 1963.

Bloch, Marc L. *French Rural History: An Essay on Its Basic Characteristics*, trans. Janet Sondheimer. Berkeley: University of California Press, 1966.

Bloch. Maurice. *Marxism and Anthropology: The History of a Relationship*. Oxford: Clarendon, 1983.

Bloomfield, Leonard. *Language*. New York: Holt, Rinhart and Winston, 1961.

Bonner, Philip. *Kings, Commoners and Concessionaires, The Evolution and Dissolution of the Nineteenth Century Swazi State*. Johannesburg: Ravan Press, 1983.

Borcherds, Petrus Borchardus. *An Autobiographical Memoir*. Cape Town, 1861.

Boserup, Ester. *The Conditions of Agricultural Growth: The Economics of Agrarian Change Under Population Pressure*. Chicago: Aldine, 1965.

Bozzoli, Belinda. "Marxism, Feminism and South African Studies." *Journal of Southern African Studies* 9:2 (April 1983): 140-71.

Brenner, Robert. "The Origins of Capitalist Development: A Critique of Neo-Smithian Marxism." *New Left Review* 104 (1977): 25-92.

Breutz, P. -L. "Ancient People in the Kalahari Desert." *Afrika und Ubersee* 42 (1958): 49-68.

_____. "Stone Kraal Settlements in South Africa." *African Studies* 15:4 (1956): 157-75.

_____. *The Tribes of Marico District*. Pretoria, 1953.

_____. *The Tribes of Rustenburg and Pilansberg Districts*. Pretoria, 1952.

_____. *The Tribes of the Districts of Taung and Herbert*. Pretoria, 1968.

_____. *The Tribes of the Mafeking District*. Pretoria, 1955.

_____. *The Tribes of Vryburg District*. Pretoria, 1959.

British Parliamentary Papers. Further Correspondence Relative to the State of the Orange River Territory. Colonies. Africa. London, 1854.

Brown, Barbara B. "The Impact of Male Labour Migration on Women in Botswana." *African Affairs* 82:328 (July 1983): 368-88.

_____. *Women, Migrant Labor and Social Change in Botswana*. Boston: African Studies Center, Boston University, 1980.

Brown, J. Tom. *Among the Bantu Nomads*. London: Seeley, Service, 1926.

_____. *Setswana Dictionary*. Gaberones: Botswana Book Centre, 1968.

Bryce, James. *Impressions of South Africa*. London, 1899. Reprint. New York: Negro Universities Press, 1969.

Bundy, Colin. "The Emergence and Decline of a South African Peasantry." *African Affairs* 71:285 (October 1972): 369-88.

_____. *The Rise and Fall of the South African Peasantry*. Berkeley: University of California Press, 1979.

Burchell, William J. *Travels in the Interior of Southern Africa*. 2 vols. London, 1822 and 1824. Reprint. Cape Town: C. Struik, 1967.

Campbell, Alec and Graham Child. "The Impact of Man on the Environment of Botswana." *Botswana Notes and Records* 3 (1971): 91-110.

Campbell, John. *Travels in South Africa*. London, 1815. Reprint. Cape Town: C. Struik, 1974.

_____. *Travels in South Africa*. 2 vols. London, 1822.

Carneiro, Robert L. "Slash-and-Burn Agriculture: A Closer Look At Its Implications For Settlement Patterns." In *Men and Cultures*, ed. Anthony F. C. Wallace. Philadelphia, 1960.

Chamberlin, David, ed. *Some Letters from Livingstone 1840-1872*. London, 1940. Reprint. New York: Negro Universities Press, 1969.

Chapman, James. *Travels in the Interior of South Africa 1849-1863*. 2 vols. London, 1868. Reprint. Ed. Edward C. Tabler. Cape Town: A. A. Balkema, 1971.

Child, G. "Ecological Constraints on Rural Development in Botswana." *Botswana Notes and Records* 3 (1971): 157-64.

Chirenje, J. Mutero. *A History of Northern Botswana 1850-1910*. Rutherford, New Jersey: Fairleigh Dickinson University Press, 1977.

Clark, Colin and Margaret Haswell. *The Economics of Subsistence Agriculture*. London: Macmillan, 1964.

Cole, Desmond T. *An Introduction to Tswana Grammar*. London: Longman's, Green, 1955.

Comaroff, Jean. *Body of Power, Spirit of Resistance, the Culture and History of a South African People*. Chicago: University of Chicago Press, 1985.

Comaroff, Jean and John. *Of Revelation and Revolution: Christianity, Colonialism, and Consciousness in South Africa*. 1. Chicago: University of Chicago Press, 1991.

Comaroff, John L. and Jean. *Ethnography and the Historical Imagination*. Boulder: Westview Press, 1992.

_____. "On the Founding Fathers, Field Work and Functionalism: A Conversation with Isaac Schapera." *American Ethnologist* 15:3 (1988): 554-65.

Comaroff, John L. and Simon Roberts. *Rules and Processes: The Cultural Logic of Dispute in an African Context*. Chicago: University of Chicago Press, 1981.

Cooley, William Desborough. "A Memoir on the Civilization of the Tribes Inhabiting the Highlands near Dalagoa Bay." *Journal of the Royal Geographical Society of London* 3 (1833): 310-24.

Copans, Jean and David Seddon. "Marxism and Anthropology: A Preliminary Survey." In *Relations of Production: Marxist Approaches to Economic Anthropology*, ed. David Seddon. London: Frank Cass, 1978.

Coquery-Vidrovitch, Catherine. "Recherches sur un mode de production africain." *La Pensee* 144 (1969): 61-78.

Crisp, William. *The Bechuana of South Africa*. London, 1896.

Cumming, Roualeyn Gordon. *Five Years of a Hunter's Life in the Far Interior of South Africa*. 2 vols. London: John Murray, 1850.

Dachs, Anthony J. *Khama of Botswana*. London, 1971.

_____. "Missionary Imperialism -- the Case of Bechuanaland." *Journal of African History* 13:4 (1972): 647-58.

Dalton, George, ed. *Tribal and Peasant Economies: Readings in Economic Anthropology*. New York: Natural History Press, 1967.

Dalton, George and Paul Bohannan. *Markets in Africa*. Garden City, New York: Anchor Books, 1965.

Delius, Peter. *The Land Belongs to Us, the Pedi Polity, the Boers and the British in the Nineteenth Century Transvaal.* Berkeley: University of California Press, 1984.

Denbow, James R. and Edwin N. Wilmsen. "Advent and Course of Pastoralism in the Kalahari." *Science,* 19 December 1986, 1509-15.

_____. "Iron Age Pastoralist Settlements in Botswana." *South African Journal of Science* 79 (1983): 405-08.

Doke, C. M. "A Preliminary Investigation Into the State of the Native Languages of South Africa With Suggestions as to Research and the Development of Literature." *Bantu Studies* 7:1 (March 1933): 1-98.

Dolman, Alfred. *In the Footsteps of Livingstone.* London: John Lane, 1924.

Dornan, S. S. *Pygmies & Bushmen of the Kalahari.* London, 1925. Reprint. Cape Town: C. Struik, 1975.

Duggan, William. *An Economic Analysis of Southern African Agriculture.* New York: Praeger, 1986.

Dupre, Georges and Pierre Philippe Rey. "Reflections on the Relevance of a Theory of the History of Exchange." In *Relations of Production: Marxist Approaches to Economic Anthropology,* ed. David Seddon. London: Frank Cass, 1978.

Eldredge, Elizabeth A. *A South African Kingdom: The Pursuit of Security in Nineteenth Century Lesotho.* Cambridge: Cambridge University Press, 1993.

Ellenberger, Vivien. "Di Robaroba Matlhakola -- tsa ga Masodi-a-Mphela." *Transactions of the Royal Society of South Africa* 25:1 (1937-38): 1-72.

_____. "History of the Batlokwa of Gaberones (Bechuanaland Protectorate)." *Bantu Studies* 13:3 (September 1939): 165-98.

Elphick, Richard. *Kraal and Castle: Khoikhoi and the Founding of White South Africa.* New Haven: Yale University Press, 1977.

Farini, G. A. *Through the Kalahari Desert: A Narrative of a Journey With Gun, Camera, and Note-book to Lake N'gami and Back.* Cape Town: C. Struik, 1973.

Firth, Raymond. *Primitive Polynesian Economy.* London: Routledge, 1939.

Fosbrooke, H. A. "Land and Population." *Botswana Notes and Records* 3 (1971): 172-87.

Geertz, Clifford. *Agricultural Involution.* Berkeley: University of California Press, 1963.

Godelier, Maurice. *Rationalite et irrationalitie en economie.* Paris: F. Maspero, 1966.

Gray, Richard and David Birmingham, eds. *Pre-Colonial African Trade.* London: Oxford University Press, 1970.

Guy, Jeff. "Analysing Pre-Capitalist Societies in Southern Africa." *Journal of Southern African Studies* 14:1 (October 1987): 18-37.

_____. "Gender Oppression in Southern Africa's Precapitalist Societies." In *Women and Gender in Southern Africa to 1945,* ed. Cherryl Walker. Cape Town: David Philip, 1990.

Hammond-Tooke, W. D., ed. *The Bantu-speaking Peoples of Southern Africa.* London: Routledge & Kegan Paul, 1974.

Harris, William Cornwallis. *Narrative of an Expedition into Southern Africa.* Bombay, 1838.

_____. *The Wild Sports of Southern Africa.* London, 1852. Reprint. Cape Town: C. Struik, 1963.

Henderson, Willie. "A Note on Economic Status and Village House Types."
    Botswana Notes and Records 6 (1974): 228-30.
Henige, David P. "Oral Tradition and Chronology." *Journal of African History*
    12:3 (1971): 371-89.
_____. *The Quest for a Chimera, The Chronology of Oral Tradition.* Oxford,
    1974.
Hepburn, J. D. *Twenty Years In Khama's Country and Pioneering among the
    Batuana of Lake Ngami.* London: Hodder & Stoughton, 1895.
Herskovits, Melville J. *Economic Anthropology.* New York: Knopf, 1940.
Hill, Polly. *Studies in Rural Capitalism in West Africa.* London: Cambridge
    University Press, 1970.
Hindess, Barry and Paul Q. Hirst. *Mode of Production and Social Formation.*
    London: Macmillan, 1977.
_____. *Precapitalist Modes of Production.* London: Routledge, 1975.
Hodson, Arnold W. *Trekking the Great Thirst: Sport and Travel in the Kalahari
    Desert.* London: T. Fisher Unwin, 1912.
Holden, Wm. Clifford, ed. *Reminiscences of the Early Life and Missionary
    Labours of the Rev. John Edwards.* Grahamstown, 1883.
Hopkins, A. G. *An Economic History of West Africa.* New York: Columbia
    University Press, 1973.
Izzard, Wendy. "Migrants and Mothers: Case-studies from Botswana." *Journal of
    Southern African Studies* 11:2 (April 1985): 258-80.
Jeffreys, M. D. W. "Sibello." *Africana Notes and News* 16:1 (March 1964): 33-
    36.
Keegan, Timothy. "Trade, Accumulation and Impoverishment: Mercantile Capital
    and the Economic Transformation of Lesotho and the Conquered
    Territory, 1870-1920." *Journal of Southern African Studies* 12:2 (April
    1986): 196-216.
Kinsman, Margaret. "'Beasts of Burden': The Subordination of Southern Tswana
    Women, ca.1800-1840." *Journal of Southern African Studies* 10:1
    (October 1983): 39-54.
_____. "Notes on the Southern Tswana Social Formation." In *Africa Seminar:
    Collected Papers.* no. 2, ed. K. Gottschalk and C. Saunders. Cape Town:
    Centre for African Studies, University of Cape Town, 1981.
Kirby, Percival R., ed. *The Diary of Dr. Andrew Smith.* 2 vols. Cape Town,
    1939 and 1940.
Knobel, Louis. "The History of Sechele." *Botswana Notes and Records* 1 (1968):
    51-63.
Krupp, Sherman Roy. "Equilibrium Theory in Economics and in Functional
    Analysis as Types of Explanation." In *Functionalism in the Social
    Sciences*, ed. Don Martindale. Philadelphia: American Academy of
    Political and Social Science, 1965.
Kuper, Adam. *Kalahari Village Politics.* Cambridge: Cambridge University Press,
    1970.
_____. "The Kgalagadi in the Nineteenth Century." *Botswana Notes and Records*
    2 (1969): 45-51.
Language, F. J. "Die Verkryging en Verlies van Lidmaatskap tot die Stam by die
    Tlhaping." *African Studies* 2:2 (1943): 77-92.
_____. "Herkoms en Geskiedenis van die Tlhaping." *African Studies* 1:2 (1942):
    115-33.

LeClair, Edward E., Jr. and Harold K. Schneider, eds. *Economic Anthropology: Readings in Theory and Analysis*. New York: Holt, Rinehart and Winston, 1968.

Lee, Richard B. and Irven DeVore, eds. *Kalahari Hunter-Gatherers: Studies of the !Kung San and Their Neighbors*. Cambridge: Harvard University Press, 1976.

Leepile, M. "The Impact of Migrant Labour on the Economy of the Kweneng 1940-1980." *Botswana Notes and Records* 13 (1981): 33-43.

Legassick, Martin. "The Sotho-Tswana Peoples Before 1800." In *African Societies in Southern Africa*, ed. Leonard Thompson. New York: Praeger, 1969.

Lestrade, G. P. "Some Notes on the Political Organisation of the Bechwana." *South African Journal of Science* 25 (December 1928): 427-32.

Levy, Norman. *The Foundations of the South African Cheap Labour System*. London: Routledge & Kegan Paul, 1982.

Lewis, Jack. "*The Rise and Fall of the South African Peasantry*: A Critique and Reassessment." *Journal of Southern African Studies* 11:1 (October 1984): 1-24.

Lichtenstein, Henry. *Travels in Southern Africa*. 2 vols. Cape Town: van Riebeeck Society, 1928-30.

Lister, Margaret Hermina, ed. *Journals of Andrew Geddes Bain*. Cape Town: van Riebeeck Society, 1949.

Little, James Stanley. *South Africa*. London, 1887.

Livingstone, David. *Missionary Travels and Researches in South Africa*. London: John Murray, 1857.

Lloyd, Edwin. *Three Great African Chiefs*. London: T. Fisher Unwin, 1895.

London Missionary Society. *The Masarwa (Bushmen), Report of an Inquiry*. Lovedale: Lovedale Press, 1935.

Long, Una, ed. *The Journals of Elizabeth Lees Price*. London: Edward Arnold, 1956.

Mackenzie, John. *Austral Africa: Losing It Or Ruling It*. 2 vols. London: Sampson Low, Marston, Searle & Rivington, 1887.

_____. *Ten Years North of the Orange River*. Edinburgh: Edmonston & Douglas, 1871.

Maingard, L. F. "The Brikwa and the Ethnic Origins of the Batlhaping." *South African Journal of Science* 30 (October 1933): 597-602.

Malinowsky, Bronislaw. *Argonauts of the Western Pacific*. London: Routledge, 1922.

Marks, Shula and Anthony Atmore, eds. *Economy and Society in Pre-Industrial South Africa*. London: Longman, 1980.

Martin, Annie. *Home Life On An Ostrich Farm*. New York: C. Appleton, 1891.

Marx, Karl. *Pre-Capitalist Economic Formations*. Ed. E. J. Hobsbawm. New York: International Publishers, 1964.

Mason, R. J. "Background to the Transvaal Iron Age -- New Discoveries at Olifantspoort and Broederstroom." *Journal of the South African Institute of Mining and Metallurgy* 74:6 (January 1974).

_____. *Prehistory of the Transvaal*. Johannesburg, 1962.

Massie, R. H. *The Native Tribes of the Transvaal*. London, 1905.

Mautle, Gaontatlhe. "Bakgalagadi-Bakwena Relationship: A Case of Slavery, c.1840-c.1920." *Botswana Notes and Records* 18 (1986): 19-31.

Meillassoux, Claude. *Anthropologie economique des Gouro de la Cote d'Ivoire.* Paris: Mouton, 1964.

_____. "From Reproduction to Production: A Marxist Approach to Economic Anthropology." *Economy and Society* 1:1 (February 1972): 93-105.

Methuen, Henry H. *Life in the Wilderness.* London, 1846.

Moffat, Robert. *Apprenticeship at Kuruman.* Ed. I. Schapera. London: Chatto & Windus, 1951.

_____. *Missionary Labours and Scenes in Southern Africa.* London: John Snow, 1842.

Molema, S. M. *The Bantu Past and Present.* Edinburgh: W. Green & Son, 1920.

Moyo, E. E. E. *Tswana Settlement Structures.* Kampala, 1975.

Mudzinganyama, N. S. "Articulation of the Modes of Production and the Development of a Labour Reservoir in Southern Africa -- 1885-1944: The Case of Bechuanaland." *Botswana Notes and Records* 15 (1983): 49-57.

Munger, F. S. *Bechuanaland: Pan-African Outpost or Bantu Homeland?* London: Oxford University Press, 1965.

Neumark, S. Daniel. *Economic Influences on the South African Frontier 1652-1836.* Stanford, 1957.

Okihiro, Gary Y. "Genealogical Research in Molepolole: A Report on Methodology." *Botswana Notes and Records* 8 (1976): 47-62.

_____. "Precolonial Economic Change Among the Tlhaping, c.1795-1817." *International Journal of African Historical Studies* 17:1 (1984): 59-79.

_____. "Resistance and Accommodation: baKwena-baGasechele 1842-52." *Botswana Notes and Records* 5 (1973): 104-16.

Omer-Cooper, J. D. *The Zulu Aftermath.* Evanston: Northwestern University Press, 1966.

Palmer, Robin and Neil Parsons, eds. *The Roots of Rural Poverty in Central and Southern Africa.* Berkeley: University of California Press, 1977.

Parson, Jack. *Botswana: Liberal Democracy and the Labor Reserve in Southern Africa.* Boulder, Colorado: Westview Press, 1984.

Parsons, Q. N. "The Economic History of Khama's Country in Southern Africa." *Africa Social Research* 18 (Decmeber 1974): 643-75.

Peires, J. B. *The Dead Will Arise: Nongqawuse and the Great Xhosa Cattle-Killing Movement of 1856-7.* Johannesburg: Ravan Press, 1989.

_____. *The House of Phalo: A History of the Xhosa People in the Days of Their Independence.* Berkeley: University of California Press, 1982.

Philip, John. *Researches in South Africa.* 2. London: James Duncan, 1828.

Polanyi, Karl, Conrad M. Arensberg, Harry W. Pearson, eds. *Trade and Market in the Early Empires.* New York: Free Press, 1957.

Ranger, Terence. "Growing from the Roots: Reflections on Peasant Research in Central and Southern Africa." *Journal of Southern African Studies* 5:1 (October 1978): 99-133.

Rey, Pierre Philippe. *Colonialisme, neo-colonialisme et transition au capitalisme.* Paris: F. Maspero, 1971.

Ridsdale, Benjamin. *Scenes and Adventures in Great Namaqualand.* London, 1883.

Roux, Edward. *Grass: A Story of Frankenwald.* Ed. Winifred M. Roux. Cape Town: Oxford University Press, 1969.

Sahlins, Marshall. *Stone Age Economics.* Chicago: Aldine-Atherton, 1972.

Salisbury, R. F. *From Stone to Steel.* Victoria: Melbourne University Press, 1962.

Saunders, A. R. *Maize in South Africa*. Johannesburg, 1930.

Schapera, Isaac, ed. *The Bantu-Speaking Tribes of South Africa*. London: George Routledge, 1937.

_____, ed. *David Livingstone Family Letters 1841-1848*. 1. London: Chatto & Windus, 1959.

_____, ed. *David Livingstone Family Letters 1849-1856*. 2. London: Chatto & Windus, 1959.

_____, ed. *David Livingstone South African Papers 1849-1853*. Cape Town, 1974.

_____, ed. *Ditirafalo Tsa Merafe ya Batswana*. Lovedale: Lovedale Press, 1954.

_____. *The Ethnic Composition of Tswana Tribes*. London: London School of Economics, 1952.

_____. "Ethnographical Texts of the Bolongwe Dialect of Sekgalagadi." *Bantu Studies* 12:3 (September 1938): 157-87.

_____. *A Handbook of Tswana Law and Custom*. London: Oxford University Press, 1938.

_____, ed. *Livingstone's Missionary Correspondence 1841-1856*. Berkeley: University of California Press, 1961.

_____, ed. *Livingstone's Private Journals 1851-1853*. Berkeley: University of California Press, 1960.

_____. *Married Life in an African Tribe*. Harmondsworth: Penguin Books, 1940.

_____, ed. *Mekgwa le Melao ya Batswana*. Lovedale: Lovedale Press, 1938.

_____. *Migrant Labour and Tribal Life*. London: Oxford University Press, 1947.

_____. *Native Land Tenure in the Bechuanaland Protectorate*. Lovedale: Lovedale Press, 1943.

_____. "Notes on the Early History of the Kwena (Bakwena-bagaSechele)." *Botswana Notes and Records* 12 (1980): 83-87.

_____, ed. *Praise-Poems of Tswana Chiefs*. Oxford: Clarendon, 1965.

_____, ed. "The Present State and Future Development of Ethnographical Research in South Africa." *Bantu Studies* 8:3 (September 1934): 219-342.

_____. *Rainmaking Rites of Tswana Tribes*. Leiden: Afrika-Studiecentrum, 1971.

_____, comp. *Select Bibliography of South African Native Life and Problems*. London, 1941.

_____. *A Short History of the Bakgatla-bagaKgafela of Bechuanaland Protectorate*. Cape Town, 1942.

_____. "A Short History of the Bangwaketse." *African Studies* 1:1 (March 1942): 1-26.

_____. "The Social Structure of the Tswana Ward." *Bantu Studies* 9:3 (September 1935): 203-24.

_____. *Tribal Innovators 1795-1940*. London: Athlone Press, 1970.

_____. *Tribal Legislation Among the Tswana of the Bechuanaland Protectorate*. London, 1943.

_____. *The Tswana*. London: International African Institute, 1953.

_____, ed. *Western Civilization and the Natives of South Africa*. London: Routledge & Kegan Paul, 1967.

Schapera, I. and D. F. v. d. Merwe. *Notes on the Tribal Groupings, History, and Customs of the Bakgalagadi*. Cape Town: School of African Studies, University of Cape Town, 1945.

Schneider, Harold K. *Economic Man: The Anthropology of Economics*. New York: Free Press, 1974.

Schwarz, E. H. L. *The Kalahari and Its Native Races*. Cape Town, 1928.

Seddon, David, ed. *Relations of Production: Marxist Approaches to Economic Anthropology.* London: Frank Cass, 1978.

Shaw, William. *Memoir of the Rev. William Shaw.* London, 1874.

Shaw, William, ed. *Memoirs of Mrs. Anne Hodgson.* London, 1836.

Shillington, Kevin. *The Colonisation of the Southern Tswana 1870-1900.* Johannesburg: Ravan Press, 1985.

Shineberg, Dorothy. *They Came for Sandalwood.* Victoria: Melbourne University Press, 1967.

Silberbauer, George B. *Hunter and Habitat in the Central Kalahari Desert.* Cambridge: Cambridge University Press, 1981.

Sillery, A. *The Bechuanaland Protectorate.* Cape Town: Oxford University Press, 1952.

_____. *Botswana: A Short Political History.* London: Methuen, 1974.

_____. *Founding a Protectorate: History of Bechuanaland 1885-1895.* London: Mouton, 1965.

_____. *John Mackenzie of Bechuanaland, 1835-1899.* Cape Town: Balkema, 1971.

_____. *Sechele, The Story of an African Chief.* Oxford: George Ronald, 1954.

Smith, Alan. "Delagoa Bay and the Trade of South-Eastern Africa." In *Pre-Colonial African Trade*, ed. Richard Gray and David Birmingham. London, 1970.

Smith, Andrew. *Journal of His Expedition into the Interior of South Africa, 1834-6.* Ed. William P. Lye. Cape Town: A. A. Balkema, 1975.

Smith, Andrew B. *Pastoralism in Africa: Origins and Development Ecology.* London: Hurst & Company, 1992.

Smith, Edwin W. *Great Lion of Bechuanaland: The Life and Times of Roger Price, Missionary.* London: Independent Press, 1957.

Smith, Thornley, ed. *Memoir of the Rev. Thomas Laidman Hodgson.* London, 1854.

Steedman, Andrew. *Wanderings and Adventures in the Interior of Southern Africa.* 2 vols. London, 1835. Reprint. Cape Town: C. Struik, 1966.

Stevens, Richard P. *Lesotho, Botswana, & Swaziland.* London: Pall Mall Press, 1967.

Stevenson, Robert F. *Population and Political Systems in Tropical Africa.* New York: Columbia University Press, 1968.

Stow, George W. *The Native Races of South Africa.* Ed. George McCall Theal. London, 1905. Reprint. Cape Town: C. Struik, 1964.

Tabler, Edward C. *The Far Interior.* Cape Town: Balkema, 1955.

_____. *Pioneers of Rhodesia.* Cape Town: Struik, 1966.

Taylor, H. W. *Tobacco Culture.* Johannesburg, 1924.

Terray, Emmanuel. *Marxism and "Primitive" Societies.* New York: Monthly Review Press, 1972.

Theal, George McCall. *The Beginning of South African History.* London, 1902.

_____. *History and Ethnography in Africa South of the Zambesi.* 1. London: George Allen & Unwin, 1907.

_____. *The Yellow and Dark-Skinned People of Africa South of the Zambesi.* London, 1910.

Thomas, David S. G. and Paul A. Shaw. *The Kalahari Environment.* Cambridge: Cambridge University Press, 1991.

Thompson, George. *Travels and Adventures in Southern Africa.* 3 parts. Ed. Vernon S. Forbes. Cape Town, 1967-68.

Thompson, Leonard, ed. *African Societies in Southern Africa*. New York: Praeger, 1969.
_____. *Survival in Two Worlds: Moshoeshoe of Lesotho, 1786-1870*. Oxford: Clarendon, 1975.
Tlou, Thomas. *A History of Ngamiland, 1750-1906: The Formation of an African State*. Madison: University of Wisconsin Press, 1985.
_____. "The Nature of Batswana States: Towards a Theory of Batswana Traditional Government -- The Batawana Case." *Botswana Notes and Records* 6 (1974): 57-75.
_____. "Servility and Political Control: Botlhanka Among the BaTawana of Northwestern Botswana." In *Slavery in Africa*, ed. S. Miers and I. Kopytoff. Madison: University of Wisconsin Press, 1979.
Tlou, Thomas and Alec Campbell. *History of Botswana*. Gaborone: Macmillan Botswana, 1984.
Transvaal Native Affairs Department. *Short History of the Native Tribes of the Transvaal*. Pretoria, 1905.
Vansina, J. *Oral Tradition*. Trans. H. M. Wright. Chicago: Aldine, 1965.
Vengroff, Richard. *Botswana: Rural Development in the Shadow of Apartheid*. Cranbury, New Jersey: Associated University Presses, 1977.
Wallis, J. P. R., ed. *The Matabele Journals of Robert Moffat 1829-1860*. 2 vols. London: Chatto & Windus, 1945.
_____. *The Matabele Mission*. London: Chatto & Windus, 1945.
Warren, Charles. *On the Veldt in the Seventies*. London, 1902.
Weare, P. "The Influence of Environmental Factors on Arable Agriculture in Botswana." *Botswana Notes and Records* 3 (1971): 165-68.
Wellington, J. H. "Some Geographical Factors Affecting Agriculture in South Africa." *South African Geographical Journal* 6 (December 1923): 41-66.
_____. "Some Physical Influences in the Human Geography of South Africa." *South African Journal of Science* 26 (December 1929): 80-94.
Westphal, E. O. J. "The Linguistic Prehistory of Southern Africa: Bush, Kwadi, Hottentot, and Bantu Linguistic Relationships." *Africa* 33:3 (July 1963).
Williams, D. *An Account of a Journey into Transorangia and the Potchefstroom-Winburg Trekker Republic in 1843 by the Rev. John Bennie*. Cape Town, 1956.
Wilmsen, Edwin N. *Land Filled with Flies: A Political Economy of the Kalahari*. Chicago: University of Chicago Press, 1989.
Wilson, Monica. "Changes in Social Structure in Southern Africa: The Relevance of Kinship Studies to the Historian." In *African Societies in Southern Africa*, ed. Leonard Thompson. New York: Praeger, 1969.
_____. "The Sotho, Venda, and Tsonga." In *The Oxford History of South Africa*. 1, ed. Monica Wilson and Leonard Thompson. New York: Oxford University Press, 1969.
Wolf, Eric R. *Sons of the Shaking Earth*. Chicago: University of Chicago Press, 1959.
Wolpe, Harold. "Capitalism and Cheap Labour-Power in South Africa: From Segregation to Apartheid." *Economy and Society* 1:4 (November 1972): 425-56.
Woodburn, James. *Hunters and Gatherers*. New York: St. Martin's Press, 1988.
Wookey, A. J. *Dinwao Leha E Le Dipolelo Kaga Dico Tsa Secwana*. Vryburg: South African District Committee of the London Missionary Society, 1921.

Wrigley, C. C. "Population in African History." *Journal of African History* 20:1
        (1979): 127-31.
Wylie, Diana. *A Little God: The Twilight of Patriarchy in a Southern African
        Chiefdom.* Hanover: University Press of New England, 1990.
Yudelman, Montague. *Africans on the Land.* Cambridge: Harvard University
        Press, 1964.

AFRICAN STUDIES

1. Karla Poewe, **The Namibian Herero: A History of Their Psychosocial Disintegration and Survival**

2. Sara Joan Talis (ed. and trans.), **Oral Histories of Three Secondary School Students in Tanzania**

3. Randolph Stakeman, **The Cultural Politics of Religious Change: A Study of the Sanoyea Kpelle in Liberia**

4. Ayyoub-Awaga Bushara Gafour, **My Father the Spirit-Priest: Religion and Social Organization in the Amaa Tribe (Southwestern Sudan)**

5. Rosalind I. J. Hackett (ed.), **New Religious Movements in Nigeria**

6. Irving Hexham, **Texts on Zulu Religion: Traditional Zulu Ideas About God**

7. Alexandre Kimenyi, **Kinyarwanda and Kirundi Names: A Semio-linguistic Analysis of Bantu Onomastics**

8. G. C. Oosthuizen, (*et al*), **Afro-Christian Religion and Healing in Southern Africa**

9. Karla Poewe, **Religion, Kinship, and Economy in Luapula, Zambia**

10. Mario Azevedo (ed.), **Cameroon and Chad in Historical and Contemporary Perspectives**

11. John E. Eberegbulam Njoku, **Traditionalism Versus Modernism at Death: Allegorical Tales of Africa**

12. David Hirschmann, **Changing Attitudes of Black South Africans Toward the United States**

13. Panos Bardis, **South Africa and the Marxist Movement: A Study in Double Standards**

14. John E. Eberegbulam Njoku, **The Igbos of Nigeria: Ancient Rites, Changes and Survival**

15. Aliyu Alhaji Idrees, **Domination and Reaction in Nupeland, Central Nigeria: The Kyadya Revolt, 1857-1905**

16. Kenoye Kelvin Eke, **Nigeria's Foreign Policy Under Two Military Governments, 1966-1979: An Analysis of the Gowan and Muhammed/Obasanjo Regimes**

17. Herbert Ekwe-Ekwe, **The Biafra War: Nigeria and the Aftermath**